Watts, Eugene J.

The social bases
of city politics

The Social Bases
of City Politics

Recent Titles in
Contributions in American History
Series Editor: Jon L. Wakelyn

In the Almost Promised Land: American Jews and Blacks, 1915-1935
Hasia R. Diner

Essays in Nineteenth-Century American Legal History
Wythe Holt, editor

A Right to the Land: Essays on the Freedmen's Community
Edward Magdol

Essays on American Music
Garry E. Clarke

Culture and Diplomacy: The American Experience
Morrell Heald and Lawrence S. Kaplan

Voting in Provincial America: A Study of Elections in the Thirteen
Colonies, 1689-1776
Robert J. Dinkin

The French Forces in America, 1780-1783
Lee Kennett

Cold War Political Justice: The Smith Act, the Communist Party,
and American Civil Liberties
Michal R. Belknap

The Many-Faceted Jacksonian Era: New Interpretations
Edward Pessen, editor

Manning the New Navy: The Development of a Modern Naval
Enlisted Force, 1899-1940
Frederick S. Harrod

Riot, Rout, and Tumult: Readings in American Social and Political
Violence
Roger Lane and John J. Turner, Jr., editors

The Long Shadow: Reflections on the Second World War Era
Lisle A. Rose

The Politics of Wartime Aid: American Economic Assistance to
France and French Northwest Africa, 1940-1946
James J. Dougherty

The Oil Cartel Case: A Documentary Study of Antitrust Activity in
the Cold War Era
Burton I. Kaufman

THE SOCIAL BASES
OF CITY POLITICS

ATLANTA, 1865-1903

EUGENE J. WATTS

Contributions in American History, Number 73

Greenwood Press
Westport, Connecticut . London, England

Library of Congress Cataloging in Publication Data

Watts, Eugene J
  The social bases of city politics : Atlanta, 1865-
1903.

  (Contributions in American history ; no. 73
ISSN 0084-9219)
  Bibliography: p.
  Includes index.
  1. Atlanta—Politics and government. 2. Atlanta—
Social conditions. 3. Politicians—Georgia—Atlanta—
History. I. Title.
JS552.A2W37   301.5'92'09758231   77-94756
ISBN 0-313-20322-9

Library of Congress Catalog Card Number: 77-94756
ISBN: 0-313-20322-9
ISSN: 0084-9219

First published in 1978

Greenwood Press, Inc.
51 Riverside Avenue, Westport, Connecticut 06880

Printed in the United States of America

10 9 8 7 6 5 4 3 2 1

À Françoise, qui m'a apporté le soutien
nécessaire pour terminer ce livre

Contents

Tables   ix

Acknowledgments   xi

1   Introduction   3
2   The Emergence of Candidates   12
3   Social Components of Atlanta's   45
    Political Culture
4   Social Roots of Political Aspiration   71
5   Victory and Defeat   114
6   Conclusion   160

Bibliographic Essay   177
Index   183

Tables

1 Occupation of Candidates by Office and by Subperiod 72

2 Property of Candidates by Office and by Subperiod 75

3 Median Property-Holdings of Vocational Groups within Contests for Each Office 77

4 Region of Birth of Candidates by Office and by Subperiod 81

5 Residence Areas of Candidates by Office and by Subperiod 86

6 Period of Arrival in Atlanta of Candidates by Office and by Subperiod 89

7 Ten Years' Length of Residence in Atlanta of Candidates by Office and by Subperiod 91

8 Age of Candidates by Office and by Subperiod 94

9 Previous Minor Officeholding of Candidates by Office and by Subperiod 97

10 Previous Membership on Political Committees of Candidates by Office and by Subperiod 98

11 Political Persistence of Candidates by Office and by Subperiod 101

12 Percentage of Victorious Candidates within Vocational Groups by Office and by Subperiod 116

13 Average Property-Holdings of Winning and Losing Candidates by Office and by Subperiod 120-21

14 Percentage of Victorious Candidates within Each Quartile of the Property Distribution by Office and by Subperiod 124

15 Percentage of Victorious Candidates by Region of Birth, by Office, and by Subperiod 126

16 Percentage of Victorious Candidates within the Center and Outskirts of Atlanta by Office and by Subperiod 129

17 Percentage of Victorious Candidates by Period of Arrival, by
    Office, and by Subperiod   132-33
18 Percentage of Victorious Candidates by Length of Residence, by
    Office, and by Subperiod   135
19 Age of Winning and Losing Candidates by Office and by
    Subperiod   138-39
20 Percentage of Victorious Candidates within Each Quartile of the
    Age Distribution of Candidates by Office and by Subperiod   140
21 Percentage of Victorious Candidates with and without Previous
    Minor Officeholding by Office and by Subperiod   141
22 Percentage of Victorious Candidates with and without Previous
    Membership on Political Committees by Office and by
    Subperiod   143
23 Percentage of Victorious Candidates within Categories of the
    Number of a Candidate's Campaign by Office and by
    Subperiod   145
24 Summary Results of a Multiple Discriminant Analysis
    for Mayoral Candidates with Won-Lost as the Dependent
    Variable by Subperiod   148
25 Summary Results of a Multiple Discriminant Analysis
    for Aldermanic Candidates with Won-Lost as the Dependent
    Variable by Subperiod   151
26 Summary Results of a Multiple Discriminant Analysis
    for Councilmanic Candidates with Won-Lost as the Dependent
    Variable by Subperiod   153

Acknowledgments

Many people provided assistance and encouragement for this project. At the most basic level, my parents, unable to obtain education for themselves, instilled in me the desire to learn and the drive to succeed that enabled me to complete this study. My mentor and good friend J. Harvey Young urged me as a young graduate student at Emory University to explore new approaches to history. Although not a practicing quantifier, Harvey has attended several services, giving me his gentle guidance at every stage of research and writing. Jerome M. Clubb, University of Michigan, and Robert P. Swierenga, Kent State University, unselfishly donated their time and considerable expertise in advising me about necessary improvements in an earlier draft; this book is immeasurably better because of their help. My colleagues—Ellen Dwyer and David Pace of Indiana University and Michael Les Benedict, Peter Hoffer, Richard J. Hopkins, Gary Reichard, and Merritt Roe Smith of The Ohio State University—generously read parts of the manuscript, often helping to translate my analysis into the English language. Professors Benedict and Reichard labored beyond the call of duty, reading several sections more times than they care to remember. Bronwyn Mellquist rendered invaluable aid under incredible pressure in the last stages of editing and polishing the manuscript. The office staff of the Department of History of The Ohio State University, ably directed by Phyllis Teitzel, typed several versions of the study; my appreciation of their effort is real. As a reader, I had wondered why writers thank their spouses in such front matter; as an author, I understand. Francoise sustained me in so many ways that a true acknowledgment would require a separate chapter. Fortunately, I can express my gratitude in better ways.

ABOUT THE AUTHOR

Eugene J. Watts is Associate Professor of History at Ohio State University, Columbus. A specialist in U. S. urban history and quantitative methodology, he has published articles in the *Journal of Southern History*, the *Journal of Negro History*, and the *Journal of Urban History*.

The Social Bases
of City Politics

1

Introduction

Political history should also be social history. This merger of interests cannot be based on the outcome of unique events or on a preoccupation with particular people; it must be based on persistent social patterns of political behavior. Traditional political histories have been overly concerned with episodic, sensational, and well-publicized aspects of politics. But a growing group of scholars, inspired by the possibilities of quantitative analysis and new directions taken in the social sciences, has gained a fresh appreciation for the social bases of politics. Practitioners of the "new political history" search the voting returns and analyze the performance of various groups of office-seekers for evidence of social conflict and cohesion.[1]

This book analyzes the social bases of politics in Atlanta, Georgia, between 1865 and 1903. It ranges beyond the political commentary of the period, weighing the relative importance of group-defining characteristics of candidates, examining possible paths of political recruitment, and, in general, taking advantage of a perspective that few Atlantans at the time could have enjoyed. Conventional tactics of historical research in an exploratory examination of Atlanta's political system proved inadequate, since the picture of city politics presented in printed sources was incomplete. Newspapers generally emphasized personalities and short-term issues during campaigns and portrayed the outcome in terms of personal victory or defeat, overlooking the possibility of more fundamental preferences of the body politic. Any long-range view of the social aspects of the political process, including any relationships among candidates, issues, and voting, became diffused in this blow-by-blow presentation. Moreover, this type of coverage focused narrowly on the political story, negating politics as part of community conflict or concensus or as illustrative of social change.

Yet a careful perusal of the press for a thirty-eight-year period clearly indicated that the political spotlight focused on the candidates. Even more important, both office-seekers and other political participants and observers believed that certain characteristics of candidates deserved and perhaps commanded the public's attention. Claims that contestants should be elected because they were large property-holders, workers or business-men, long-time residents of the city, inhabitants of a particular area, and so on, received frequent mention throughout this period. Consequently, the basic premise of this work is that the social bases of politics can best be revealed through analysis of the major actors in the political drama—the candidates.

A well-known methodology using this premise is *political prosopo-graphy,* the investigation of the common background characteristics of political actors by means of a collective study of their lives. Information amassed about individuals is juxtaposed and tested both for internal rela-tionships and for associations with other forms of political behavior. Scholars have used this technique to attack two basic problems in history: the changing roots of political action and the role in society of specific groups such as officeholders.[2] Historians have produced prosopographic studies of numerous groups but only sociologists and political scientists, investigating the question of "who governs" in American society, have studied social patterns of urban public leadership over extended periods. Along with describing political elites, some of these latter studies connect the social backgrounds of politicians to some form of behavior, either in terms of elections or public policy.[3]

The assumption that democratic societies, in choosing their leaders, may base their choices upon certain attributes of potential officeholders underlies many of these later works. Atlantans in the late nineteenth century frequently expressed this same notion. Thus the outcome of a number of elections considered together should reveal a continual sorting and sifting of citizens who entered the quest for political position.[4] Ex-amination of this *social filter*—the analysis of the social characteristics of candidates and their relationship to political success—should bring the political picture presented by contemporary sources into sharper focus as well as indicate what social trends in city politics were obscured, distorted, or excluded by political pundits and participants.[5]

As explained in chapter two, Atlanta during this period provides a use-ful case for developing and refining an analytical model of the social filter

in urban politics. Good reasons exist for this effort. The theoretical concept of a social filter, although a generally accepted notion, has not been
clearly defined, measured, or subjected to systematic tests. Most studies
exploring a social filter in politics have suffered from certain methodological deficiencies. Many of the best-known works on urban public leadership have examined only mayors and not other elected officials. This presents problems not only because of the small number of observations, but
also because mayors may be atypical of candidates in terms of their characteristics. To avoid these shortcomings, this study includes aspirants for
all major elective offices in Atlanta—mayor, alderman, and councilman.

Another methodological deficiency of many "social-filter" studies is
that rarely have writers proceeded beyond the examination of a few attributes, typically occupation, ethnic background, and some indicator of
wealth. A number of conceivably important characteristics, all subject to
historical documentation, have not been analyzed. To correct this over-
sight, this book included eight group-defining social characteristics—
amount of assessed property, occupation, race, ethnic background and
region of birth, residence, age, period of arrival, and length of residence
in the city—and three political variables—political persistence (number
of campaigns), prior political experience in municipal appointive offices,
and previous membership on partisan or nonpartisan citizens' nominating
and executive committees.

An even more serious drawback of previous studies is that most have
dealt with only the winners of elections. This has been true particularly
in studies of public leadership, which usually analyze only officeholders.
But all who aspired to public position, regardless of their eventual victory
or defeat, deserve attention. The emergence, disappearance, and failure
to participate of various groups of citizens reveal much about the social
patterns underlying competition for city office.

The situation in which all candidates share the same social backgrounds
and the case in which contestants have diverse backgrounds that differen-
tiate the victors from the vanquished produce quite different social filters.
Exclusive examination of officeholders reflects only the end result of the
underlying social filter and substitutes inference for a systematic evaluation of the social basis of past politics. Analysis of all candidates may reveal a prior stage of screening that prevents some groups from becoming
candidates at all or in numbers approximate to their proportion of the
population. Such proscriptions may be formal—through law—or informal,

and by producing a homogeneous body of contestants may be the crucial factor in the under—or over—representation of certain groups in public positions.

The fact that such a preliminary filter operated to some extent in late nineteenth-century urban politics is not new, but its implications must be amplified by the measurement of the theoretically more impor- tant and more visible social filter at the elections level. Elected officials generally won their positions in competition with others. The identifica- tion of attributes important in politics, therefore, must be made in this context of competition or by comparing characteristics of winners with those of losers.[6] Is the frequently noted domination of city government by businessmen simply the result of their preponderance among contes- tants, or do their disproportionate chances for success at the polls com- pared to the chances of other candidates suggest some deeper belief that such people should rule?[7] If the attributes of office-seekers consistently influenced the voters' choices, patterns of political preference for certain types of contestants should emerge from the analysis in this book.

If the posited social bases of politics is to stand the test of scholarship, the analysis must be quantitative. The description of over eight hundred candidates, based on eleven of their characteristics, and the examination of the relationship between those attributes and political success demand some kind of statistical presentation. The important element here, as else- where in historical research, is how imaginative, relevant, and theoretically important are the questions asked, and how appropriate are the methods used to answer these queries. Previous studies seldom proceeded beyond describing one attribute of officeholding at a time, at least in any system- atic fashion; yet such individual relationships may not be particularly meaningful. A more complex analysis, for example, might reveal not only that certain kinds of businessmen were officeholders, such as those who were wealthy or who lived in the central section of the city, but also, perhaps, that wealthy people or inner-city dwellers, regardless of occupa- tion, held the reins of city government. Only multivariate statistical pro- cedures, in which a number of characteristics are examined simultaneous- ly for their relationship to political success, can provide such insights.

In addition to the consideration of individual characteristics of con- testants, this study analyzes the relationship of each attribute with the others. Examination of pairs of attributes revealed several cases of mod- erately and at times highly correlated characteristics. For example, vocational groups among candidates differed according to political persistence, and both occupation and political repeating were related to other factors such as property-holding. To judge whether the first distinction was superficial and trivial—the product of the second, more fundamental association—or meaningful by itself, multiple discriminant analysis (discussed below) was employed. Although analysis of the candidates in chapter four is presented in a style similar to the reading of percentage tables (indeed, hundreds of such tables and measures of statistical association had to be examined to discuss the precise nature of interrelationships), it is based on findings from the multivariate analysis. In this way the reader does not have to search through a labyrinth of statistical notation to learn the final results.

Similarly, chapter five discusses the relationship between each characteristic of candidates and the outcome of elections. Any connections must then by qualified by other qualities of political hopefuls. Varying rates of political success for vocational groups, for example, may be modified when other factors associated with occupation are introduced into the analysis. Were only businessmen with substantial property-holdings victorious, while other contestants with substantial holdings were not? Was the association (or lack of association) between occupation and the outcome of elections the fortuitous result of the relationship of both with one or more attributes? Cross-tabulation of each characteristic of candidates with winning and losing, controlling for relevant third and fourth variables, forms the core of chapter five.[8]

Such a strategy helps to relate the findings to contemporary comment concerning each characteristic presented in chapter three. More important, this tactic permits a precise picture of the associations between each attribute and political success that could not be easily seen from the multiple discriminant analysis. It is also essential to uncover the relative political importance of all attributes considered in this study. In what way can scholars reasonably conclude that occupation had a greater or lesser political impact than property, nativity, or period of arrival in Atlanta? Multiple discriminant analysis is used in chapter five to gauge the *relative* weight of each attribute and the *cumulative* political significance of all characteristics. In the latter case this tool provides a quantitative measure of the social filter in Atlanta's elections.

Multiple discriminant analysis is a variant of multiple regression analysis with the dependent variable—in this case the outcome of elections—expressed in categories.[9] The social characteristics of candidates are the independent variables, the presumed "cause" of variations in victory and defeat. The advantage of this technique, which is analogous to the multi-variate approach used with tabular arrays, is that all characteristics can be scrutinized simultaneously for their association with the outcome of elections, whereas even with very large numbers of cases such as arrangement would be practically impossible to interpret in an extremely large percentage table. In short, the relationship of each group-defining characteristic with the outcome of elections emerges, through an involved weighting procedure, after its association with other attributes is taken into account. Several statistical measures of the combined political impact of all important attributes are also generated. Finally, comparison of actual political performance with "predicted" victory or defeat derived from the discriminant equation provides another empirical measure of success in discrimination and thus the magnitude of the social filter.[10] With this statistical tool we can determine rather rigorously what factors were associated with political victory and defeat and their degree of influence, and with this information infer the theoretical and historical significance behind the results.

The purpose of this project, however, is not to explain the outcome of individual contests. The reality of Atlanta's politics, and presumably of most political systems, was not so simple.[11] The results of individual elections depend on many factors that exist in a particular sequence of events. These situational elements, of course, are conditioned by various structural factors—the relatively unchanging aspects of the polity such as electoral rules and nomination systems. Existing concurrently with these structures, providing them with meaning and legitimacy, is the political culture of the city, which at least partly is reflected in attitudes towards desirable and undesirable qualities for officeholders. The political structures and cultural norms may permit situations that favor one or more social groups with political advancement. But knowledge of these facets of politics does not always reveal who is likely to win in a unique sequence of events. The central concern of this study, therefore, is on those factors that affected a wide variety of electoral situations.[12]

Many proponents of prosopography have unduly neglected cultural and structural elements of the political system.[13] The formal analysis—the bedrock of social-scientific history and the potential basis for the systematic comparative study of several cities—should be placed in its political setting. The second chapter discusses the general structure of Atlanta city politics and the emergence of candidates, including the changing process of nominations. Chapter three considers in detail the political culture as it pertained to the characteristics of political aspirants. After the analysis of the social filter in the fourth and fifth chapters, chapter six summarizes and discusses the wider implications of this study. The organization of this book, therefore, follows the chronology of research and analysis, a tactic that might prove helpful to other historians of urban politics interested in applying the model used here.

NOTES

1. For a discussion of the recent directions taken by political historians, see Allan G. Bogue, "United States: The 'New' Political History," in Robert P. Swierenga, ed., *Quantification in American History* (New York, 1970), 274-87. Forceful arguments for the historical analysis of the social bases of politics have been presented by Lee Benson, "Research Problems in American Political Historiography," in Mirra Komarovsky, ed., *Common Frontiers of the Social Sciences* (Glencoe, 1957), 113-83; and by Samuel P. Hays, "New Possibilities for American Political History: The Social Analysis of Political Life," in Seymour Martin Lipset and Richard Hofstader, eds., *Sociology and History: Methods* (New York, 1968), 181-227, and "Historical Social Research: Concept, Method, and Technique," *Journal of Interdisciplinary History* (Winter, 1974), 475-82.

2. For a good discussion of prosopography, see Lawrence Stone, "Prosopography," *Daedalus* (Winter, 1971), 46-79.

3. Bogue mentions a number of collective biographies written by historians in a footnote to his essay, "United States: The 'New' Political History," Swierenga, *Quantification in American History,* 38. Among the most important studies dealing with the social backgrounds of political leaders written by political scientists or sociologists are: Robert A. Dahl, *Who Governs* (New Haven, 1961); Donald S. Bradley and Mayer N. Zald, "From the Commercial Elite to Political Administrator: The Recruitment of the Mayors of Chicago," *The American Journal of Sociology,* LXXI (1965), 153-67; Mayer N. Zald and Thomas A. Anderson, "Secular Trends and Historical Contingencies in the Recruitment of Mayors: Nashville as Compared to New Haven and Chicago," *Urban Affairs Quarterly,* III (1968), 53-68; Robert T. Daland, *Dixie City: A Portrait of Political Leadership* (Tuscaloosa, 1956); Robert S. Schulze, "The Role of Economic Dominants in Community Power Structure," *American Sociological Review,* XXIII (1958), 3-9, and "The Bifurcation of Power in a Satellite Community," in Morris Janowitz, ed., *Community Political Systems* (Glencoe, 1961), 19-80; and Donald A. Clelland and William H. Form, "Economic Dominants and Community Power: A Comparative Analysis," in Willis D. Hawley and Frederick M. Wirt, eds., *The Search for Community Power* (Englewood Cliffs, 1968), 78-92.

4. For a more elaborate exposition of this idea, see Lester G. Seligman, "Elite Recruitment and Political Development," *Journal of Politics*, XXVI (1964), 612, and "Political Mobility and Economic Development," in Neil J. Smelser and Seymour Martin Lipset, eds., *Social Structures and Mobility in Economic Development* (Chicago, 1966), 341. Also see Donald R. Matthews, *The Social Background of Political Decision-Makers* (New York, 1954), 4.

5. The voting preferences of particular groups cannot be recovered to complement this discussion. Atlanta's wards were large and extremely heterogeneous, similar to slices of pie carved out of the circular city, with only one voting precinct in each throughout most of the period. Except for the relatively exclusive Seventh Ward, annexed in 1893, no wealthy or working-class wards existed; nor were there any significant social distinctions in the kinds of candidates residing in the respective wards.

6. For example, although one student of Atlanta claims the economic elite withdrew from politics after 1873, his exclusive examination of Atlanta's elected officials demonstrates only that they no longer were represented in office, not that they ceased their political activity. James H. Russell, "Atlanta, Gate City of the South, 1847-1885" (unpublished Ph.D. dissertation, Princeton, 1972), 279-80, 335-42.

7. See, for example, Robert H. Salisbury, "Urban Politics: The New Convergence of Power," *Journal of Politics,* XXVII (1964), 778-80; and Peter H. Rossi, "Power and Community Structure," in Hawley and Wirt, eds., *The Search for Community Power,* 310.

8. Paul F. Lazarsfeld, "Interpretation of Statistical Relations as a Research Operation," in Paul F. Lazarsfeld and Morris Rosenberg, eds., *The Language of Social Research* (New York, 1955), 115-24, is a standard discussion of multivariate analysis.

9. Although the winning and losing of elections are the primary concerns of the study, political success also can be measured by the percentage of votes received by candidates. Multiple regression analysis, with "percent vote" as the dependent variable, produced results similar to findings from the discriminant analysis. For my use of regression analysis, see Eugene J. Watts, "Property and Politics in Atlanta, 1865-1903," *Journal of Urban History* (May, 1977), 295-322.

10. For a full discussion of the mechanics of multiple discriminant analysis, see William Klecka, "Discriminant Analysis," *Statistical Package for the Social Sciences* (New York, 1975), 434-67. Those basic comments that are appropriate will be offered as notes later in the discussion of the findings.

11. In seeking the extent to which the characteristics of candidates "explain" political success, we confront all the hazards of ex post facto research. In this case, the outcome of elections is known, and then ensues a retrospective search for attributes expected to have been associated with those results. However, assumptions regarding causality should be handled with caution and may well be outdated. For a good discussion of this type of research, see Fred N. Kerlinger, *Foundations of Behavioral Research* (New York, 1965), 359-74. On the other hand, this study could produce lawlike generalizations regarding such associations, that is, the ex-

istence of a social filter. For a good treatment of this kind of historical explanation, read Murry G. Murphey, *Our Knowledge of the Historical Past* (Indianapolis, 1973), 67-100.

12. For a good discussion of factors that influence elections, see Robert R. Alford, "The Comparative Study of Urban Elites," in Leo F. Schnore and Henry Fagin, eds., *Urban Research and Policy Planning* (Beverly Hills, 1967), 263-302. The concept of "political culture" used in this study is taken from Gabriel Almond, "Comparative Political Systems," *Journal of Politics,* XVIII (1956), 391-409.

13. Stone, "Prosopography," 64-65.

2

The Emergence of Candidates

Although the citizens of Atlanta through their franchise fundamentally decided who would govern the city, their choice could not be entirely open. Then as now voters had a limited group from which to choose—those candidates who presented themselves for office. The emergence of office-seekers, in turn, did not occur within a political vacuum. The structure of Atlanta's social and political systems set limits on participation. While certain forces contributed to an open, even frenzied, atmosphere in which many groups had potential access to political power, other pressures placed constraints on citizens' choices. In short, the nature of the political process served to advance the campaigns of some contestants and to retard those of others, and, although not clearly revealed by contemporary discussion, it also affected the social filter. This chapter explores the political pathways used by members of various social groups to win elective office.

Atlanta, Georgia, in the period from 1865 to 1903 is especially suited for investigation of the social bases of politics. First, Atlanta provides a different perspective from more frequently studied northern cities. Two basic demographic facts distinguished Atlanta: the foreign-born population during these years never exceeded 5 percent of the total, and the black proportion of the population remained fairly stable at approximately 40 percent. Such social factors had a definite impact on Atlanta municipal politics.[1] Also, the city's political structure differed from that of its northern counterparts. During most of the period, Atlanta's municipal political system eschewed competition between the two major political parties, relied almost exclusively on the general-ticket procedure (citywide elections) rather than on ward elections, and prohibited city officials from succeeding themselves in office. These macrocharacteristics undoubtedly contributed to differences in the types of people who sought and won office in Atlanta in comparison with other cities.

Second, certain historical events and available source materials in Atlanta clearly define the beginning and end points of this time period. The end of the Civil War provides a natural starting point since the city had been virtually destroyed, forcing the citizens to rebuild the political system and the physical city. Likewise, 1904 serves as a useful terminal point since several events in that year altered the political structure. New wards were added to city government, the system of at-large election of alderman was changed to one of ward representation, and a long, involved struggle over political reform of the Police Department reached its denouement. In addition, much crucial source material, particularly city directories, tax lists, and major newspapers, are not available for Atlanta before 1865, and the identity of defeated candidates in that period cannot be determined. Also, the systematic analysis underlying this study could not be sustained past the first few years of the twentieth century because new figures who could not be located in earlier manuscript censuses rose to local political prominence.[2]

Third, certain aspects of Atlanta's political system make it an interesting one to study. Within this period the formal framework of municipal politics was significantly restructured by adoption of a new city charter in 1874. This charter, which remained substantially unaltered until 1908, was a "reform" produced by some of Atlanta's wealthiest and most prominent citizens. Frustrated in their attempt to capture city office in 1873, these wealthy reformers proposed a set of charter revisions allegedly designed to curb the power of a corrupt political ring and to stop extravagant expenditures by City Council in a time of depression.[3] The 1874 charter created a bicameral legislature through the addition of aldermen and proscribed all incumbents from succession in office. It also lengthened the term of office for mayor and councilman from one to two years; that of alderman was to be three years. Mayors continued to be representatives of the city at-large, as were aldermen; each councilman, as before, had to reside in the ward he represented. All officials were elected, however, by the general-ticket system. The number of alderman ranged from three in 1874 to seven by the end of the period. Two councilmen represented each ward, the number of which varied from five to seven during the period. After the election of 1974, one councilman per ward and one or two aldermen at-large were elected each year; the mayoral election occurred every two years.[4]

The mayor and members of the Board of Aldermen and City Council held joint responsibility for creating and maintaining city services. With one minor exception, these officers were the only popularly elected public officials in Atlanta until 1894. They appointed all other city officeholders until that year, when several minor positions became elective. In short, the mayor, aldermen, and councilmen constituted an important political elite, and for most of the period they were the only elected public officeholders in Atlanta that can be examined.[5]

For most of the period from 1865 through 1903, Atlanta had an open political system. By 1868 the lingering doubt concerning the eligibility of former southern sympathizers to hold municipal office had been removed. Also in that year blacks were declared eligible to vote and hold office in Atlanta, a situation that would continue, at least legally, until 1908. Universal male suffrage was the rule, and the only prerequisite for holding city office was that an individual be a qualified voter. Thus an officeholder had to be twenty-one years of age, a resident of the city, and he had to have lived in Fulton County generally six months and in Georgia for one year.[6]

Some citizens felt the path to office was too wide and agitated for a voter-registration law that would include such restrictions as a tax-paying qualification. Proponents of this position justified their stand as a method to reduce the number of black voters, to prevent fraud, and to protect "citizens with property and business interests at stake." The tax-paying provision surfaced as soon as blacks became eligible to vote and hold office in 1868, but Republican Governor Bullock was able to prevent the necessary state approval. Not until 1872, after the Democrats had driven the Republicans out of the statehouse, did Atlanta receive permission from the state to require registration, and only under the 1874 city charter were ordinances created to implement this restriction. From 1874 to 1881, each citizen, in order to vote, had to pay ". . . all legal taxes that may have been required of him, and which he has had an opportunity of paying. . . for the year preceding the one in which he may apply. . . ." Beginning in 1882, voters were required to have paid all taxes required of them since 1877, except for the year of registration.[7]

In addition to the age, residency, and tax-paying requirements, other rules restricted the potential range of office-seekers. The city charter of

1874 made it illegal for any mayor, alderman, or councilman to be interested in, either directly or indirectly, any contract with the city. For this reason, George Sciple, whose firm sold sewer pipes to the city, was forced to retire from the 1896 campaign. As previously mentioned, the new charter also declared incumbents ineligible to succeed themselves in office, although they could campaign for a different city position. This loophole was partly closed in 1896, when incumbent councilmen were proscribed from running for alderman and aldermen were made ineligible for council. The stipulation did not apply to campaigns for mayor, and in 1902 this became a minor issue. Evan P. Howell, councilman from the Seventh Ward, resigned his seat to seek the mayoralty, but one opponent, Alderman James G. Woodward, did not follow his example. These political restrictions, of course, had no direct bearing on a candidate's social position.[8]

Although virtually any eligible voter could compete for Atlanta city office, relatively few decided to make the race. Those who did underwent a campaign process, sometimes simple and on other occasions elaborate, that separated the bona fide contenders from the hopeless also-rans and dropouts.

Self-determination and declaration for office were usually the first steps in the making of a candidate. Would-be contestants would sound out their prospects and jockey for position with politicians—a toe-testing of the political waters that might occur months before the official opening of the campaign. The press provided few hints of this undercover process until near election time. Although announcements for the 1883 contest did not appear until early November, the Atlanta *Constitution* reported in December that "For the past two months busy candidates and sympathetic friends have been hurrying to and fro working with a view to legislating for the city for the next two years." In 1902 the Atlanta *Journal* acknowledged that although public campaigns had not yet begun, they nevertheless were being "quietly prosecuted with much animation."[9]

Several Atlantans doubtlessly were discouraged by their timid forays and never appeared publicly as candidates. Those who ventured on eventually declared their intentions, usually by publicizing their candidacy in the "Announcements" section of the newspapers. That politics could be a risky venture was underscored by the *Constitution's* heading for this section: "All announcements under this head must be paid for in advance."[10]

Some individuals had to be persuaded by other citizens to contest city office. This phenomenon, or perhaps fiction, was particularly noticeable after 1883, when the emerging citizens' reform movement allegedly nominated men without personal political ambition. In 1884 the *Constitution* approvingly declared that no man on the Citizens' Ticket had sought the place, but all had been induced to become candidates by the citizens' committee. Unsought nominations seemed to indicate virtue. In 1873 the *Constitution,* strongly supporting John Collier, said the office "had sought him," while his opponent was seeking the position. Those individuals who accepted unsought nominations generally coupled a statement of their personal disinterest for public position with an acknowledgment that when duty called they would not refuse. Despite such disclaimers, real or otherwise, the individual had to decide to make the race, and at some point had to proclaim that fact. The personal announcement, even for drafted candidates, was the normal mode of throwing one's hat into the ring.[11]

Personal announcements were only the prelude to the elections. Construction of informal slates of candidates was generally the second step in the campaign process. This stage, usually occurring well after individual declarations had been made, took many forms. Specifically, there were two major types of combinations: those published in the press by anonymous sources and those produced by political parties, citizens' nominating committees, or ad hoc groups of citizens and candidates.

The publication in the press of slates or tickets for city office was a prominent part of the political process in Atlanta. Only rarely did such combinations fail to appear during city campaigns. Because the success of particular tickets was often exaggerated, their political impact is difficult to judge. More often than not they were too numerous and contained too much overlap of candidates to be decisive. They often seemed to confuse matters rather than to clarify them.[12]

The origin of many of these tickets is unknown although the probable source was the candidates themselves. The *Constitution* complained in 1897 that the "tickets and combinations galore" were both "mysterious and annoying." Although the press sometimes admitted its inability to name the derivation of slates, they frequently were eager to point accusing fingers. The most common and self-serving claim alleged that behind-the-scenes political bosses, called cliques or rings, had formed combinations in their own interests. This was an eternal campaign cry in Atlanta politics.

In 1876 the *Constitution* noted: "The cry of ring, which seems now to have become quite fashionable. . . was heard on every side."[13]

The press rarely was able to identify members of rings, although later in the period the leaders of two such factions and some of their alleged followers were named. These two political alignments supposedly consisted of the supporters of two police commissioners—William H. Brotherton, a wealthy dry goods merchant, and James English, former mayor and one of Atlanta's leading financiers. According to some accounts, they formed combinations of candidates for council on the basis of each contestant's pledge to support certain people for police commissioner. It is difficult to determine the extent to which this occurred, however, since the principals denied it, and the press was highly prone to political puffery. No individual candidate or group of office-seekers, of course, ever acknowledged a connection with a clique or ring. On the contrary, several slates for city office labeled themselves "Anti-Ring" and, in some contests, the making of that assertion became a mandatory campaign issue. Nearly all candidates in 1878, for example, publicly declared their independence from any ring. Political aspirants freely suggested, however, that their opponents had such connections.[14]

At times the press and other accusers were more specific in their identification of sources supporting various slates, pointing to particular groups such as the Mutual Aid Brotherhood or the American Protective Association. The MAB was the earliest undercover organization to appear in Atlanta politics. This secret society, which had apparent connections with organized labor and a decided bias against prohibition, initially gained public attention in 1886 as the reputed political arm of the Knights of Labor; it disappeared five years later. The American Protective Association first appeared in the 1895 campaign as the prime mover behind the Progressive Labor League Ticket. The APA also reportedly led the opposition to the obviously upper-class Star Chamber Ticket of 1896, although the association reportedly split into factions that year. The APA's connection to labor, and secondarily to prohibition groups, appeared more important than its affinity with nativists in Atlanta. Although no candidate publicly admitted membership in either the MAB or the APA, various citizens, candidates, and the press eagerly linked their rivals to the organizations.[15]

Secret clubs and other organizations with concealed memberships also claimed certain tickets as their creation. Two mysterious, oath-bound clubs—the upper-class Conservative Club and the 1890 Club, a temperance organization closely tied to labor, presented tickets in 1890. The latter club also was a factor in several subsequent campaigns. The Dracoes and the Atlanta Prohibition Club appeared only in the 1894 campaign, when both selected a slate of candidates from among those already in the field. The Liberal Club, which achieved prominence in 1897, consisted of several hundred young members who wanted a "more liberal city government." It held a mass meeting attended by three hundred people and endorsed a ticket for city office.[16]

Various well-identified special interest groups were a more important source of combinations than these clubs. Even though some, such as the Atlanta Liquor Dealer's Association, were relatively inconsequential, the several workers' and businessmen's associations constituted influential political forces. Labor Union No. 1 of Atlanta, in 1869, was the first worker's organization to select a slate for city office and represented the only attempt in the period to organize unskilled workers. For a time after 1869, workingmen pressed their demands through other channels, usually the Democratic party. Organized labor reappeared as a separate force in the 1880s, leading the opposition to the tickets of the citizens' reform movement in 1884 and, under the aegis of the Knights of Labor, again in 1886. The Railroad Men's League offered tickets in 1891 and 1892, and in the latter year the first Ticket of the Industrial Union Council also appeared. The Industrial Union Council consisted of committees from twenty-nine different labor organizations. All had clauses in their constitutions stating they were nonpolitical but allowing the formation of a committee to suggest to laboring people "how they may vote with benefit to themselves." The council suffered a serious split in its ranks while selecting another ticket in 1894. The Atlanta Federation of Trades made an inauspicious political debut in 1896, when some of its members unsuccessfully tried to capture a citizens' meeting to name a ticket and promote a pro-labor platform.[17]

Leaders of the business community generally preferred to capture existing political structures or, as in the case of the citizens' reform movement of the 1880s, to construct their own. Particularly in the 1890s, however, businessmen acted in smaller groups to promote candidates of their choice. In 1892 five important bankers and financiers, led by T. B. Neal, appointed a committee to select a slate. A similar small gathering of "representative citizens" again gave Neal the authority to name a nominating committee in 1896. Both resultant slates were popularly called

the Star Chamber Ticket. Businessmen sometimes used their own associations for political purposes. In 1894 thirty prominent members of the
Chamber of Commerce formed a nominating committee, and in 1899
the presidents of the Chamber of Commerce and Atlanta Business Men's
League initiated the formation of another.[18]

In the era of the partisan press, newspapers played a large role in city
politics. Often they seemed to be prime movers in political movements.
On several occasions tickets of unknown origin appeared and were supported by the papers that published them. Early in the period some
newspapers carried tickets on their mastheads. In 1871 and 1874 the
Daily News asked its readers to elect the ticket it had constructed. The
Daily Herald presented its recommendations in 1873, and from 1868
to 1877 the *Constitution* always supported the "regular" (as opposed
to "independent") Democratic Ticket. In 1869 the *Constitution* battled
with the *Daily Intelligencer* over the authenticity of the different Democratic tickets they carried on their mastheads. The *New Era* displayed the
People's Ticket or Citizens' Ticket, both synonymous for Republican
early in the era.[19]

Whatever the origins of the tickets published in the press, implicit in
their advertisement was that they represented a collective effort of certain
candidates. This was not necessarily, or even generally, the case. If they
were not constructed by an identifiable, formally constituted group,
such as the Democratic party, then they were advertised only as suggestions to the voters. The *Constitution's* comment regarding two tickets
in the 1895 contest was representative: "As neither ticket was regularly
nominated, but merely recommended, there will doubtless be much
scratching done."[20]

In Atlanta, as elsewhere, institutionalized nominations were the most
important element in the political filter. Debates over the propriety and
fairness of various procedures for nominations, and the different types of
candidates produced by these methods, were integral features of Atlanta
campaigns. In theory the overriding purposes of nominations were to
promote harmony, establish order, and avoid disruptive contests. In practice the real objectives were to settle the outcome of elections before
they occurred and to prevent the possible victory of certain kinds of undesirable office-seekers. This desire to compel voters and candidates to
support a regularly nominated ticket for city office resulted in considerable concern with voter acceptability of selected candidates. As dis-

cussed in the subsequent chapter, certain characteristics of contestants, such as occupation, property, age, and residence, clearly demanded attention. Atlantans openly discussed these and other qualifications of nominees in the process of making nominations and during the course of campaigns.

A number of options for nominations were available to Atlantans in the late nineteenth century. Some citizens favored ward selections, and others advocated citywide modes of choosing candidates. Some Atlantans preferred the direct selection of nominees, and others promoted indirect procedures. Citizens could and did change their position when they felt their own personal or group interest would be better served. For example, a candidate might favor nomination by committee when this would advance his campaign but oppose this procedure when the committee appeared stacked against him. Few political hopefuls wanted to beat a dead horse, or to ride one into battle. The press and "better class of citizens" appeared to favor indirect, citywide nominations, although this alignment was not always distinct. In contrast, lower-class citizens and those politicians who most assiduously courted their votes supported direct, ward-based procedures. Some Atlantans opposed the notion of nominations completely, believing office-seekers should place their fates directly with the voters without any intermediate attempt to influence the contest. Over the course of this period, indirect methods of selecting candidates, either by elected delegates or committees, fell into disuse, as did ward-based systems of both direct and indirect nominations. At the end of the period a white primary became the effective election, and regular nominations vanished from the Atlanta political arena.

Debate over the form of nominations took place within two distinct periods. The emergence in 1884 of the citizens' reform movement as the controlling influence in Atlanta municipal politics demarcated the boundary. Before that year partisan political organizations provided the framework for nominations, as Republicans and Democrats battled to control city government. With the disappearance of both parties in the 1870s, the task of nominations and voter mobilization fell to less formal groups. Through the explicitly nonpartisan citizens' reform movement, Atlantans primarily of the upper class sought to place city affairs firmly in their own hands rather than in the hands of "politicians," a goal that aroused opposition from the white working class. Blacks were a pivotal group in these battles between the warring white factions throughout much of the late

nineteenth century. But increased black militance in the 1880s, especially
demands for direct representation in city office, led to a strong white reaction and to the final major political development of the period—the
white citizens' primary. This system, however, preserved nonpartisanship
and continued political activism of Atlanta's business elite begun by the
citizens' reform movement.

The appearance of the city Republican party, which surfaced in 1867,
was a major cause of the extreme disruption and dislocation characteristic
of municipal politics early in the era. Competition between parties, normal
in northern cities and having precedent in Atlanta's brief history, was
nevertheless considered illegitimate by the majority party in Atlanta. This
was doubtlessly due to the Republican connection with Radical Reconstruction and the black vote, even though in most years blacks did not
vote as a unified bloc. Lack of black unity, in fact, eventually helped to
produce the Republican downfall.[21]

More important to the Republican demise was the development of the
general-ticket system. Before 1866 Atlanta held citywide elections, but in
that year a citizens' meeting successfully petitioned the legislature for
ward elections. In 1868, when blacks became citizens, the Georgia
Assembly reenacted the general-ticket system. Since black voters were a
majority or near majority in the Third and Fourth wards, any chance for
Republican victory depended on each ward electing its own representatives. The Republican-controlled legislature in 1870 again ordered ward
elections, but in the next year the Democrats regained the reins of state
government and promptly reversed the situation. Thereafter there were
no further changes, and the general-ticket system remained in effect
throughout the rest of the period.[22]

The city Republican party developed slowly and cautiously; not until
1870 did it become a visible and potent political force. Before that year
Republicans did not run black candidates for office and had difficulty
persuading white members of the party to campaign. Republicans held
mass rallies and constructed a full ticket for municipal office, including
three blacks as well as seven whites, in 1870. Ward elections enabled
two black and two white Republican councilmanic candidates to win,
while schism within the Democratic party led to victory for the Republi-
can-backed Independent Democratic candidate for mayor. The election
was so violent that United States troops had to restore order around the
polls.[23]

Republican success was short-lived. Open Republican nominations were not held after 1870, although a Republican slate, again containing several black candidates, unexpectedly appeared at the polls in 1871 and met disasterous defeat. The Atlanta GOP remained underground until 1875, when it launched a last-ditch effort to capture city office. Republicans held ward meetings to secure registration of black voters and to ratify the secret choices of the Republican executive committee. Several nominees declined, and the all-white Independent Ticket sponsored by the Republicans challenged the Democratic slate in only a few contests. The black vote reportedly was divided between the two slates, and the Democratic Ticket smashed its opposition at the polls.[24]

The Republicans disappeared from city politics thereafter, except for a brief return in 1888. The continuation of citywide elections, the voting by some blacks for Democratic candidates, the unwillingness of prominent white Republicans to campaign for city office, the failure of determined Republican efforts to enlist large numbers of white workers—through inclusion of their representatives on tickets, and strong Democratic unity in the face of Republican opposition in general elections led to the disappearance of the minority party from the municipal political arena. Many prominent politicians with an early connection to the city Republican organization, such as John H. James and Nedon Angier, also had defected to the majority party during the mid-1870s.[25]

The Democratic party, which had dissolved in Atlanta during the Civil War, reappeared on the city level in 1868 as the dominant political institution. Historians frequently have asserted that the Democratic party in the late nineteenth-century South was anything but democratic, that party politics was the private preserve of a few citizens known by the disaffected as the "ring."[26] To some extent this was true, but turbulence and disruption within the Atlanta Democratic organization often belied that notion. Claims of party solidarity were loudest in times of bitter internal division and almost always were exaggerated. Fierce intraparty battles took place between proponents of ward sovereignty and those who urged citywide centralization of nominations as well as between supporters of primaries and advocates of delegated conventions. Such debate divided the Democrats most noticeably along class lines, but less publicized differences between early settlers and recent arrivals, residents of the center and outskirts, political novices and established politicians, Southerners and non-Southerners, also contributed to dissension. The actual maneuvers and manipulations in Democratic decision-making that fomented disharmony, however, were not clearly revealed in contemporary sources.

Dissension within the majority party was so intense that the only apparent cement holding the organization together was the fear of significant black participation. Party leaders and loyalists openly and shamelessly used the threat of black rule to keep Democratic voters in line, even though at times some Democrats sought to use black voters to advance their campaigns. The attempt to maintain a solid front, even in the face of Republican opposition, sometimes failed. Some dissidents disavowed Democratic proceedings and struck out on their own—a situation that eventually would lead to the complete collapse and disappearance of the Democratic party in Atlanta politics.

In response to the Republican challenge, in 1868 the Democrats organized ward clubs and a central executive committee to oversee party nominations for mayor and councilmen. Assembled members of each ward club chose two candidates for City Council by acclamation or show of hands from 1868 to 1870 and by ballot in 1871 to 1873 and in 1875. This use of ward voting for councilmanic nominees, as intended, nullified the impact of general-ticket voting. Thus Democrats were able to maintain "home rule" for whites only while limiting black political power in general elections. Democrats also healed internal class divisions and countered the Republican appeal to white workers in 1868 by devising a "formula" for representation of all "interests" on their tickets for City Council.[27]

Selection of a Democratic standard-bearer for mayor caused considerable friction in early years, especially in 1869 and 1870. Black participation in the traditional citywide primary meeting in 1869 led to a break in Democratic ranks; a second Democratic mayoral contender subsequently was chosen by a convention of delegates elected at ward meetings. Use of the delegate convention in 1870 again led to open rupture and one "regular" and one "independent" Democratic mayoral candidate. Initiation of the citywide mayoral primary in 1871, however, managed to end maverick candidacies and still maintain hotly contested elections.[28]

Democrats never questioned the propriety of some form of citywide nomination for mayor, but attempts to modify the system of ward elections for City Council candidates provoked bitter debate, eventually leading to a full-scale battle in 1873. Three factions formed at an extremely disruptive mass meeting called to decide the form of nominations. After advocates of ward meetings were defeated, supporters of a citywide primary won a narrow victory over proponents of a delegate convention. The *Constitution* admitted "that our business men generally preferred the delegate plan, while the laboring classes seemed to center on the other . . . ." At least five tickets, albeit with considerable overlap, were advertised in 1873. Supporters of the delegate system, calling themselves "reformers," published one of these slates. This was referred to by the opposition, popularly named the "wool hat boys," as the "kid-gloves" or Chamber of Commerce Ticket. No slate won a clear-cut victory, although John Collier, mayoral candidate on the reformers' ticket, narrowly lost to Samuel B. Spencer, the foremost opponent of the "silk-stocking" Democrats.[29]

Debate over the manner of Democratic nominations continued past 1873, usually within the increasingly important City Executive Committee. In 1874 the committee decided in favor of a *white* Democratic general primary. The discussion in committee suggested that upper-class citizens had triumphed over representatives of the lower classes who favored ward elections, with both groups supporting the first specific exclusion of blacks. This latter point appeared as a new issue, for blacks reportedly had taken part in Democratic deliberations only in 1869. The committee again excluded blacks from the separate ward primaries in 1875 but, significantly, did not stipulate race as a condition for voting in the 1876 citywide primary. Apparently some Democrats, particularly partisans of citywide nominations, had begun to consider cooperation with the black vote, possibly in the belief that this tactic might offset challenges from working-class white supporters of ward nominations. Subsequent elections, however, demonstrated more than one Democratic faction could appeal to black voters.[30]

The Democratic general primary in 1877, again open to "all Democrats," was a tame affair, basically because many Democrats refused to participate. Candidates cooperated with one another within the various wards, in some cases leaving the field open only to one office-seeker. Although charges of rigged nominations had been voiced in preceding primaries, the compromises of 1877 were so blatant that dissidents within the party were no longer willing to accept the maneuvers. Independents proclaiming themselves "true democrats seeking reform in local affairs," offered an opposition ticket in the general election. Their platform stated:

The time has come when the people of Atlanta are determined
to throw off the yoke of nominations and assert the right of
free opinion on the subject of municipal representation.[31]

The dissidents sought the black vote to overthrow party machinery;
the stalwarts recognized that more than one faction could play that game
and competed for black support. Blacks, according to the *Constitution,*
were divided in their preferences, but the Independents received their
strongest support in the heavily black Fourth Ward. When the results were
in, the independents had won three of the six places.[32]

Although it was not immediately evident, the death knell of the Democratic party on the municipal level had been sounded. By the next year
the Democratic organization was smashed beyond repair. According to
the *Constitution,* "The leading spirits of the democratic party were so
divided and so confident of the strength of their man before the people
that all propositions to have a nomination. . . were howled down. . . ."
Threats of eventual independent candidates appeared with the initial
suggestion for a primary, and supporters of the Greenback party, which
had successfully organized for the county and state elections, marshalled
their forces for the municipal contest even though no greenback issue
was at stake. The campaign assumed "heated personal features," and the
election was one of the most disruptive in Atlanta's history.[33]

The demise of the Democratic party in city politics, although sudden
and in a way unexpected, did not occur without warning. Although the
party disintegrated into bitter division, to some extent that bitterness and
division had existed for some time. Tensions within the party—particularly
class differences, arguments over black participation, and factional dis-
putes—continually threatened to wreck Democratic unity. The rhetoric
of mass rallies and ward meetings indicated that other ill-defined alignments appeared among citizens and candidates divided by social factors
such as age and location and length of residence in the city. Cries for and
against practiced politicians also punctuated city campaigns. The realiza-
tion after 1875 that a Republican takeover was unlikely, and the willing-
ness of some white Democrats to work with blacks to secure their own
elections, further explains the decline of Democratic ascendancy. Democratic solidarity depended on partisan opposition, and when the outside
threat no longer existed, the fragile nature of the Democratic coalition
was exposed.

An organizational vacuum existed in Atlanta municipal campaigns for several years following the era of partisan politics. No nominations occurred from 1878 through 1883; candidates simply presented themselves to the voters at the general elections. Critics suggested that some "combinations" of candidates evolved from behind-the-scenes maneuvers, described by the *Constitution* as the "I-tickle-you-and-you-tickle-me" policy. This was a common complaint of the disaffected in Atlanta elections, but if true, the nature of the process provided no proof. Although city campaigns, for whatever reasons, were considerably less rambunctious after 1878, contestants continued to canvass the electorate, to hold rallies, and to publish notices in the press.[34]

The *Constitution,* and those Atlantans whose opinions it reflected, were strongly opposed to a free-wheeling political system, which in their view catered far too much to the lower classes, rewarded an unidentified group of politicians, inhibited participation by the "better class of citizens," and promoted political opportunities of men "unfit for office." About one hundred Atlantans, mostly prominent men of wealth, met in early August 1884 to change the course of city government. According to the Atlanta press and the assembled citizens, a reform movement aimed at installing the "best people" in city office, regardless of party affiliation, was necessary to "prevent rings and cliques from taking the city's affairs into their own hands." Then as now, the term *best people* had no clearer meaning, but several connotations. Generally it seemed to indicate wealthy business and professional men who previously had not sullied their hands in politics, although other attributes may have been important.[35]

Citizens at the meeting searched for the proper technique to encourage "good men" to seek city office, and equally important, to guarantee political success for their choices through elimination of competition. The inauguration of the citizens' nominating committee as the appropriate device occurred at a second meeting sponsored by the reformers. By a method that became standard, the nominating committee included representatives elected by wards and at-large members appointed by the chairman of the mass meeting. However, since the committee met as a whole, the range of ward influence was lessened considerably. The committee had authority to name a ticket that would be presented to another mass meeting "for its ratification or rejection." Although the size of the committee varied, the legitimacy of its nominations apparently depended on repetition of this ritual.[36]

A large attendance at the ratification meeting obviously was desirable to demonstrate that the selected slate had the support of Atlantans and to discourage any potential opposition. Thus all Atlantans were invited to these gatherings. The ratification meeting, typically, was neither as restrained nor as harmonious as the initial gathering and frequently posed problems for the citizens' reform movement. In 1884 a minority report claiming the ticket discriminated against workingmen met a "sustained wild uproar" from the large number of mechanics in the audience. Although the ticket constructed by the citizens' committee was adopted, dissent soon took harder lines.[37]

The citizen's reform movement did not always succeed in binding all Atlantans to its ticket. Tension between ward and citywide selections sometimes led to open rupture, but the major source of dissension followed class lines. In 1884 a meeting "representing the labor interest of the city" presented its own slate—the People's Ticket. This was an alarming development to the original reformers. The *Journal,* hoping to "restore the harmony and fraternity so desirable in our municipal affairs, and which it was the object of a majority of our citizens to establish through the citizens reform movement," encouraged a compromise whereby two workers would be included on the Citizen's Ticket. No compromise emerged, however, and soon the press openly and repeatedly attacked the People's Ticket. The *Constitution* argued that working men had no special interest except a wisely managed city, and freely admitted that the purpose of the reform movement had been "to bring into the management of city offices the best class of our business men." The *Journal* declared it had "no sympathy with those who would array capital against labor." Reuben Arnold, a lawyer associated with workingmen's groups and mayoralty candidate on the People's Ticket, continually lashed out at the Citizen's Ticket for its "exclusion of the working class" and derisively described his opponents as people born with a "gold spoon" in their mouths. Arnold's opponent for the mayoralty, George Hillyer, a wealthy lawyer, strongly defended the citizens' movement's attempt to interest "the best and busiest and interested people" in city government.[38]

The Citizens' Ticket, with only one exception, was elected in 1884. The *Constitution* considered this proof that the "good people" finally controlled city affairs and that any attempt to array classes against each other would fail. The paper also noted that an "astonishingly large number of Negroes voted the straight Citizens Ticket." The link between these two statements appeared more than coincidental. Black votes at this time aided elite reformers and helped frustrate the challenge based in the white lower classes.[39]

The overall success of the citizens' reform venture prompted the continuance of the movement throughout the 1880s. Although it was not apparent then, the movement marked a fundamental change in city politics by sealing the coffin on partisan politics and guaranteeing a continual political activism among Atlanta's leading citizens. Indeed, subsequent attempts to reintroduce partisan organization or party considerations into municipal politics inevitably met strong condemnation, especially since prominent white Republican leaders in Atlanta were allied with the citizens' reform movement. The injection of the prohibition issue into city politics, beginning in 1885, provided another early impetus for the movement. This question exerted considerable pressure on nominations for several years and forced political leaders to devise strategies to smooth over the resultant bitterness. On the other hand, the press and some politicians also used the prohibition issue as a smokescreen to cover more fundamental opposition to citizens' tickets based on class conflict and increasing black militancy.[40]

For a brief period, representatives of white workers and politically active black Atlantans attempted to form a coalition to challenge the citizens' movement. In 1884 and 1885 blacks had been limited to voting at ratification meetings and in elections. Beginning in 1886, however, black Atlantans organized to gain representation on the nominating committee and to press for black candidates. In the same year the Knights of Labor reportedly organized the opposition People's Ticket, which differed from the Citizens' Ticket by including two white workers as candidates. W. A. Pledger, a prominent black politician, and J. S. Lester, a white worker, submitted the new slate to the press. The resignation from the race of J. W. Asbury, an independent black candidate, in favor of a candidate on the People's Ticket gave further evidence of unusual public cooperation between blacks and working-class whites. The Knights, supported by the Mutual Aid Brotherhood, formed a well-organized and active political force. The results for the two contested spots were very close, but the Citizens' Ticket was triumphant.[41]

Several black politicians and representatives of the white working class again attempted to form a unified front in 1888. By this time, how-

ever, blacks were not willing to surrender their demand for direct representation in city office, and whites were not willing to acquiesce. During the course of the extremely bitter, class-conscious contest, the attempted coalition disintegrated. The comments of contemporaries and
the wide margin of victory for all candidates on the Citizen's Ticket suggest that neither blacks nor white workers cared for such an alliance. Indeed, most leading black figures by the end of the 1888 campaign had
thrown their weight behind the "better element" of Atlanta.[42]

The conduct of the 1888 campaign undoubtedly reinforced the de-
sires of many for conflict-free campaigns. In fact, a proposal to continue the citizens' reform movement in 1889 raised a groundswell of
approval. A petition signed by over one thousand citizens resulted in a
meeting attended by twice that number to choose a nominating committee. No organized opposition to the Citizens' Ticket developed in
1889. A leading figure in the movement presented one reason for this
unprecedented unity: "There are no party lines in the ticket, no class
lines, no sectional lines, and they are all good men." This time the committee had included several representatives of workingmen as well as a
prominent white Republican on the ticket. When one maverick announced
his opposition to the Republican, he was roundly chastised for attempt-
ing to "bring party politics in on the city elections." Atlanta voters apparently agreed, for the entire slate was swept to victory.[43]

Despite the spectacular success of the citizens' reform movement in
1889, and generally throughout the 1880s, the use of nominating committees was gradually superceded in the next decade. The press and
many substantial members of the community fought a rearguard action
to preserve nominating committees, while representatives of Atlanta's
white working class, rebuffed in their efforts to enlist black voters to
their cause, became the main supporters of the white primary.[44]

Battles over the form of nominations in the 1890s were waged within
the City Executive Committee. This institution, established initially at
the 1884 ratification meeting to conduct the campaign and to arrange
for similar mass meetings in subsequent years, had disappeared by 1886.
The citizens' ratification meeting in 1889 resurrected the committee,
which dutifully arranged details for selection of a nominating committee
of one hundred persons for the 1890 campaign. Dissent developed immediately, however, and the committee eventually acceded to demands
for a primary in which only white Atlantans could participate. Several

slates contested the 1890 primary, establishing a pattern that became commonplace. No matter how bitter the struggle, white Atlantans always closed ranks for the general election. The last serious, organized opposition to winners of primary elections appeared in 1890, when discontented black Atlantans attempted a democratic coup d'etat. Hoping to catch white voters napping on election day, they kept the all-black Anti-Primary Ticket a secret. Unfortunately for the organizers, the press discovered the ruse the day before the election. White voters turned out "under the circumstances," and administered a sharp defeat to black aspirations.[45]

After its faltering start in 1890, the City Executive Committee assumed paramount importance in deciding the form of nominations in succeeding campaigns. A majority of the committee in 1891, supported by the press and by a meeting of about one hundred "substantial citizens," resisted pressures for a white primary generated mainly by working-class supporters of a ticket already in the field. Instead, the committee called ward meetings to elect delegates to a nominating committee that included several black Atlantans. The resultant Citizens' Ticket easily defeated its opposition in the extremely bitter, class-conscious campaign. Blacks reportedly played a major role in that victory.[46]

Because of the bitterness of the 1891 contest, and the large part played by blacks, the movement for a white primary arose again in 1892. James G. Woodward—a noted representative of workingmen, one of the most powerful politicians of the period, and in 1892 a candidate for mayor— first demanded the white primary. After hearing opposing arguments from a delegation of well-known black Atlantans and supporting statements from a representative of "the legislative body of twenty-one labor organizations" and from a "selected spokesman of the political committees of each Ward," the City Executive Committee overwhelmingly voted for a white primary. By election time a great variety of tickets greeted the voters, but no one slate won a clear victory. John B. Goodwin, a prominent lawyer, defeated Woodward in a very heated campaign.[47]

Although the use of a direct primary was not yet firmly established, the exclusion of blacks from the political process appeared well accepted by 1893. The Executive Committee in that year finally decided that all white citizens would vote in their own wards for delegates to a citizens' nominating committee. Despite various contrivances and machinations

at ward meetings and at the nomination session, only minor opposition
to the Citizens' Ticket developed. Two other slates that appeared on
election day received only token support. If anything, their defeat demonstrated the unwillingness of Atlantans to challenge a nominated ticket.
No comparable effort would be made for the rest of the period.[48]

The City Executive Committee, again amid considerable consternation
and debate, vetoed the anticipated plan for a white primary or any other
nomination in 1895. A majority argued that nominations were an unnecessary duplication and would lead to unwelcome strife when the city was
filled with guests for the Piedmont Exposition. Despite a very agitated and
close campaign, candidates did not publicly solicit support from eligible
black voters. To have done so apparently would have invited defeat. Blacks
did not endorse any candidate, but a good number of black registered
voters went to the polls. This election marked the last occasion for black
participation in Atlanta city politics during this period.[49]

The white primary returned in 1896 and remained the mainstay of Atlanta city politics well past the turn of the century. This form of nomination did not end controversy or excited campaigns; it simply moved conflict ahead in the calender. A variety of tickets, always with considerable
overlap, continued to contest primary elections. At times either organized
labor or prominent businessmen backed individual tickets, but generally
the origins of combinations remained unknown.[50]

Even when slates were chosen through formal nominations or by more
informal construction of combinations, each contestant generally conducted his own campaign. Much of this activity, particularly in the early
stages, was devoted to maneuvers that by their very nature were not openly reported or discussed at length. Promises of patronage appeared particularly important as one of these maneuvers. In 1877 the *Constitution*
claimed that "putting certain persons in the offices to be filled by the next
council" was a matter of major importance. All city officials beginning in
1893 had to swear, as part of their oath of office, that they had not promised any city position in exchange for votes or support in the city election. It is doubtful whether this disclaimer had its desired effect. The
Journal discussed some aspects of the "quiet campaign" in 1896: "Small
jobs around the city hall are promised, 'undertakings' are had about certain contracts and the attitude of new candidates on the question of de-
posit for the city's money or toward street railway corporations—but the
question of supreme importance. . . is the old police board fight. . . ."

The stomping ground for candidates, politicians, and ward heelers—the area where all could meet and discuss such aspects of the campaign—was the block on Pryor Street between Block's candy factory and city hall, popularly called "Politician's Row."[51]

Candidates also canvassed the electorate. Reports that political hopefuls and their supporters were circulating around the city in search of votes generally indicated the opening of the feverish activity associated with campaigning. In 1866 the *New Era* noted that "Electioneering has been somewhat lively for some days. Candidates have been stirring around some, and the friends of candidates have been moving things." In 1897 the *Constitution* reported that the candidates in the preceding few weeks "have been in the streets, stores and shops" appealing for votes. Person-to-person appeals by candidates, called *button-holing,* continued through the voting process.[52]

A candidate also was expected to attend various ward meetings, presumably to discuss the issues of the day but more often than not simply to generate enthusiasm among his supporters. In this latter regard, candidates were often so successful that the 1874 city charter required office-seekers and other politicians to notify the mayor and chief of police before the meeting so one or both of them could attend "with a sufficient police force to preserve peace and order." Late in the period, when candidates often seemed more concerned with capturing prominent newspaper space than votes at a meeting, various contestants reportedly resorted to such subtle tricks as transporting supporters from one ward to another and hiring small halls, so the press would report that he had talked to an overflow crowd.[53]

Another device for arousing interest and support of the citizenry were the mass meetings held throughout the period. These gatherings frequently had a carnival-like atmosphere, complete with a band and fireworks. The press often disparaged these public rallies. In 1869 the *Constitution* advised its readers: "Keep away from the mass meeting tonight. . . . It inaugurates an excited campaign, that every body must deprecate. . . ." This paper in 1883 described the crowd at one colorful meeting: "The gathering was such as usually congregates at a fire or brings up the rear end of a street parade." Although the "best citizens" made these rallies an object of scorn, they were the equal of anyone in Atlanta in planning them. In 1884 the *Journal* reported "A brass band in a wagon pulled by four beautiful horses, paraded the streets yesterday afternoon . . . ." distributing handbills announcing a grand rally in support of the Citizens' Ticket. These rallies, of course, did provide one way for candidates to take to the "stump" with their platforms and reasons why they should be elected, although in several years critics claimed that "whiskey was the chief argument used."[54]

Speeches presented at these mass meetings attempted to show the voters where each candidate stood on the "issues." Issues in which the electorate were interested could not be safely ignored by office-seekers, but in the time-honored practice of politicians, positions on these matters often were so obfuscated that distinguishing among candidates is difficult. Every politicial aspirant in Atlanta favored better streets and sewers, increased police and fire protection, improved public schools, and, of course, lower taxation, and they all condemned corrupt politics in the strongest terms. Some candidates appeared to be more in favor of "retrenchment and reform," while others urged increased city services; but these divisions, as reflected in their speeches and platforms, were far from distinct. Even in those campaigns that featured the prohibition issue, a highly visible and divisive topic, other issues served to confuse alignments. Although newspaper coverage by the turn of the century indicated a greater tendency for candidates to state publicly their positions on innumerable issues regarding taxation, railway franchises, the sale of the Water Works, and so on, clear differences among office-seekers rarely existed.[55]

It is possible, of course, that subtle emphases in the speeches of political hopefuls may have been more apparent to Atlantans then than to readers of the papers now, although there is little reason to assume this was the case. Moreover, a major source on the "positions" of candidates came from their opponents and a highly partisan press, and neither was trustworthy. Public stances assumed by contestants on the issues of the day simply did not appear as fundamental as the qualifications and the qualities of office-seekers and the traditional political expressions regarding class conflict and reform.

The part of the campaign devoted to speech-making and public rallies was usually quite brief. Economy may have been one reason, for the cost of the campaigns was borne by the candidate and his friends and supporters. In addition to the hiring of bands and renting of halls, these costs might include payment to ward heelers and poll workers, the printing of campaign material, and the use of carriages and other conveyances to bring voters to the polls. Late in the period, candidates for the white citizens' primary also were assessed fees as their share of general campaign costs. These assessments generally amounted to twenty-five dollars for councilmanic candidates, thirty-five dollars for alder-manic aspirants, and fifty dollars for mayoral contestants.[56]

Although not a major campaign cost, the printing of tickets for the use of voters at the polls was an important responsibility of each candidate, since these tickets served as the actual ballots. Until late in the period, candidates were able to design tickets as they preferred; some adopted the extreme tactic of distributing tickets with the names of all contestants except that of their opponent. The printing of tickets appeared to have been an easy matter, as this 1866 advertisement suggested: "We are prepared to print Election Tickets in any quantity needed. Candidates can be served promptly and reasonably by leaving their orders in time." Such service might well have contributed to the proliferation of slates. The 1876 contest witnessed an extreme case: "Tickets of all descriptions, with eagles, roosters, cupids and American flags were printed upon all colors of paper, and distributed by the tens of thousands." The unlucky candidate who did not print tickets was severely handicapped. In 1882 the *Constitution* cited this reason to explain the poor showing of M. M. Brannan. Office-seekers who neglected this important practice had to hope that voters would write their name on someone else's ballot. This process, known as *scratching* in Atlanta, was commonplace in city elections. In 1887 it was reported that "The lead pencil, that breaker of slates and terror to the heart of the politicians, was out in force yesterday and the scratched tickets were abundant."[57]

Not until 1896 did the standardization of ballots occur in Atlanta: after this time the candidates had to distribute tickets that contained the names of all contestants. Voters then would scratch out the names of their candidates' opponents. Another major departure came in 1898 with the introduction of the Australian ballot into Atlanta politics. For the first time, voters were guaranteed anonymity in their selections. Even under this system, the candidates continued to supply tickets to voters until a new primary rule in 1903 forbade the practice.[58]

Attempts to directly influence voters or to secure additional support when the contest hung in the balance provided good reasons for candidates and other politicians to circulate around the polling places on election day. There was only one polling place in each ward, and all were located in the center of the city, within easy walking distance of each other. Although convenient for contestants "making the rounds," and for business and professional men and voters who lived near the city's center, this arrangement was disadvantageous for those who worked and lived in areas more distant from the polls. Since most elections in this period were scheduled on working days and during working hours, the problem was particularly acute for blue-collar workers who frequently agitated for additional polling places and voting at night. The "better citizens" often opposed these proposals on the grounds they were conducive to fraud.[59]

The use of carriages to bring voters, particularly workers employed in shops away from the city's center, to the polls provided at least partial amelioration. This was a common part of the electoral process before 1890, and in some contests "Almost every available team in the city" was engaged in this practice. The *New Era* provided this description in 1866: "Carriages and wagons were busily engaged throughout the day transporting voters to the polls. Everyone who was entitled to a vote was hunted up and urged to go and exercise the duties of a free American citizen." Candidates were imaginative in their use of conveyances. The contestants in 1882 used "hacks, buggies and carriages with placards on them." In the following year the *Constitution* condescendingly noted: "The usual number of carriages and various mongrel turnouts, improvised for the occasion, dipped around gathering up voters hither and yon. . . ."[60]

Generally, the press and upper-class Atlantans, who favored "orderly" and "dignified" proceedings—more likely, of course, with a lower turn-out—treated these tactics with scorn. At times, however, upper-class candidates also used this technique. Tom Glenn, mayoral candidate of the "conservative citizens" in 1888, was bitterly assailed by his opponent, Walter Brown, who claimed that one of Glenn's carriages was known throughout the city as the "pay train." Glenn claimed he had not spent any money ". . . beyond carriage hire and other legitimate expenses of campaigns. . . ."[61]

In the 1890s the City Executive Committee instituted a number of reforms for the electoral process. In 1890 an anticarriage motion passed by a vote of thirteen to twelve over the strong objections of workingmen on the committee. The City Executive Committee also passed a rule in 1890 forbidding the hiring of poll workers by candidates, but these hustlers were back at their posts the next year. Another attempt in 1896 to ban the use of poll workers did not even last the duration of the campaign. Beginning in 1900 the workers were segregated from the voters at the polls, but they simply took their station the prescribed distance from the ballot box and continued their trade. The *Journal* provided a colorful description of these people in 1902:

> Workers with badges, with tickets, with cards, with megaphones; some hoarse from the constant cries of victory that they have been making for their candidates and all full of energy, have jostled voters, pulled their coats out of shape and stepped on their toes in the contest that has been made over nearly everyone who has approached the polls.

From this account it appears that poll workers truly earned their money, but according to the press in most cases such activity was wasted, for the voters already had firm convictions before going to the polls.[62]

Strategies employed or neglected during campaigns, including the formation of combinations as well as the character of the canvass, undoubtedly affected the outcome of elections. But whatever process preceded it, it should not be forgotten that ultimately a citizen could forsake any influence and cast his vote as he wished. In the final analysis, the fate of candidates was settled at the ballot box, and while they and other political actors exerted pressures on the electorate, the collective weight of the voters in turn placed pressures on them. The successful office-seeker had to understand the attitudes and behavior of citizens, and to practice the arts by which their votes could be won. Certainly he had to have qualities that the citizens approved. The next chapter examines these characteristics of candidates that Atlantans in the late nineteenth century expressly considered important.

NOTES

1. Several general histories of Atlanta exist for this period: the most recent is Franklin M. Garrett, *Atlanta and Environs: A Chronicle of the People and Events* (3 vols., New York, 1954). Several dissertations on Atlanta history are more helpful: Richard J. Hopkins, "Patterns of Persistence and Occupational Mobility in a

Southern City: Atlanta, 1870-1920" (unpublished Ph.D. dissertation, Emory, 1973); James M. Russell, "Atlanta, Gate City of the South, 1847-1885" (unpublished Ph.D. dissertation, Princeton, 1972); Arthur Reed Taylor, "From the Ashes: Atlanta During Reconstruction, 1865-1876" (unpublished Ph.D. dissertation, Emory, 1973); and Grigsby H. Wooten, Jr., "New City of the South: Atlanta, 1843-1873" (unpublished Ph.D. dissertation, Johns Hopkins, 1973). For a good, concise summary of census information, see Hopkins, "Patterns of Persistence," 8-9. A comparison between Atlanta and other southern cities is presented by Howard N. Rabinowitz, "Continuity and Change: Southern Urban Development, 1860-1900," in Blaine A. Brownell and David R. Goldfield, eds., *The City in Southern History: The Growth of Urban Civilization in the South* (Port Washington, 1976), 92-122.

2. The changes of 1904 are described in Garrett, *Atlanta and Environs,* II, 455. Although legislation enabling aldermen to be elected by wards was passed in 1901, the change was not put into practice until 1904. Georgia General Assembly, *Acts and Resolutions . . . . 1901* (Atlanta, 1901), no. 255, p. 311. The political struggle over the police department is presented in Eugene J. Watts, "The Police in Atlanta, 1890-1905," *The Journal of Southern History,* XXXIX (May, 1973), 165-82.

3. For a condensed version of this reform movement, see Russell, "Atlanta, Gate City of the South," 109-13, 276-81.

4. The changes in the structure of city government can be seen in the comparison of *The Code of the City of Atlanta* (Atlanta, 1873), cited hereafter as *City Code, 1873;* and *The Code of the City of Atlanta* (Atlanta, 1875), cited hereafter as *City Code, 1875.* See also *The Code of the City of Atlanta* (Atlanta, 1891), cited hereafter as *City Code, 1891; The Code of the City of Atlanta* (Atlanta, 1899), cited hereafter as *City Code, 1899;* and *The Charter and Ordinances of the City of Atlanta, Code of 1910* (Atlanta, 1910), ch. III, sec. 24, sec. 31; ch. VI, sec. 56; ch. VII, sec. 77; and ch. LXXIV, sec. 2134, cited hereafter as *City Code, 1910.*

5. *City Code, 1899,* ch. XII, sec. 195. Several city officials previously appointed by the mayor, aldermen, and councilmen became subject to direct election on December 19, 1893; moreover, members of the Board of Water Commissioners also were elected in the 1870s.

6. Atlanta *Constitution,* November 11, 28, 1868; *City Code, 1873,* ch. 1, sec. 2, required voters to be white, a situation that changed in 1868. *City Code, 1875,* ch. XVI, sec. 102, required a residence in Fulton County for only thirty days and in Georgia for six months. The return to the initial residency requirements came in 1882. *City Code, 1886,* ch. XLII, sec. 675.

7. Atlanta *Journal,* November 29, 1885; Atlanta *Constitution,* November 11, 1868; December 3, 1869; November 9, 1870; *City Code, 1873,* ch. XXXVI, sec. 171; *City Code, 1875,* ch. XLVII, sec. 454-57; *City Code, 1886,* ch. XLII, sec. 674-75; *City Code, 1891,* ch. XLVI, sec. 960-63; and *City Code, 1899,* ch. IV, sec. 337-40. The 1891 legislation designed to protect primary elections did not require registration. Georgia General Assembly, *Acts and Resolutions . . .* 1891 (Atlanta, 1891), no. 778, pp. 210-11. Generally, however, all rules governing general elections also applied to primaries. One exception occurred in 1893, when the

primary election manager in each ward was ordered to use registration lists "as far as possible." Atlanta *Constitution,* October 19, 1903. Also see September 4, 1876; December 3, 1877; October 16, 1888; November 21, 1891; and the Atlanta *Journal,* November 26, 1883, for a contemporary discussion of registration procedures.

8. *City Code, 1875,* ch. III, sec. 18; Atlanta *Journal,* August 7, 1896; Atlanta *Constitution,* December 5, 1883; *City Code, 1899,* ch. III, sec. 29; Atlanta *Journal,* September 9-10, 1902; and Atlanta *Constitution,* September 27, 1902. A similar issue had appeared earlier, in 1890, when A. L. Kontz, an outgoing councilman, campaigned for mayor. Ibid., November 19, 1890. In addition to the question of succession, beginning in 1889 mayors, aldermen and councilmen were prohibited from holding any other city office during their tenure. *City Code, 1891,* ch. XXIV. In 1895 this regulation was broadened to include the holding of any appointive or elective office in the county, state, or national government, or a position on more than one city administrative board. *City Code, 1899,* ch. IV, sec. 61.

9. Atlanta *Constitution,* December 4, 1883; Atlanta *Journal,* September 5, 1902. Also see Atlanta *Constitution,* December 8, 1878; October 3, 1883; October 18, 1892; and Atlanta *Journal,* November 6, 1890.

10. Atlanta *Constitution,* November 2, 1883.

11. Ibid., August 6, December 2, 1884; and October 24, 1873. Some citizens declined persistent offers to seek city office; see, for example, Ibid., November 18-19, 1868; Atlanta *New Era,* November 20, 27, 1870; Atlanta *Constitution,* September 21, 1874; Atlanta *Journal,* December 2-3, 1885; and Atlanta *Constitution,* December 1, 1885; November 30, 1887. This study does not include those who withdrew before election day, primarily because it is not possible to relate the social backgrounds of such people to the outcome of campaigns. Moreover, to include persons given consideration by a reasonably sizeable minority of voters, but to exclude objects of inconsequential "drafts" or the victims of a few voters' whimsy, only people receiving at least seventy-five votes were defined as "candidates," regardless of their intentions. Fewer than fifty individuals were dropped from the analysis by this requirement.

12. The final appearance of only two slates occurred in the general elections from 1870 to 1872, and in 1875, 1886, 1891, 1896, and 1901. Atlanta *Constitution,* December 8, 1870; December 7, 1871; December 4, 1872; November 30, 1875; December 2, 1886; November 22, 1891; August 28, 1896; and September 26, 1901.

13. Atlanta *Constitution,* October 7, 1897; October 14, 1876; also see Atlanta *Daily News,* September 27, 1874.

14. For a detailed discussion of these two factions, and the connection between the police and politics, see Watts, "The Police in Atlanta," 176-82. Anti-Ring tickets appeared in 1878, 1882, 1890, and 1897. Atlanta *Constitution,* November 30, 1878; December 6, 1882; Atlanta *Journal,* November 20, 1890; and Atlanta *Constitution,* October 7, 1897; November 27, 30, December 1, 1878. Later in the period candidates would allege their opponents belonged to the local "Tammany." Atlanta *Journal,* September 18, 1899.

15. Atlanta *Constitution,* December 1-2, 1886; September 23, 1888; Atlanta *Journal,* November 20, 1890; Atlanta *Constitution,* November 3, 1891; and Atlanta *Journal,* November 14, 19, 25, 1895; August 10, 11, 1896.

16. Ibid., November 19, 20, 1890; Atlanta *Constitution,* November 19, 20, 1890; October 28, 1891; Atlanta *Journal,* November 14, 1892; Atlanta *Constitution,* September 6, 9, 26, 1894; and Atlanta *Journal,* September 27, October 1-4, 1897.

17. The *Constitution* once complained at length about special interest groups:

> There is no organization in the city composed of citizens resolved to put men on who will protect the city. We have a perfect organization of liquor men. The contractors and all who have an eye to the distribution of office and the money of the city are perfectly organized. This is natural. . . . But who is to look after the city?

Atlanta *Constitution,* November 18, 1883. The Atlanta Liquor Dealer's Association actually published a ticket in 1890. Ibid., September 25, 1900. For a discussion of separate working-class tickets, see Ibid., November 12, 16, 1869; Atlanta *Journal,* November 4, 1884; Atlanta *Constitution,* December 1-2, 1886; November 3, 10, 1891; November 8, 14, 1892; Atlanta *Journal,* November 14, 1892; October 2, 3, 1894; August 11, 12, 25, 1896; and Atlanta *Constitution,* August 11, 1896.

18. Ibid., October 19, 20, 1892; Atlanta *Journal,* July 30-31, August 4-5, 19, 1896; Atlanta *Constitution,* July 31, August 5, August 21-22, 1896; Atlanta *Journal,* August 7, 9, 1894; Atlanta *Constitution,* September 13, 1894; and Atlanta *Journal,* September 12-19, 1899.

19. Atlanta *Daily News,* October 10, 1871; October 8, 10, 1874; Atlanta *Daily Herald,* October 25, 1873; Atlanta *Constitution,* November 2, 23, 25, 1869; Atlanta Daily *Intelligencer,* November 25-28, December 1, 1869; and Atlanta *New Era,* November 27, 1870; December 6, 1871. The *Constitution,* which called itself "the organ of the Democratic party," decided which Democratic ticket was "regular" in those years in which more than one Democratic slate competed.

20. Atlanta *Constitution,* December 4, 1895. *Scratching* consisted of crossing out names on a ticket and substituting names of opponents. See p. 34.

21. Wooten, "New City of the South," 346-47; Russell, "Atlanta, Gate City of the South," 274; and Judson C. Ward, Jr., "The Republican Party in Bourbon, Georgia, 1872-1890," *The Journal of Southern History,* IX (March, 1943), 197-209. For a detailed discussion of the role of blacks in Atlanta municipal politics, see Eugene J. Watts, "Black Political Progress in Atlanta, 1868-1895," *Journal of Negro History,* LIX (July, 1974), 268-86; and Clarence A. Bacote, "The Negro in Atlanta Politics," *Phylon,* XVI (December, 1955), 333-50, and "William Finch, Negro Councilman and the Political Activities in Atlanta During Early Reconstruction," *Journal of Negro History,* XL (October, 1955), 341-64.

22. Atlanta *New Era,* November 9, 1866; *City Code, 1873,* ch. XX, sec. 90; Georgia, General Assembly, *Acts and Resolutions. . . 1866* (Macon, 1867), no. 250, pp. 180-81; Atlanta Daily *Intelligencer,* February 8, 1867; Georgia General Assembly, *Acts and Resolutions . . . 1868* (Macon, 1868), no. 14, pp. 166-67; *City Code, 1873,* ch. XXI, sec. 95; Georgia, General Assembly, *Acts and Resolutions. . . 1870* (Atlanta, 1870), no. 379, p. 486; and *City Code, 1873,* ch. XXVII, sec. 147. For a brief account of maneuvers in the legislature see Bacote, "The Negro in Atlanta

Politics"; Georgia General Assembly, *Acts and Resolutions . . . 1871* (Atlanta, 1872), no. 1, p. 87; *City Code, 1873,* ch. XXX, sec. 154; Atlanta *Constitution,* October 27, 1871; Atlanta *New Era,* December 7, 1871; Georgia General Assembly, *Acts and Resolutions . . . 1874* (Atlanta, 1874), no. 111, p. 119; *City Code, 1875,* ch. III, sec. 2; Atlanta *New Era,* November 12-13, December 8, 1870; and Atlanta *Constitution,* December 1, 9, 1870. The later defeat of two black candidates—Mitchell Cargile in 1879 and Augustus Thompson in 1880—who carried their own wards underscored the significance of the general-ticket system. Ibid., December 4, 1879; and December 2, 1880. Other southern cities at this time relied principally on the gerrymandering of ward boundaries, also done in Atlanta at this time. Howard N. Rabinowitz, "From Reconstruction to Redemption in the Urban South," *Journal of Urban History* (February, 1976), 169-94.

23. Atlanta *Constitution,* December 3, 1868; November 12, 16, 1896; Atlanta *New Era,* November 3-4, 10-13, 27, December 1, 8, 1870; Atlanta *Daily Sun,* November 12-15, 1870; and Atlanta *Constitution,* December 9, 1870.

24. Atlanta *New Era,* October 22, 24, December 7, 1871. The all-white Citizens' Ticket of 1872 supported by the Atlanta *Daily Herald* had a clear connection to the Republican party. Atlanta *Daily Herald,* November 16, 24, December 4, 1872; and Atlanta *Constitution,* November 26, 30, December 4, 1872; November 21, 23-24, 28, 30, December 1, 1875.

25. Wooten exaggerates the Republican appeal to white workers and mistakenly states that fourteen of nineteen Republican candidates for council in 1870 and 1871 were blue- and white-collar workers. Wooten, "New City of the South," 354. Republican city organizations also disappeared in other southern cities about this time. Rabinowitz, "Continuity and Change," 101.

26. C. Vann Woodward, *The Origins of the New South, 1877-1913* (Baton Rouge, 1951), 52. For similar interpretations regarding Atlanta, based on highly partisan newspaper accounts, see Russell, "Atlanta, Gate City of the South," 275-77; and Wooten, "New City of the South," 360-64.

27. Atlanta *Constitution*, November 7, 11-12, 17, 27, 1868; October 26, 31, 1869; November 11, 1870; October 22, 27-28, November 14, 16, December 4, 1871; Atlanta *Daily Herald,* October 2, 7-8, 1872; October 8, 1873; October 21, 1875; and Atlanta *Constitution,* November 21, 1875; November 14, 1868.

28. Ibid., November 2, 4, 7, 18, 21-24, 26, December 1, 3, 1869; Atlanta *Daily Intelligencer,* November 25, 28, December 1, 1869; Atlanta *Daily Sun,* November 11, 1870; Atlanta *New Era,* November 11, 1870; Atlanta *Constitution,* November 11, 27, December 1, 1870; Atlanta *Daily Intelligencer,* October 30-31, 1871; and Atlanta *Constitution,* December 6, 1871.

29. Atlanta *Daily Herald,* October 2, 7-8, 27, 1872; October 8, 11, 17-19, 25, 1873; Atlanta *Constitution,* October 7-11, 17, 22, 24, December 4, 1873; Russell, "Atlanta, Gate City of the South," 277-78.

30. Atlanta *Constitution,* September 13, 1874; Atlanta *Daily News,* October 10, 1874; Atlanta *Constitution,* October 16, 20, 1875; Atlanta *Daily Herald,* October 21, 1875; and Atlanta *Constitution,* September 12-13, 17, 1876.

31. Ibid., October 30, November 7, December 1, 4, 1877. For some earlier claims of rigged nominations, see Atlanta *Daily Herald,* October 8, 1872; Atlanta *Daily*

News, September 29, 1874; Atlanta *Daily Herald,* October 21, 1875; and Atlanta *Constitution,* October 4, 1876.

32. The Independent challenge to the Democratic party was widespread in Georgia at this time. See Alex Arnett, *The Populist Movement in Georgia* (New York, 1922), 33-45, for an account of this movement from 1874 to 1882. Members of both Democratic factions were not clearly identified by name or social position. The *Constitution* reported that the heavy black vote was about evenly divided for both sides. Atlanta *Constitution,* December 3-7, 1877.

33. Ibid., November 28, 30, December 1, 4-5, 1878.

34. Newspaper coverage of municipal campaigns, for no apparent reason, slackened considerably for several years after 1878. For brief accounts of campaigns, see ibid., November 30, December 1-4, 1879; November 20-21, 24, 28, 30, December 1-2, 1880; December 8, 1881; December 6-7, 1882; and November 18, 28-29, December 4-6, 1883.

35. The *Constitutions'* advocacy of greater participation by the "best people" had surfaced several years before (see ibid., November 10, 1879; December 1, 1880; and November 18, 1883), but was more determined in 1884. Ibid., August 6, November 23, December 2, 1884. The new city daily newspaper joined in the chorus. Atlanta *Journal,* November 27, 1884. It, no doubt, was not coincidental that this movement was conceived the year a new and more restrictive registration law took effect. *City Code, 1886,* ch. XLII, sec. 675. The authors of *The American Voter* have argued that "The psychological economy of the individual demands parties as an organizing principle, and if bereft of this, there might be more straightforward dependence on other groups. In situations of this sort, secondary groups with quite apolitical origins have in fact come to function as political parties." Angus Campbell et al., *The American Voter, An Abridgement* (New York, 1964), 182.

36. Atlanta *Constitution,* August 8, 1884.

37. Ibid., August 15, 1884.

38. Ibid., November 2, 1884; Atlanta *Journal,* November 4, 1884; Atlanta *Constitution,* November 2, 23, December 2, 1884; and Atlanta *Journal,* November 18, 21, 27, 1884.

39. Atlanta *Constitution,* December 3-4, 1884. Unfortunately, the changing configuration of Atlanta's few large, heterogeneous wards proscribe precise estimates of the size of black support for the Citizens' Ticket. Even after substantial realignment of boundaries in 1883, blacks reportedly maintained a narrow majority among registered voters in the Fourth Ward, which delivered a slight majority to the mayoral and one councilmanic contender on the Citizens' Ticket and to one aldermanic and five councilmanic contestants on the People's Ticket. That the mayoral candidate on the Citizens' Ticket garnered 69 percent of the votes across the city but only 51 percent in the Fourth Ward suggests that blacks may have been more likely than whites to vote for the People's Ticket. Challengers to the Citizens' Tickets in the 1880s, however, pinned their hopes for success on the solid support of black and white workers.

40. For a summary of the prohibition campaigns, read John Hammond Moore, "The Negro and Prohibition in Atlanta, 1885-1887," *South Atlantic Quarterly,* LXIX (Winter, 1970), 38-57. Moore and other writers uncritically accepted press

opinion regarding the central importance of prohibition in municipal politics, ignoring statements of other contemporaries that class and race were more fundamental. Rabinowitz, "Continuity and Change," 120, propogates this myth. See, for example, Atlanta *Journal,* November 4, December 2-3, 1885; and Atlanta *Constitution,* November 27, December 1-3, 1885; December 6, 1887.

41. Atlanta *Journal,* October 23, 27, 30, November 5-6, 29, December 2, 1886; and Atlanta *Constitution,* October 26-29, November 6, 25, 30, December 2, 1886. The response of black politicians to the citizens' movement is presented in Watts, "Black Political Progress," 275-76. The Knights were more successful in other southern cities at this time. Woodward, *Origins of the New South,* 228-32.

42. Atlanta *Constitution,* September 21-29, October 2-6, 9, 16-25, November 2, 15-16, 28, 30, December 2-4, 5-7, 1888. See Watts, "Black Political Progress," 279-81, for a discussion of black organization under auspices of the Republican party in this campaign.

43. Atlanta *Constitution,* November 2, 12, 14-17, 20-21, 24, December 4, 5, 1889.

44. The white primary was adopted in several cities at this time, including Nashville, Memphis, Jackson, and Chattanooga. See Rabinowitz, "Continuity and Change," 120. Rabinowitz, however, failed to note that support for this change in Atlanta came from the white working class and not from the "local elite."

45. Atlanta *Journal,* November 5, 7-8, 17, 18-20, 22, December 1-3, 1890; and Atlanta *Constitution,* November 9, 19-20, December 2-3, 1890.

46. Ibid., October 27-28, 30, November 3, 5, 10, 13, 22, 1891; Atlanta *Journal,* November 12, 1891; Bacote, "The Negro in Atlanta Politics," 336-37; Watts, "Black Political Progress," 283-84; and Savannah *Tribune,* August 6, November 12, 1892.

47. Atlanta *Constitution,* October 18, December 7-8, 1892; and Atlanta *Journal,* November 14-15, 1892. For a capsule description of Woodward, see Lucian Lamar Knight, *History of Fulton County, Georgia* (Atlanta, 1930), 167.

48. Atlanta *Constitution,* October 18-19, 21, 24-26, 28-31, November 1, 5, 7, 1893; and Atlanta *Journal,* October 14, November 1, 7-9, December 6-7, 1893. In 1894 the Executive Committee decided upon a white primary even though thirty members of the Chamber of Commerce tried to prevent the decision by organizing a nominating committee of one hundred. Their ticket and several others competed in the primary, but none won a clear victory. Ibid., August 7, 9-10, 16, 23, 1894; and Atlanta *Constitution,* September 13, October 2, 4, 1894.

49. Ibid., October 25, 28, November 30, December 3-5, 1895; and Atlanta *Journal,* October 25, November 14, 15, 18, 25-26, December 2-3, 1895. The *Constitution* thought it was curious that two blacks actually voted in the 1900 general election. Atlanta *Constitution,* December 6, 1900. Black voters briefly returned as an important force in the 1908 municipal election that momentarily abrogated the white primary's decisive influence. *The Outlook,* 90, December 19, 1908, 848.

50. Atlanta *Journal,* July 28, 1896. Party considerations, in spite of the Populist challenge and continued efforts of Atlanta Republicans in state and national elections, were irrelevant in the primaries throughout this period. The City Executive Committee at the turn of the century, when confronted by the question whether a

"white Democratic primary" or a "white primary" would be held, reaffirmed that national party politics had no connection with city elections. Atlanta *Constitution,* September 15, 1900. Also see Atlanta *Journal,* October 6, 1904.

51. Atlanta *Constitution,* November 6, 1877; *City Code, 1899,* ch. II, sec. 26; Atlanta *Journal,* August 10, 11, 1896; and Watts, "The Police in Atlanta," 165-82.

52. Atlanta *New Era,* December 5, 1866; and Atlanta *Constitution,* October 7, 1897. The character of the canvass often provoked the ire of the press and other citizens. See ibid., October 30, 1875; November 27, 1878; and November 30, 1879.

53. *City Code, 1875,* ch. XXXIX, sec. 331. Charles Collier, candidate for mayor in 1896, made this charge against his opponent, Albert Howell. Atlanta *Journal,* August 22, 1896.

54. Atlanta *Constitution,* November 26, 1869; November 29, 1883; Atlanta *Journal,* November 21, 1884; Atlanta *Constitution,* November 28, 1888; and Atlanta *New Era,* December 5, 1870.

55. Issues in Atlanta were common to local politics in the South. See Woodward, *The Origins of the New South,* 58-9, 79-85, 171. Certain matters were debated among candidates, such as what should be done about the Peters Street viaduct, or the selling of Ogletree Park, or cutting off city water to Clark University. No one issue completely dominated any campaign, however, including contests that featured prohibition. The extent of obfuscation on the street railway question in 1901 was captured in this remark by Mayor Livingston Mims, "Competition!— How much miserable devilment has been done in thy name!" Atlanta *Journal,* September 25, 1901.

56. Candidates were first assessed for costs of the white primary in 1896, and many complained that the fees were too high. Ibid., July 28, August 14, August 24, 1896; Atlanta *Constitution*, September 15, 1900; September 19, 23, 1901; and Atlanta *Journal,* September 19, 1902; September 16, 1903.

57. Atlanta *Constitution,* December 8, 1887; Atlanta *New Era,* November 30, 1866; and Atlanta *Constitution,* December 5, 1878; December 7, 1882; December 7, 1887. In 1896 workingmen notified candidates that the union label had to be on their tickets to capture their support, and nearly all candidates complied with this demand. Atlanta *Journal,* August 8, 1896.

58. Ibid., August 20, 1896; Atlanta *Constitution,* August 15, October 5-6, 1898; Atlanta *Journal,* October 5, 1899; and Atlanta *Constitution,* September 18, 1903.

59. The Democratic and white citizens' primaries used the same polling places as those regularly authorized by the city. Atlanta *Daily Intelligencer,* February 8, 1867; *City Code, 1873,* ch. XXIII, sec. 306; *City Code, 1875,* ch. XXV, sec. 237; *City Code, 1886;* ch. XXIII, sec. 405; *City Code, 1891;* ch. XXIV, sec. 537; and *City Code,* 1899, ch. III, sec. 333. General elections were held on weekdays, from 7:00 a.m. to 6:00 p.m. Primary elections in the late 1860s and early 1870s often were held at night, and sometimes on Saturdays, but these elections imitated rules for regular elections in the 1890s, as they were required by law in 1891. Georgia General Assembly, *Acts and Resolutions . . . 1891* (Atlanta, 1892), no. 778, pp. 210-11. For one bitter debate over the time for voting, see Atlanta *Constitution,* November 14, 1868.

60. Atlanta *Journal,* December 5, 1883; Atlanta *New Era,* December 6, 1866; and Atlanta *Constitution,* December 7, 1882; December 6, 1883.

61. Ibid., December 7, 1888.

62. Ibid., July 22, November 21, 1890; December 3, 1891; Atlanta *Journal,* July 8, August 27, 1896; Atlanta *Constitution,* September 25, 1900; and Atlanta *Journal,* October 1, 1902. Some poll workers were friends and supporters of candidates presumably working for free. This was not the case with a related political activist—the ward heeler—who simply worked for pay. See Atlanta *Journal,* August 24, 1896.

3

Social Components of Atlanta's Political Culture

Judging from contemporary opinion, citizens' attitudes toward candidate characteristics constituted one of the most important components of Atlanta's political culture, often deciding the outcome of elections. Indeed, the attributes of political aspirants were more easily identifiable and became as much if not more a point of contention than other elements of political discourse. The speeches and statements of candidates and their supporters, the comments and demands of citizens at nominating meetings and political rallies, and the analyses and reporting of newspaper and other commentators repeatedly referred to these attributes in the appraisal of campaigns and elections. Another indicator of the political importance of these characteristics was the various "Communications," "Cards," and "Notices" published in the press, often by anonymous sources such as "A Tax-Payer" or "Many Citizens," which urged support for particular candidates. These brief, bold-faced announcements appeared in the newspapers just before the election. Examples of such advertisements are given below in the discussion of each variable, but one illustration, referring to the previous political experience of a perennial candidate, is appropriate here:

> Frank P. Rice is no novice in city government. He will
> go into the Mayor's office fully equipped in every respect.[1]

In addition to these appeals on the behalf of aspirants, the press often prepared more "factual" biographical sketches of candidates. Presentation of this information indicates possible reader interest.

> Jones, the nominee for alderman, is an old citizen, a man
> of public spirit and executive ability.[2]

Possession of certain characteristics, such as maturity or a long identification with the city, often was considered politically important or desirable in itself, without further argument or explanation. During this
period several qualities, such as occupation, also demarcated self-conscious
groups, and the political salience of a characteristic is often high when a
candidate is recognized as a fellow member of a group. Other characteristics, such as age, did not define actual "groups" so clearly, but certainly
divided the office-seekers in a meaningful way.[3] Differences among contestants based on such attributes formed real and concrete issues that
allegedly influenced voter choices. Some attributes also had functional
significance. For example, those candidates with political experience or
large property-holdings conceivably could wage more effective campaigns
as well as be considered those most or least fit for public position.

As mentioned in chapter one, eight social characteristics—occupation,
amount of property, race, ethnic background and region of birth, residence, period of arrival, length of residence in the city, and age—and
three political variables—prior political experience in municipal appointive
offices, previous membership on either city executive committees (partisan or nonpartisan) or citizens' nominating committees, and previous
campaigns were chosen.

These attributes were selected for the theoretical or postulated
likelihood of their importance, the frequent contemporary mention of
their significance, and the possibility of their documentation. This last
point provides a greater limitation upon historians than upon students
of present-day politics since the availability of evidence varies widely.
Several other characteristics were initially included in the research design,
but problems in data collection precluded their evaluation for a sufficient
number of candidates. Although attributes such as religion, membership
in fraternal organizations, and military service during the Civil War received mention during city campaigns, none attained the frequency given
the social variables that are included. Others, such as education and membership in one or more exclusive social organizations, were rarely discussed by Atlantans. These characteristics had to be dropped from consideration, since such data could be gathered only for a relatively few
people, generally the most well-known and socially prominent.[4] It is

commonly the case that many things are known about some candidates and almost nothing about others, and different information generally is available for each contestant. Although not a happy situation, it is a necessary one. Nonetheless, the variables considered certainly can be examined for their political significance even if others cannot.[5] Moreover, the eleven characteristics used in this study were the most politically visible in late nineteenth-century Atlanta.

Other problems besides unrecoverable data must be considered to analyze these attributes. Even though the selected characteristics may have political significance, the construction of categories in the analysis might disguise the true situation.[6] For example, occupation might have been significant in the electoral process, but the way certain jobs are categorized could hide the association. Also, in rare cases it may be more important to know that an office-seeker was a carpenter in the employ of a politically important person than that he was a skilled worker. Nevertheless, to describe the political participation and performance of hundreds of people, historians are forced to classify. Retention of information on specific occupations would not only make systematic analysis impossible, but would be incompatible with the historical situation. In Atlanta workers' organizations did not want a carpenter to represent them but someone from the working class; residents from the north end of a ward did not want a councilman from a particular address but someone from their general area.[7]

Another problem is whether the surviving historical record may be an unreliable indicator of attitudes and beliefs. All of these characteristics could have been part of the posited social filter but in ways that could not be deduced from conventional historical sources. There is, of course, good reason to suspect some statements of contemporaries. Politicians often attempt to present a picture favorable to their cause, and their pronouncements and newspaper editorials could have been deliberately self-serving and misleading. It is also possible that they were unknowingly wrong, as, for example, in the oft-stated claim that the citizenry preferred public officials who were men of property. A related and larger difficulty with reconstructing from traditional sources the ideational patterns regarding the social filter is that disagreement was the hallmark of Atlanta politics, and conflicting opinions on the value of certain attributes were standard. Some Atlantans espoused the virtues of a younger contestant, and others championed the desirability of a more mature man. Counting the frequency of such statements to measure contemporary evaluations is of little worth.

Analysis of the behavior of Atlanta's voters provides a better guide to past public opinion.[8] Examination of the preferences of the electorate for certain types of office-seekers over a fairly long sweep of Atlanta's history suggests what kind of attributes were valued in local politics. Information presented in this chapter, therefore, should be evaluated with the actual description of the candidates and the analysis of the relationship between their characteristics and political success in subsequent chapters. The concept of the social filter is the theoretical bridge connecting candidacy, political performance, and contemporary attitudes.[9] Examining the eleven characteristics individually constitutes the first stage in the analysis of the social bases of Atlanta politics, establishing the grounds for later comparison between beliefs and behavior.

OCCUPATION

By far the most frequently mentioned characteristic, the occupation of an office-seeker was often cited as if it had a distinct relevance to the campaign. The newspapers rarely failed to connect a contestant to his job or general class standing, and candidates and their friends and supporters also frequently noted this attribute in their public speeches and various published "communications."

Thus J. S. Garmany was the "candidate of the mechanics and the laboring men of Atlanta" in 1874, and D. A. McDuffie was the "workingmen's candidate" in the following year. In 1878 E. A. Baldwin was described as a ". . . mechanic, one of the town boys, and ready at any moment to support the old flag and an appropriation for the fire department." According to the newspaper, "such a combination in city politics is hard to beat." The anonymous announcements, signed by "Many Working Men" or "A Mechanic" in support of a candidate who also was a worker, were almost as numerous as those in support of the "Friend of the Workingmen"—who could have been, as was often the case, a lawyer or businessman. Class seemed so important in Atlanta politics that candidates from the upper reaches of society frequently tried to assume affiliation with the lower classes to attract voters. Such a theme was captured in this 1902 campaign advertisement: "Who is Labor's best friend?

The man who creates for it new and larger opportunities. That is what
Evan P. Howell has done for the workingmen of Atlanta. That is what
he will do as mayor."[10]

Frequently announcements supporting candidates drew attention to
business experience to demonstrate fitness for office. A recommendation
in behalf of O. H. Jones for alderman in 1875 read: "One of the best as-
surances that he will manage the affairs of the city well is in the fact that
he has managed his own business well." A letter to the editor in support
of H. I. Kimball for mayor in 1880 emphasized his business ability and
reminded the *Constitution:* "In your editorial on the 'mayoralty question'
you advise the people 'to vote for the man to manage the affairs of the
city to whom they would trust their own business.'" A supporter of J. L.
Richmond wrote to the *Constitution* in 1883, pointing out that the council post Richmond was seeking was being vacated by a businessman, and
asked: "Is it not right that his successor should also be a businessman. . .?"
Both Richmond's opponent and the continuing councilman from that
ward were lawyers, and the writer felt that ". . . two lawyers at the same
time from the same ward is not just to the many other vocations."[11]

The relationship among occupation and candidacy and election demands investigation in the study of Atlanta politics for reasons other than
frequent contemporary reference. Overt class conflict was a regular feature
of city politics, and the most visible variable in this regard was the vocation of office-seekers. Workers, a loosely defined term in the press, were
an organized force in city politics from the days of Labor Union No. 1 in
1869 to the Industrial Union Council and the Atlanta Federation of
Trades in the 1890s. Political organizations not created specifically for
the betterment of workers, such as the Mutual Aid Brotherhood and the
American Protective Association, were described as partaking of a strong
labor identification. One of the major concerns of such groups, as well
as of those workers who crowded into the various nominating meetings
of the period, was the direct representation of workingmen in municipal
office. To cite just one example, a "great many mechanics were in the
company" for a citizens' meeting in 1884, where a "representative of
several labor organizations" insisted on the nomination of candidates from
the working class. When this demand was not met, a "meeting of citizens
representing the labor interest of the city" adopted a resolution saying:
"The laboring and working element of the city do not feel that their interests have been regarded, or will be sufficiently protected, and that

many of the persons proposed are not in sympathy with them. . . ." One
of the two tickets contested for city office that year was "specially put
in the field by the labor organizations."[12]

Businessmen seemed equally insistent upon nominating and electing
men from their ranks. In 1896, for example, the Atlanta *Journal* approvingly reported that businessmen were "determined to make the next municipal council a body of business men." The leader of this group declared:
". . . We want representative business men . . . securing a dignified, busi-
ness-like administration of the city's affairs." One constant theme throughout the period expressed the propriety, if not the right, of the upper occupational class to control city government. Frequently the Atlanta press
was the leading proponent of this position. In 1871 the Atlanta *New Era*
bluntly suggested: "Let us choose the best businessmen. . . ." The Atlanta
Constitution, in a typical editorial statement, declared in 1888 that "The
governing of the city is a business. . . . Therefore in voting for your officers, vote precisely as you would vote if you were selecting men to manage your own business. . . ."[13]

This idea, of course, has a long and respectable lineage in American
politics. The frequent reiteration of this sentiment in Atlanta suggests this
notion received widespread acceptance. Atlanta's political aspirants thus
would parallel those of other cities examined for this period. Occupation
has been a prominent variable in all studies of public officials, primarily
because it often has been assumed that the most useful indicator of social
status is occupation, and that such status plays an important role in the
political process. The "overrepresentation" of upper occupational groups,
relative to their proportion in the population, is well established; to what
extent was this true in Atlanta in the late nineteenth century?[14]

To assess the alleged significance of occupation requires the description
of all candidates according to this characteristic and the analysis of its
association with political success. To undertake this dual task, scores of
diverse occupations were distilled into meaningful groupings. The examination of such sources as newspapers led to the impression that only a
few broad categories of occupation had political relevance in Atlanta.
Although complete agreement upon classification schemes for occupation rarely exists, other writers have agreed generally on some conventional categories, and these basically conform to the contemporary record.
Thus occupation was divided into these commonly used classifications:
professional (doctor, lawyer), proprietor (businessman, official, manager),

clerical employees, and blue-collar workers (skilled, semiskilled, and unskilled).[15]

PROPERTY

From 1865 through 1903, the amount of property owned by candidates was a commonly discussed political topic. According to the newspapers and other contemporary commentators, property ownership, presumably the more the better, was a sign of suitability for public office.
Those candidates with the "most stake" in the community, and thus
those who paid the most taxes, at times were portrayed as the only people
fit to rule in Atlanta. An Atlantan writing in favor of W. H. Brotherton
for alderman in 1883 stated, "That he is a freeholder and a heavy tax-
payer; therefore a fit guardian for the property interests of our citizens
. . . ." A card from a candidate for council in 1900 provided an interesting viewpoint: "Judge Kontz says that he has no apology to offer for
having some taxable property which would cause him to bear some share
of the burden he might as councilman place on others." A more direct
advertisement for another candidate in the same year stated: "Vote for
Branch Lewis. . . . He has property to be taxed in the city." Few decisions
of city government fail to involve property rights in some way or another,
and political appeals in Atlanta, and in the South generally at this time,
frequently and forthrightly advocated the political advancement of the
propertied class.[16]

Most expressions, in fact, echoed this sentiment, but not all Atlantans
agreed. Mayor James E. Williams declared in 1867 that "more people
than the property holders have a right in public movements." An opponent of the Citizens' Ticket in 1884 objected that apparently "a reform
in municipal matters means only the selection of men of wealth to ad-
minister the affairs of the city." A detractor of a later Citizens' Ticket,
in 1888, argued that members of the slate paid taxes on $500,000 worth
of city property. Other Atlantans worried about the consequences of a
democratic system when the lower classes held such sentiments. In 1892
the *Constitution* supported J. B. Goodwin instead of James G. Woodward
for mayor at least partly because of Goodwin's considerably greater property-holdings. The paper also issued this strange warning to voters without
property:

It may happen that men who have no property will feel that
they are free to vote according to their prejudices. . . . But
they could not make a more serious error. Management in
municipal matters. . .falls more heavily on those who are poor
than on the rich. . . .It is the poorer classes . . . who are ground
beneath the heels of the city tax collector.[17]

As this passage suggests, a prominent indicator of class or social position in Atlanta was the amount of property ownership. Indeed, an individual's property, albeit an imperfect indicator of wealth, was perhaps
a better key to socioeconomic status and prestige than occupation. Professional men and businessmen could vary widely in wealth, but people
with large amounts of property more clearly represented a certain type
of professional man or businessman. Conflict between "classes" in Atlanta
politics was expressed as a battle between the rich and the poor, although
no specific level of property-holdings was suggested by Atlantans as an
appropriate demarcation point. In 1873, for example, the editors of the
Atlanta *Daily Herald* lamented: "There is a vast amount of this sort of
stuff being bandied about, the object being to create an impression on the
minds of the poorer classes that all the disaffection in the Democratic party
comes from wealthy men who aim to keep poor men out of office." Such
conflict was frequently heralded in Atlanta city politics, and unquestion-
ably was an overriding matter for some participants. The later investigation of the amounts of property owned by office-seekers and its relationship to political success indicates the nature and outcome of the struggle.[18]
Wealth also has a functional importance, since individuals with more
financial resources can wage more expensive and effective campaigns.
Campaign expenses could include the costs of advertisements and the
printing of tickets, the payment of poll workers and the hiring of carriages,
and, later in the period, actual campaign assessments. These kinds of costs
were discussed in a *Constitution* editorial in 1878: "It now means business to run for office, and it is fast approaching a point in politics when a
poor man will have no showing whatsoever. It will depend more on money
than the merit of the candidate." Men of wealth also had more subtle
means of influencing elections. Charges of bribing voters were frequently
hurled during Atlanta contests. Walter Brown, a candidate for mayor in
1888, claimed that one carriage used by his opponent to cart voters to the
polls was popularly called the "pay train."[19]

The exact amount of a candidate's property, both real and personal, is used for most of the analysis. For some purposes, however, classification of this characteristic is helpful. Unfortunately, contemporary sources provide no clue to what level of property-holding separated larger and smaller owners. The quartiles of the frequency distribution of property owned by all candidates in the period, which divide contestants into four numerically equal groups ranked from lowest to highest, are taken as a useful and conventional cutting point for analysis. Other distinctions include those candidates who owned no property and the *economic elite,* defined as those whose property holdings placed them in the top 10 percent of all candidates by this criterion.[20]

RACE

The issue of race, which, like that of class, was an important part of city politics, was featured in the preceeding chapter and has been discussed in detail in other studies.[21] Here it is sufficient to recall that black Atlantans attempted organization for municipal contests, and that a major goal was direct representation in city office. The black proportion of registered voters ranged from 10 percent to 39 percent, and a number of black politicians enjoyed high visibility in the political arena. White Atlantans could tolerate, and even solicit, black ballots for most of the period, but they never conceded that Afro-Americans were full participants in the political process. The white majority always opposed a black voice in the actual administration of city affairs and especially representation in city office.

This characteristic obviously defined two self-conscious social groups. Consequently, whenever black men competed for city office, their race was called to the attention of the electorate. Perhaps the clearest example occurred in the 1879 contest. Mitchell Cargile, a black man competing against three white opponents, had been heralded as the likely winner. In response to this threat a multitude of cards published in the press urged voters to support the apparent white frontrunner, using as the argument: "This is the only way to defeat Cargile, colored." The *Constitution,* commenting on the 1880 campaign of David Mapp, stated: "The city will not have a colored Mapp in the council room."[22]

If the color of a black candidate's skin disturbed whites, it nevertheless seemed to whet the political appetites of blacks. Republican voters, a synonym for blacks in Atlanta, marched firmly and solidly to the ballot box in 1870 and elected two black men to city office. In 1874 the *Constitution* decried the alleged "assaults by negroes upon the negroes that vote or express a desire to vote the democratic ticket." According to this paper, "The colored churches, societies, schools, and all the humble but potent social machinery of the colored population have been openly used to intimidate the negroes who desired to vote against radicalism."Black voters in the 1878 campaign reportedly favored a white worker, B. F. Longley, for councilman from the Fourth Ward, but the late announcement of W. H. Bird, a black Atlantan, considerably weakened this prior attachment. In that same campaign, "A Citizen" published this blurb in the paper: "Vote for W. W. Wall, the white man's candidate for councilman from the fifth ward," even though all of Wall's opponents were white. The *Constitution* in 1879 explained that blacks voted in large numbers because of the candidacies of Cargile and William Finch for council, but "the negroes did not vote solidly for either him [Cargile] or Finch, many of the most influential politicians among them being engaged for other candidates." Both black men received roughly the same number of ballots per ward, and contrary to the claims of the newspaper, the size of the vote strongly suggested blacks solidly supported both men. Cargile in 1879 and Augustus Thompson in the next year both carried their own wards, a fact that underscored the significance of the general-ticket system in city elections.[23]

Black politicians were more insistent in their demands for direct representation in the 1880s, and even in the next decade, when blacks were no longer a potent political force in Atlanta, this desire was expressed. The Negro Press Association of Georgia, meeting in Atlanta in 1892, advised blacks to refuse to support any ticket that "failed to recognize that Negroes were entitled to representation in public office." In 1894 Rev. E. R. Carter wrote on black political aspirations: "All he asks is a citizen's privilege, the rights of a tax-payer and free access to the public positions of the city." Carter also complained that black Atlantans had "so little recognition in the government of the city."[24]

REGIONAL-ETHNIC BACKGROUND

Four categories were considered for the regional-ethnic attribute: birth in Georgia, in the South other than Georgia, in states outside the South (no candidate came from states west of the Mississippi), and in foreign countries. Birth in Atlanta also may have been politically significant, and certainly some candidates were advertised this way, but for most cases this could not be determined.[25]

One crucial distinction among these categories appeared to have been identification with the South by birth and at times an even more specific connection to Georgian birth. This characteristic sometimes seemed to define Southerners as a conscious social group, and single out one or more negative reference groups—Northerners or foreigners. Candidates born in northern states are of special interest in the post-Civil War South, since they often have been portrayed as speculators and carpetbaggers coming to the city in the wake of war either to seek their fortunes or to further their political ambitions. It seemed reasonable to assume that candidates from the North would have had different opportunities for political success than those with bona fide Southern pedigrees, if only because the antipathy of native Southerners to the carpetbaggers is part of our political folklore.[26]

Northern birth was mentioned in the biographical sketches of candidates provided by the press and at times during city campaigns. For example, during the 1874 campaign, the *Constitution,* in support of C. C. Hammock, stressed the point that he was a "native Georgian" and his opponent, N. L. Angier, was from New Hampshire. Even so, northern birth did not appear to have been a major issue in Atlanta politics. Perhaps the reason for this was that native Southerners so dominated campaigns for city office that there was little reason for controversy. Careful inspection of the empirical evidence will clarify this situation. Moreover, analysis of the reactions of the electorate, as judged by their voting, will determine if they differed from the responses of their more articulate leaders.[27]

Foreign birth often denotes self-conscious groups in American politics. Robert Dahl, in his study of New Haven, concluded that immigrant office-holders rose to political power on the strength of numbers and political consciousness of their compatriots. Donald Bradley and Mayer Zald, in their investigation of Chicago's mayors, supported this finding. Unlike these cities, however, Atlanta had a very small ethnic population and thus no base upon which candidates sharing the same foreign background could build a political following. In Atlanta, therefore, as elsewhere in the South, the potential functional significance of this factor was minimal. In 1870, however, a card signed by "Many German Citizens" stated: "The German citizens of Atlanta . . . consider themselves entitled to representation in the City Council by one of their own countrymen, and propose to the nominating parties the name of Dr. Ch. Rauschenberg. . . ." Two years later the Citizens Reform Club, a group of foreign-born Atlantans who organized regardless of "wealth, religion or nationality," attempted to persuade both Democrats and Republicans to include members of the city's immigrant population on tickets for city office.[28]

The biographical sketches of candidates in the newspapers sometimes identified ethnic background, and this information alone indicates that barely a handful of foreign-born men ever competed for city office. The 1874 contest experienced an outbreak of "Know-Nothingism" aimed at John H. Flynn, a northern-born Catholic of Irish descent, and Aaron Haas, a German-born Jew. The Atlanta *Daily News* attacked this "bigotry and intolerance" and denounced "anything like a war upon individuals because of their nationality or religion." In 1890 a speaker at a political gathering was widely chastised and labeled a "Know-Nothing" for his attack on P. J. Moran, a Canadian-born man of obvious Irish descent, as an "outsider" who should not be elected. Although the American Protective Association (APA) in Atlanta during the 1890s was not openly nativist, Irish Catholics reportedly joined together in the 1895 campaign to defeat the alleged APA ticket.[29]

Despite these examples, Atlanta was not notable for its nativism. Ann Mebane, in her study of Atlanta's immigrants, noted a high level of assimilation of the foreign-born into the city's culture, especially through intermarriage. Richard Hopkins, in his analysis of occupational mobility in Atlanta, convincingly demonstrated that immigrants persisted and advanced upward in much the same manner as native-born whites. Furthermore, several immigration societies were organized in Atlanta during the late 1860s and 1870s to attract foreign migrants to the Gate City of the South. The political campaigns and success of those individuals with a discernible ethnic background later provides additional evidence on the acceptance of such people in a Southern city.[30]

RESIDENCE

A candidate's residence was important in city politics since crucial questions included the placement of sewers, the location of paved streets, and fire and liquor limits. This, perhaps, was particularly true in Atlanta, where a few irregular wedge-shaped wards, carved from the circular city, were so large and heterogeneous that the election of ward representatives gave residents of certain areas good cause to complain. Comments concerning the residence of candidates, either by disgruntled citizens or candidates seeking to improve their own chances, were regular features of Atlanta political campaigns.

Typical of the appeals for equality in representation among sections of wards was this 1883 letter written by "Fair Play" in support of Jerome McAfee: ". . . he comes from a section of the ward which has had no representation in the general council since 1878, and as the holding over member is from the opposite extreme of the ward, fair play would seem to suggest that the other section should now be recognized." Such consideration was shown at a nomination meeting in 1885, when "Mr. Greene's part of the ward conceded that it was just that Mr. Maddox's end should have the representation." This courtesy was not extended in 1889, when opposition to Porter King in the Sixth Ward came "from the northwest portion of the ward, and the people out there say they are entitled to a representative because they never had one."[31]

Often more than fair play was involved. An irate citizen in 1885 made this connection: "We have not had representation. There is a place in four hundred yards of this place where a man can't live for the filth and stench." J. P. Trotti, in announcing his candidacy in 1888, declared: "The people are tired of putting in men from the other end of the first ward all the time. . . . It is high time the people in this part of the ward have a councilman to represent them and have their streets fixed up." In these and other instances this attribute apparently assumed paramount importance for at least some citizens.[32]

The investigation of the overall pattern of candidates' residences and the relationship between them and political success are important for other reasons. The population was heavily concentrated in the center of Atlanta early in the period, and gradually became more dispersed towards the city limits by the turn of the century. If representation were connected to human geography, the areas in which candidates lived would follow the same pattern of dispersion. James Russell, at least indirectly, suggests another possible line of inquiry. His general portrait of Atlanta, from 1848 to 1885, shows that the well-to-do inhabited the center area of the city, where rents were high and property expensive, while the poor, both white workers and blacks, lived nearer to the city's boundary, where

building costs and rents were much cheaper. This situation changed somewhat after 1885, when many wealthier Atlantans had either moved
towards the limits or lived in substantial suburban areas annexed by the
city. This clearly was the case along South Pryor and North Peachtree
streets, and in the fashionable West End area. In this situation, the residence area of candidates may have had another dimension.[33]

Finally, other writers, including Howard Chudacoff for Omaha and
Zane Miller for Cincinnati, have suggested that important differences in
urban politics were associated with the inner and outer belts of cities.
Although most such arguments hinged upon political party preference
and voting patterns, and thus do not coincide with the concerns of this
study, the questions raised are important ones. Were there significant
differences between candidates who lived in the center and those who
lived in the outskirts of Atlanta? Since contemporary discussion emphasized distinctions between the inner and outer reaches of wards, Atlanta, for purposes of this study, was divided into two such areas, approximately equal in area, by defining the core as a three-quarters of a mile
radius from the exact center of the city—the Union Depot.[34]

PERIOD OF ARRIVAL AND LENGTH OF RESIDENCE

The characteristic identified as period of arrival and length of residence
as reflected in the discussions and campaign advertisements of contemporaries, appeared to have been a very desirable quality for Atlanta's political aspirants. Indeed, few dissenting voices could be found to the notion
that a long identification with the city and its interests was an important
attribute of public officials. In a functional sense, people who resided in
the city for a considerable period would have greater opportunity to become known to more people and especially to influential political figures.
Very likely, citizens might feel their representatives should be knowledge-
able concerning the city's problems and that a reasonable term of residence would provide this.

Candidates often boasted, when possible, that they were "long identified with the city." A letter to the *Constitution* in 1878 from W. A. Fuller,
a candidate for council, stated: "I have been living in the city twenty-five
years, and am thoroughly identified with all her interests." Frank P. Rice,
in a communication to the press in 1900, observed that he "has lived in
Atlanta for over 50 years." The newspaper vignettes of candidates also
generally mentioned this characteristic. For example, the *Constitution*

in 1878 described J. J. Lynch as "the son of an old and worthy citizen of Atlanta, who has lived among us for a number of years." To some extent this attribute seemed to signify continuity with the past and a personal attachment to the city as well as the implication of greater knowledge of the city's affairs.[35]

A long period of residence helped to establish credentials for office, but a deficiency in this regard put relative newcomers on the defensive. The Atlanta *Constitution* in 1868 replied to an "unjust" attack on several candidates for their insufficient identification with the city. The paper acknowledged they had not been citizens of Atlanta before the war, but it pointed out that half of the present population also were recent arrivals. When Harry C. Stockdell, a candidate for alderman in 1883, was criticized on this score, a rejoinder stated he had been a "permanent resident of our city for the past ten years, and is thoroughly identified with every interest in the city. . . ." When the eligibility of Martin F. Amorous, in 1902, was challenged because he had a legal residence in another county, he pointed out that he also maintained a home in the city, and stated: "I came to Atlanta more than 25 years ago." His response indicated more than eligibility was at stake.[36]

Length of residence is measured in two ways for this study. When Atlantans mentioned earlier days they meant either the prewar years or at least the 1860s when Atlanta began to rebuild after the devastation of war. People who arrived in Atlanta before 1870, therefore, could lay claim to being founders of the "Capitol of the New South." Thus the distinction between those who could be considered early settlers and those who came late to the city first indicates cohort groups whose social position and political performance may have differed in interesting ways. For example, did the early settlers who sought city office resemble the "patrician elite" discussed by Dahl for New Haven? Second, since this measure of length of residence indicated one thing at the beginning of the period and quite another toward the turn of the century, an invariable and finer measure is needed to distinguish between newcomers and more established citizens. A period of ten years was deemed sufficient to identify these two groups.[37]

AGE

The variable of age is one that can be appreciated almost intuitively as having potential importance in politics. The analysis of the distribution of this characteristic among candidates generally and public officials in particular often reveals a great deal about the practice of politics. The Atlanta *Daily Herald,* in attacking the boisterous city contest of 1873, suggested a relationship between age and the conduct of campaigns: ". . . to such an extent has this thing been carried out that it has been almost impossible to get the older and more conservative citizens to take any part in municipal campaigns at all." The emphasis in the 1880s on recruiting the "best citizens" for city office also might be reflected in the greater age of candidates, since in some degree wealth and social position are functions of age. Thus the analysis of the age of candidates indicates aspects of Atlanta's political system that have definite interest for the historian.[38]

In some political cultures, and perhaps in Atlanta, the attribute of older (or younger) age is intrinsically important: for example, the belief that it is "right and proper" that the elders should rule. A person's age can denote a variety of contradictory qualities in an ideational structure, such as experience, innocence, wisdom, senility, stability, and rigidity. The ages of candidates were almost always included in the biographical summaries of the newspapers, and at times this characteristic was mentioned during campaigns, including complaints that certain candidates were either too young or too old. After the 1878 contest, the *Constitution* explained the defeat of an older man, who had not been able to be very active in the campaign, by saying that "the younger bucks rather got the 'age' on him." A supporter of John B. Goodwin for mayor in 1882 admitted his choice "is a young man, but Atlanta is a young city."[39]

Generally, letters in support of candidates that discussed this attribute emphasized youth. A communication favoring C. W. Smith in the 1883 campaign pointed out that "He is a young lawyer of twenty-eight years of age. . . ." In 1897 D. N. McCullough, addressing a meeting of citizens, emphasized that he belonged to that class of young men who had made Atlanta and that it was the "day of young men." His opponent, also at that meeting, replied that he was a "young" fifty-eight years old. Three years later, the campaign cry of McCullough was "Give a young man a showing." Also in 1897, the Liberal Club, whose ostensible purpose was to support young men for city office, achieved considerable prominence.[40]

Although the actual age for each candidate is maintained in the analysis, the classification of this attribute into categories is also useful. Unfortunately, such groupings are not self-evident, and contemporaries did not provide any hard clues. As in the case for property, the quartiles of the age distribution of all candidates during this period are used to establish four strata and to distinguish between older and younger office-seekers.[41]

MINOR CITY OFFICEHOLDING

The first of three measures of political experience and exposure in Atlanta politics is minor city officeholding. This particular variable measures political experience as the number of times a candidate for mayor, alderman, or councilman had held lesser city positions before his campaign. In Atlanta this included offices such as treasurer, engineer, and recorder and membership on administrative boards such as the Board of Education and Board of Police Commissioners. For most of the period, such officeholders were appointed by the General Council and thus were subordinate to it.[42]

The possibility that such experience constituted an apprenticeship for the major city offices and thus formed a major path of political recruitment in Atlanta is an important line of inquiry, particularly in comparative analysis. It appears almost axiomatic that cities whose major public officials rise through the ranks have political systems that differ significantly from cities where this process does not occur. Certainly the factor of previous experience looms larger in the former instance. This attribute also helps to define politicians with multidimensional political interests. The key question, then, is did such people differ in their social characteristics and political performance from other candidates. Another matter of interest is the inclusion or exclusion of certain social groups from these positions, or whether certain types of candidates were more or less likely to have had such political opportunities or interests.

Only an occasional discussion of this factor could be found in the press. In 1874 the *Constitution* stated it was pleased to support J. W. Goldsmith for councilman since he had been city treasurer and thus was acquainted with financial matters. The Atlanta *Journal,* in its description of candidates in the 1897 contest, acknowledged that W. S. Thomson was new to city campaigns, but that he had served on the Board of Education. This kind of experience sometimes was mentioned in the biographical summaries, but never seemed to have been an issue in city elections. Of course, in this case as well as others, the general electorate may have responded to attributes that were not publicized in the press. Nevertheless, the analysis of this factor represents an attempt to go beyond what traditional sources suggested was important politically.[43]

MEMBERSHIP ON POLITICAL COMMITTEES

Unlike the other characteristics, membership on political committees is specifically connected to the Atlanta context. The intent is generally to examine the political significance of prior membership on party or independent citizens' committees involved in the nomination process, and particularly to judge the access of certain types of candidates to these powerful organizations. One important committee was the City Executive Committee. Early in the period this was an integral part of the Democratic and Republican party structure. It disappeared with the demise of party politics in the 1870s but a similar body, identical in name, was created by the citizens' reform movement of the 1880s. By the next decade it had achieved its own legitimacy in city politics. This City Executive Committee was an extremely influential body; it could, for example, decide the form of nominations. Membership on this committee almost always resulted from some type of election, either by ward clubs and committees, citizens at large mass meetings, or by the electorate directly during a primary contest.[44]

Citizens' nominating committees were another political organization of major importance in Atlanta. Their function was to select a unified slate for city office that all or at least most Atlantans would support. At times these nominating committees were self-constituted, especially early in the era, but by the 1880s, the period of their greatest influence, members generally were elected by citizens in large meetings. Only committees that commanded a wide support, held open meetings, and submitted their choices to some form of ratification process were considered in this study; ad hoc groups of individuals such as the Atlanta Liquor Dealer's Association or the 1890 Club were not included.[45]

Membership on both the City Executive Committee and on citizens' nominating committees indicates prior political experience for candidates that might have been important in the electoral process. The holding of such positions could denote the esteem in which individuals were held, the power or influence they commanded, or, when elected, the vote-getting appeal they possessed. Individuals could make important political contacts and perhaps later on could collect political debts. Some persons might have been able to arrange their own nominations. A speaker at a political meeting in 1876 observed that "There has been considerable comment upon the fact that candidates for office in the past have occupied positions on the different executive committees. . . ." His motion that any member of the Executive Committee who later became a candidate would have to resign his committee position carried. In 1885 a mass meeting called to appoint a citizens' nominating committee featured a debate over a measure that would have forbidden members of the committee to stand for election. Generally, however, membership on these organizations was not a public issue during this period. Nonetheless, inclusion of this factor makes possible the consideration of a potentially important line of political recruitment.[46]

POLITICAL PERSISTENCE

The variable of political persistence represents the number of times a candidate had campaigned for the offices of mayor, alderman, and councilman including the contest being considered. Other writers have discussed previous office*holding* of elected officials, but have not examined the possibility that some officers, before their election, may or may not have *unsuccessfully* sought public position. Although the political variables indicate something of the social situation of candidates, the primary reasons for their inclusion in this study were to define certain political configurations and to analyze their association with the social characteristics. Thus this particular factor permits the identification of individuals with long political persistence rates, distinguishing perennial politicians from novices and other candidates. Were there differences in the social characteristics among such contestants? Examination of the candidates according to this variable proves illuminating in other ways. For example, a system dominated by perennials is quite different from one characterized by a constant rotation of beginners. This variable also was included to weight the effect of sustained political careers upon success at the polls. Were office-seekers competing after several prior attempts more successful than those campaigning for the first time? Multiple candidacies might have allowed a person to gain important knowledge in the art of campaigning, to cultivate important political contacts, and to gain greater recognition among the electorate.[47]

Candidates frequently were identified by this characteristic in the press, particularly if they previously had held city office. For example, the Atlanta *Journal,* describing one slate in 1894, pointed out that five of the nine candidates had such qualifications. Implications of this experience, including successful and unsuccessful previous campaigns for office, were both laudatory and derogatory. Candidates were described as practiced politicians or regulars, political hacks, members of a "ring," or even as clowns deserving ridicule—as was the case with "Soda Water" West, a perennial campaigner lampooned in the Atlanta *Daily Sun* in 1870.[48]

That individuals could succeed themselves in office from 1866 to 1873 supposedly encouraged repeating. The alleged continuation of many of the same individuals in office was one source of complaint by the reformers of the early 1870s. The Atlanta *Daily Herald* claimed in 1873 "that certain individuals in Atlanta have obtained practically a monopoly of all the city patronage, and have grown fat upon it. . . ." Complaints such as these led to the 1874 charter revision that prohibited incumbents from succeeding themselves.[49]

But this revision did not remove the issue of multiple candidacies from campaigns. An important motive for the formation of the citizens' reform movement in the 1880s was to rid the system of professional politicians and to encourage the candidacies of persons previously uninterested in city office. A letter written to the Atlanta *Journal* in 1883 urged the defeat of William H. Brotherton, an aldermanic candidate and an outgoing councilman, on the grounds that his campaign violated the spirit of the city charter. A. M. Reinhardt in 1888 boasted that he was "a new factor in politics but an old one in Atlanta." During the 1897 campaign some Atlantans strongly opposed "allowing men to stay in office who have been there ever since they were old enough to be voted for." On the other hand, other Atlantans still felt that political persistence provided valuable experience for office. A supporter of Brotherton in 1883 claimed that the candidate's primary qualification was "He has served the people often and so as to be thoroughly posted upon the history of our affairs and to have a clear understanding of our present condition and needs." Such differences of opinion in the traditional sources prevent a clear verdict on the significance of this characteristic. The political status and performance of candidates must be examined as well.[50]

In conclusion, each of the characteristics of candidates chosen for the study of Atlanta politics was discussed by contemporaries during this thirty-eight year period. Many of them appeared to have had a potentially powerful political impact. All of the attributes, including those not mentioned as frequently as others, may have constituted elements of a social filter in Atlanta's political system. Conventional sources, however, which often included conflicting claims of the political importance of attributes or confusing accounts of the activities of various groups, could not alone reveal the nature of this filter. By examining the empirical evidence, the description of contestants for city office according to their characteristics, the social bases of city politics becomes more evident.

NOTES

1. Atlanta *Journal,* October 4, 1900. This year marked Frank Rice's ninth successful race for city office.

2. Atlanta *Constitution,* November 7, 1875. The reference was to O. H. Jones, a man who had held city office several times before the Civil War.

3. Angus Campbell et al., *The American Voter, An Abridgement* (New York, 1964), 172-80.

4. Membership lists for the many fraternal organizations in Atlanta are not extant, although the city directories provided lists of officers, many of who were politicians. It is theoretically possible to search through the lists of all Confederate soldiers, but since this attribute surprisingly received little mention during campaigns, such a gargantuan task did not appear worthwhile. Although membership lists of four prestigious Atlanta social groups—the Capital City Club, the Piedmont Driving Club, the Pioneer Historical Society, and the Social Register—are extant, these organizations came into being relatively late in the period. Any relationship between candidacy and political performance and a later social status obviously would be difficult to interpret. Except for the candidacy of Harry Stockdell, a member of the Capital City Club, in 1883, such membership was not a publicized issue in Atlanta politics.

5. For a sympathetic discussion of this problem, see Lawrence Stone "Prosopography," *Daedalus* (Winter, 1971), 58-59.

6. For an introduction to operational definitions and measurement, see Hubert M. Blalock, *Social Statistics* (New York, 1972), 11-25; and Fred N. Kerlinger, *Foundations of Behavioral Research* (New York, 1965), 31-50, 411-28.

7. For a discussion of the reasons for classification, see Stephan Thernstrom, "Quantitative Methods in History: Some Notes," in Seymour Martin Lipset and Richard Hofstadter, eds., *Sociology and History: Methods* (New York, 1968), 59-78.

8. For origins of this idea, see Lee Benson, "An Approach to the Scientific Study of Past Public Opinion," in his book, *Toward the Scientific Study of History* (Philadelphia, 1972), 151-59. Since analysis of the voting of particular groups cannot be undertaken for Atlanta during this period (see chapter one, fn. 5), preference for certain kinds of candidates cannot be connected to specific subgroups of the population.

9. The best treatment of the relationship between the ideation and behavior of historical actors, and the distinction between past political culture and the viewpoint of the historian-observer, is Robert F. Berkhofer, Jr., *A Behavioral Approach to Historical Analysis* (New York, 1969).

10. Atlanta *Constitution,* October 9, 1874; Atlanta *Daily Herald,* November 6, 1875; Atlanta *Constitution,* December 1, 1878; and Atlanta *Journal,* September 28, 1902.

11. Atlanta *Constitution,* November 7, 1875; November 28, 1880; and November 23, 1883.

12. Ibid., August 15, November 2, 1884; and Atlanta *Journal,* November 4, 1884.

13. Ibid., July 28, November 15, 1896; Atlanta *New Era,* October 24, 1871; and Atlanta *Constitution,* September 30, 1888. Businessmen and professional men also had their organizations, which served to give cohesion and forum for discussion to members and to define Atlanta's occupational elite. For a discussion of these organizations, see Grigsby H. Wooten Jr., "New City of the South: Atlanta, 1843-1873" (unpublished Ph.D. dissertation, Johns Hopkins, 1973), 202-5, 220-27.

14. For example, the authors of *The American Voter,* 188-90, found that of the objective criteria of social class—income, occupation, education, and so on—that ". . . occupation tends to predict political attitudes and voting most efficiently. . . ." Also see Stephen Thernstrom, *The Other Bostonians, Poverty and Progress in the American Metropolis, 1880-1970* (Cambridge, 1973), 46. For a summary of the overrepresentation of upper occupational groups in politics, see Peter H. Rossi, "Power and Community Structure," in Willis D. Hawley and Frederick M. Wirt, eds., *The Search for Community Power* (Englewood Cliffs, 1968), 310; and Howard N. Rabinowitz, "Continuity and Change: Southern Urban Development, 1860-1900," in Blaine A. Brownell and David R. Goldfield, eds., *The City in Southern History: The Growth of Urban Civilization in the South* (Port Washington, 1977), 109-10.

15. This scheme is an adaption of the classification system developed by Richard J. Hopkins, "Patterns of Persistence and Occupational Mobility in a Southern City: Atlanta, 1870-1920," (unpublished Ph.D. dissertation, Emory, 1973), 32-45. For my handling of ambiguous cases, see Eugene J. Watts, "Characteristics of Candidates in City Politics" (unpublished Ph.D. dissertation, Emory, 1969), 23-24.

16. Atlanta *Constitution,* December 4, 1883; Atlanta *Journal,* October 4, 1900. For an overview of such political appeals in the South, see C. Vann Woodward, *Origins of the New South, 1877-1913* (Baton Rouge, 1951), 59. For one Atlanta example, see the Atlanta *Journal,* November 19, 1884.

17. Atlanta *Daily Intelligencer,* January 30, 1867; and Atlanta *Constitution,* November 2, 1884; November 20, 1888; November 5, 1892.

18. Atlanta *Daily Herald,* October 8, 1873. Most writers who have studied

social patterns of public leadership for this period also have used property as an important indicator of socio-economic status.

19. Atlanta *Constitution,* December 1, 1878; and December 7, 1888.

20. There is no alternative to accepting the amount of assessed property reported in the Fulton County Tax Digests as a "real" figure. Most historians and social scientists continue to classify variables such as property into preconceived, arbitrary categories, often with little or no real defense. These scholars fail to take advantage of an easy standardization procedure based on the distribution of the data. For a good discussion of quantiles, see John Mueller and Karl Schuessler, *Statistical Reasoning in Sociology* (Boston, 1961), 127-28.

21. For a fuller discussion of the importance of this factor, see Eugene J. Watts, "Black Political Progress in Atlanta, 1868-1895," *The Journal of Negro History* (July, 1974), 268-86; and Howard N. Rabinowitz, "From Reconstruction to Redemption in the Urban South," *Journal of Urban History* (February, 1976), 169-94.

22. Atlanta *Constitution,* December 3, 1879; and December 2, 1880.

23. Atlanta *New Era,* December 8, 1870; and Atlanta *Constitution,* November 19, 1874; December 1, 5, 1878; December 3-5, 1879; December 2, 1880.

24. For example, a black newspaper, the Atlanta *Weekly Defiance,* October 29, 1881, urged black Atlantans to unite politically, for "then we shall be able to have our people represent us . . . in the municipal capacity." Atlanta *Constitution,* December 31, 1892; and E. R. Carter, *The Black Side—A Partial History of the Business, Religious and Educational Side of the Negro in Atlanta* (Atlanta, 1894), 19.

25. The federal censuses from 1850 to 1880, and a special Atlanta city census of 1896, were the major sources for documentation of birthplace; information on city of birth, of course, was not published. The foreign-born category was further divided into country of origin; in Atlanta only three subdivisions—Ireland, Germany, and England-Scotland-Canada—were necessary. Because of the few numbers of immigrant office-seekers, and the similarity in social characteristics and political performance among the three subdivisions, all foreign-born contestants were considered as one group. Similarly, the initial search for candidates who were native-born sons of immigrants (that could only be conducted in the 1880 census and thus for only a part of all contestants) yielded such a small number that this category was discarded. See Watts, "Characteristics of Candidates," 29, 378.

26. It is at least implicitly a corollary of the concept of the "Lost Cause," discussed in Woodward, *Origins of the New South,* 156, that a southern identification was important for office-seekers in the South. Daland, in his study of public leadership in an Alabama city from 1911 to 1956, found that birth in the South, preferably in Alabama, was essential in city elections and that alien birth invariably became an important campaign issue. Robert T. Daland, *Dixie City: A Portrait of Political Leadership* (Tuscaloosa, 1956), 6-7.

27. Atlanta *Constitution,* October 6, 1874. A remarkable number of Northerners had settled in Atlanta before the war. Wooten, "New City of the South," 39-42, 101, 184, 222.

28. Robert A. Dahl, *Who Governs* (New Haven, 1961), 36-37; Donald S. Bradley and Mayer N. Zald, "From the Commercial Elite to Political Administrator: The

Recruitment of the Mayors of Chicago," *The American Journal of Sociology,* LXXI (1965), 166-67. Atlanta *New Era,* November 10, 1870; and Atlanta *Daily Sun,* August 17, 1872. Some ethnic groups had their own societies, such as the Hibernian Benevolent Society and the Hebrew Benevolent Society. Wooten, "New City of the South," 228, 366.

29. Atlanta *Daily News,* October 13, 1874; Atlanta *Constitution,* November 21, 1890; and Atlanta *Journal,* November 25, December 2, 1895.

30. Anne Mebane, "Immigrant Patterns in Atlanta, 1880 and 1896" (unpublished M. A. thesis, Emory, 1967); Hopkins, "Patterns of Persistence," 153-56; James M. Russell, "Atlanta, Gate City of the South, 1847-1885" (unpublished Ph.D. dissertation, Princeton, 1972), 167-68.

31. Atlanta *Constitution,* December 5, 1883; November 4, 1885; and November 19, 1889.

32. Ibid., November 4, 1885; and November 29, 1888.

33. Russell, "Atlanta, Gate City of the South," 263-70. Also see Franklin M. Garrett, *Atlanta and Environs: A Chronicle of the People and Events,* II (3 vols., New York, 1954), 17, and Wooten, "New City of the South," 192-97. Richard Hopkins, using quantitative techniques in his ongoing research on social mobility in Atlanta, confirms the general pattern described above, but points out, correctly, that lower- and upper-class groups could be found all over the city before and after 1884. Another recent study that discusses a rough pattern of status differences between the core and the ring is John M. Allswang, *A House for all Peoples: Ethnic Politics in Chicago, 1890-1936* (Lexington, 1971), 232.

34. Howard P. Chudacoff, *Mobile Americans: Residential and Social Mobility in Omaha, 1880-1920* (New York, 1972), 130-47; and Zane Miller, *Boss Cox's Cincinnati: Urban Politics in the Progressive Era* (New York, 1968), 9-55, 161-241. Other writers who employed similar residential distinctions include Sam Bass Warner, "If All The World Were Philadelphia: A Scaffolding for Urban History, 1774-1930," *American Historical Review,* LXXIV (October, 1968), 26-43; and Peter Knights, *The Plain People of Boston, 1830-1860; A Study in City Growth* (New York, 1971). Initially, residence areas were determined by drawing seven concentric circles, each one-quarter of a mile in width, around and out from the Union Depot, but the reduction of the seven categories to a dichotomy appeared to fit Atlanta's political situation, and did not disguise any important variation within the two broad areas.

35. Atlanta *Constitution,* December 1, 1878; Atlanta *Journal,* October 4, 1900; and Atlanta *Constitution,* December 1, 1878. Robert Dykstra used similar concepts of old settlers versus later arrivals, although the distinction was not put to any particular political test. Robert R. Dykstra, *The Cattle Towns* (New York, 1970), 109-10, 218.

36. Ibid., November 14, 1868; November 29, 1883; and Atlanta *Journal,* September 26, 28, 1902.

37. Dahl, *Who Governs,* 11-16. The manuscript censuses and the city directories, when available, were used to document this variable. The oldest extant directory was printed in 1859 and the next oldest in 1867. Thus the actual period of this minimum length of residence is longer than ten years for candidates from 1870

to 1872, and shorter than ten years for office-seekers from 1867 to 1868 and 1873 to 1876. A period of less than ten years might fail to distinguish among candidates very much, and evidence was not available for many contestants for a longer period. Research required to cover the actual length of residence for such a large number of candidates is prohibitive.

38. Atlanta *Daily Herald,* October 11, 1873. Bradley and Zald, "From Commercial Elite to Political Administrators," 160, found that age was an important criterion for distinguishing Chicago's mayors in different periods. Also see Campbell et al., *The American Voter,* 250, for a discussion of the present-day political importance of age.

39. Atlanta *Constitution,* December 5, 1878; and November 26, 1882.

40. Ibid., November 28, 1883; and Atlanta *Journal,* October 2, September 22, 1897; October 4, 1900.

41. Information on the age of candidates was taken from the censuses, with newspapers as a supplementary source. Neither is notable for absolute accuracy, although Peter Knights reported that the margin of error in the former was one year. Peter R. Knights, "Accuracy of Age Reporting in the Manuscript Federal Censuses of 1850 and 1860," *Historical Methods Newsletter* (June, 1971), 79-83. Most historians and social scientists arrange age into ten-year categories—twenty to twenty-nine and so on. Although useful for some purposes, for example, tracing cohort groups through the censuses, such a classification has little relevance to a political study.

42. Information on candidates in these positions after 1880 was taken from the Annual Reports of Council for Atlanta. Evidence for previous years was taken from Franklin M. Garrett, *Atlanta and Environs,* I; and Walter G. Cooper, *Official History of Fulton County* (Atlanta, 1934). During the 1870s the members of the Board of Water Commissioners were elected to their positions, and after 1894 most minor city officials, except members of administrative boards, also were elected. For a discussion of this change, see Atlanta *Constitution,* October 2, 1894. Each of these two avenues of political recruitment appeared to indicate the same kind of lower level political experience, even though administrative boards enjoyed some political autonomy. Little difference in social background or political performance existed between candidates with prior service on administrative boards or in other minor positions. Previous officeholding in the government of Fulton County, largely co-terminus with Atlanta, also was considered, but fewer than 7 percent of the candidates had such involvement. Hardly any competed for state or national offices.

43. Ibid., October 9, 1874; and Atlanta *Journal,* October 7, 1897.

44. For many other United States cities a comparable focus would be citywide or ward organizations of political parties. Ward organizations existed for only a few years in Atlanta, and their officers were difficult to identify. Atlanta *Constitution,* November 7, 1868; November 16, 1872; October 22, 1873; September 13, 1874; October 20, 1875; August 15, 1884; November 15, 1889; July 22, 1890; Atlanta *Journal,* November 8, 1890; Atlanta *Constitution,* October 28, November 10, 1891; November 1, 1892; October 18, November 5, 1893; September 2, 1894; October 25, 1895; Atlanta *Journal,* July 28, 1896; and Atlanta *Constitution,* September 1, 1900; September 28, 1901; October 9, 1903.

45. Definition of such organizations in a way that would fit different cities is difficult, but in Atlanta the selection was obvious. Ibid., November 18, 1868; October 26, 1869; August 6, 1884; Atlanta *Journal,* November 4, 1884; Atlanta *Constitution,* October 31, 1885; October 23, 1886; October 2, 23, 1888; November 15, 1889; Atlanta *Journal,* November 5, 1890; and Atlanta *Constitution,* November 10, 1891.

46. Ibid., September 13, 1976; and October 17, 1885.

47. Only in general elections before 1866 and in the Democratic primary of 1869 could losers not be identified. Mayer N. Zald and Thomas A. Anderson, "Secular Trends and Historical Contingencies in the Recruitment of Mayors: Nashville as compared to New Haven and Chicago," *Urban Affairs Quarterly,* III (1968), 53-68, discuss the importance of long periods of office holding in their study of Nashville.

48. Atlanta *Journal,* August 9, 1894; and Atlanta *Daily Sun,* November 1, 1870.

49. Atlanta *Daily Herald,* October 24, 1873.

50. Atlanta *Journal,* December 4, 1883; Atlanta *Constitution,* December 6, 1900; December 1, 1888; and Atlanta *Journal,* October 2, 1897; December 5, 1883.

4

Social Roots of
Political Aspiration

Examination of the social background of contestants, especially when
compared with the larger population of Atlantans, sheds light on social
patterns in politics not clearly elucidated by contemporaries.[1] Because
statistical analysis confirms suggestions in conventional sources that there
were important differences among types of candidates for mayor, alderman, and councilman, this and the subsequent chapter examine characteristics of contestants for each office. To investigate the change through
time in candidate attributes, the period has been divided into two seg-
ments that contain a roughly comparable number of elections and reflect the historical situation. Because the inception of the citizens' reform movement in 1884 marked an obvious watershed in Atlanta city
politics, the time spans of 1865-83 and 1884-1903 provided logical choices.[2]

OCCUPATION

   Political commentators placed considerable importance on the occupation of office-seekers during Atlanta's political campaigns; table 1 expands
on and clarifies that commentary by displaying the vocational backgrounds of candidates for each office. It is apparent that the municipal
political arena was largely the province of individuals from the top of the
vocational hierarchy and that candidates were far from representative of
the total population of adult male wage earners. Between 1865 and 1903
approximately three-fifths of the contestants were businessmen and another one-fifth were professional men.[3]

TABLE 1

Occupation of Candidates by Office and by Subperiod

	Mayor			Alderman			Councilman		
	I[a]	II[b]	M	I[a]	II[b]	A	I[a]	II[b]	C
Professional	63.6%	45.8%	56.1%	7.7%	17.1%	14.7%	14.7%	23.6%	18.2%
Proprietor	36.4	37.5	36.8	76.9	61.8	65.7	61.2	57.4	59.7
Clerical	0.0	4.2	1.8	11.5	14.5	13.7	11.2	9.7	10.6
Blue Collar	0.0	12.5	5.3	3.8	6.6	5.9	12.9	9.3	11.5
[c]100% =	33	24	57	26	76	102	402	258	660
Cramer's V =		0.33			0.15			0.12	
(Change through time within races for each office)									

[d]Cramer's V (between offices) = 0.18

	All Candidates		
	I[a]	II[b]	All
Professional	17.8%	23.7%	20.4%
Proprietor	60.3	57.0	58.9
Clerical	10.4	10.3	10.4
Blue Collar	11.4	8.9	10.4
[c]100% =	461	358	819[e]
[d]Cramer's V =		0.08	

[a]I = 1865-83.

[b]II = 1884-1903.

[c]Because of rounding, some totals in this and subsequent tables are equal to 99.9 percent or 100.1 percent.

[d]Cramer's V is the only chi-square-based statistic that ranges from zero to unity—independence to perfect association—regardless of the numbers of rows and columns in the tabular array. Hubert Blalock, *Social Statistics* (New York, 1972), 297. As used here, this measure of association indicates the magnitude of differences in the distribution of an attribute, in this case occupation, between the two time frames (within races for each office and overall) and among contests for each office. For example, if only professional men had campaigned for mayor before 1884, and only proprietors had competed for this office after that year, then V would have been 1.0. If an equal proportion of professionals and proprietors had run for mayor within each period, then V would have been 0.

[e]The occupation of seven candidates could not be determined.

This is not surprising, since clear reasons existed in Atlanta and in other cities for the political participation of men with these occupations. Contemporary opinion, especially self-serving pronouncements of the press and leading citizens, dictated that such people should control city government. Moreover, professional men and businessmen had obvious interests in many aspects of municipal decision-making, such as the improvement of city services in the downtown area.[4]

What may have been unusual in late nineteenth-century Atlanta was the extent of participation by other occupational groups. Approximately one-fifth of all office-seekers throughout this period were either white-collar or blue-collar employees. In general, clerical candidates did not appear to have a strong sense of group identification. They were not supported by any specific vocational organizations, although a few, such as ticket agent Albert Howell, an important politician late in the period, clearly identified themselves with working-class groups. Skilled workers, on the other hand, were well organized and possessed a definite class awareness. Thus it was no accident that all but five of the eighty-five blue-collar office-seekers had skilled trades. Of those five semiskilled or unskilled worker candidates, four were black—an identifying characteristic far more significant than occupation.[5]

Historical circumstances sometimes helped blue-collar workers become candidates. For example, the Republican party, eager to break the Democratic stranglehold on city hall, placed white workers on their municipal tickets from 1869 to 1871.[6] The Democrats responded to this threat, and to pressure from Democratic laboring men, by adopting a "formula" for representation of all "interests" on party slates. Even more significant were the several workingmen who contested Democratic primaries and thereby forced such recognition. By the 1880s the formula was interpreted as requiring inclusion of at least some working-class candidates on organized tickets. Whenever local slates did not include working men, organized opposition quickly surfaced. Worker demands at nomination meetings for direct representation could be ignored only at peril of a pitched battle.[7]

Nevertheless, blue-collar representation was not evident at all levels. Workers themselves generally seemed content with only a few places. Even the slates of the Railroad Men's League or the Industrial Union Council in the 1890s included candidates with occupations other than skilled trades. Also, the formula for representation of blue-collar citizens did not seem to include the more prestigious and powerful positions of mayor and alderman. James G. Woodward was not only the sole working-class mayoral candidate, he was also one of only four artisans who ran for alderman. Until the mayoral campaigns of Woodward and Albert Howell in the

1890s, workers even placed professional men at the head of their own tickets. Thus S. B. Spencer, an attorney, championed the working class in the early 1870s and another lawyer, Reuben Arnold, headed the maverick 1884 slate in opposition to the Citizens' Ticket.[8]

To a certain extent, political hierarchy corresponded with occupational hierarchy. Councilmanic races provided the most important avenue into city politics for blue-collar workers.[9] Competition for aldermanic races, in turn, involved more than twice as many clerical as manual workers. But the Board of Alderman, which had the greatest power of the purse in Atlanta government, remained primarily the domain of the business interest: nearly two-thirds of those who ran for alderman were proprietors. The highest prize in Atlanta city politics—the mayoralty—seemed to have a special attraction for professional men, although businessmen were also well represented. Even so, table 1 also shows clearly that no matter what the office, and particularly in the case of at-large positions, upper occupational groups provided the highest proportion of contenders.[10]

PROPERTY

Differences in average amount of property provided the only sharp distinctions, besides race, among candidates already separated by occupation. Both occupation and property ownership, of course, were primary indicators of a person's socioeconomic position. Since great emphasis was placed on such status in Atlanta politics, careful consideration should be given to these combined factors.

In 1873 some dissatisfied citizens complained that the rich monopolized public positions. The Atlanta *Daily Herald* countered the claim by saying that ". . . not one in twenty rich men of this city are aspirants for office."[11] This, no doubt, was true. A clever citizen, however, could have rejoined that not one in hundreds of poor men in the city had similar aspirations. The summary statistics presented in table 2 clearly indicate that on the whole candidates were a considerable cut above the crowd in Atlanta with regard to property-holdings. The bottom 25 percent of the contestants owned $2,500 or less in property, and the median property value for all candidates was $6,750, a considerable sum in those days. Moreover, 25 percent of the office-seekers owned property valued over $16,000. Indeed, from 1865 to 1903, 10 percent of the contestants

TABLE 2

Property of Candidates by Office a,d by Subperiod

	Mayor			Alderman			Councilman			All Candidates		
	I	II	M	I	II	A	I	II	C	I	II	Overall
Median	$ 9,270	$ 12,790	$ 10,900	$ 13,825	$ 7,950	$ 10,340.	$ 6,720	$ 5,550	$ 6,250	$ 7,150	$ 6,275	$ 6,750
Mean	36,538	29,126	33,417	29,390	22,735	24,415	12,929	17,159	14,592	15,541	19,139	17,122
Standard Deviation	57,754	42,532	51,601	35,738	58,793	53,824	20,899	39,622	29,744	27,018	44,563	35,821
Coefficient of Variability[a]	1.58	1.46	1.54	1.22	2.59	2.20	1.62	2.31	2.04	1.74	2.33	2.09
Minimum	0	0	0	645	500	500	0	0	0	0	0	0
Maximum	215,000	154,608	215,000	156,875	495,512	495,512	143,575	408,855	408,855	215,000	495,512	495,512
First Quartile	5,100	2,450	5,100	7,425	3,775	4,012	2,500	2,100	2,285	2,700	2,220	2,500
Third Quartile	45,640	27,800	45,640	37,560	19,408	25,102	13,200	15,675	14,175	14,900	18,050	16,000
Number of Cases	33	24	57	26	77	103	403	261	664	462	362	824
F Ratio[b] =	0.28 (1/55 d.f.)			0.30 (1/101 d.f.)			3.2 (1/662 d.f.)			2.05 (1/822 d.f.)		
Eta²[c] =	0.08			0.05			0.07			0.05		
F Ratio (office) =	9.90											
Eta² (office) =	0.15											

[a] V, the coefficient of variability, is the ratio of the standard deviation (S.D.) to the mean; as such V provides a standardized measure of dispersion, helpful because the size of standard deviations increases with the size of means. See Hubert Blalock, *Social Statistics* (New York, 1972), 88.

[b] Analysis of variance techniques were employed to determine if variation in property among candidates organized according to the office they sought or period of candidacy (within offices and overall) were greater or lesser than dispersion in property-holdings of contestants within separate contests or time frames. When F, the ratio of variation *between* groups to variation *within* groups, is greater than unity, then distinctions between (or among) groups are greater than differences within groups. The F ratio generally is used to indicate whether observed values are statistically significant. Since this study used an entire population, there is no question of statistical significance; degrees of freedom are presented solely for the benefit of readers who believe in 100 percent samples.

[c] Eta is a measure of association, ranging from zero to unity—independence to perfect relationship—that measures the ratio of the between-group variation to the total variance around the overall mean. Thus eta, when squared, indicates the proportion of the total variance "accounted for" by differences between subgroups (property of candidates by office or time frames). For a good introduction to F and Eta, see Fred N. Kerlinger, *Foundations of Behavioral Research* (New York, 1965), 187–256. Also see fn. 16, this chapter.

owned more than $40,000 in property, and 3 percent had holdings in excess of $100,000. At the other extreme, only 3 percent of the total 824 political hopefuls owned no property, and only 10 percent of the candidates had property worth less than $600. Although no precise figures are readily available, undoubtedly most of Atlanta's eligible voters fell somewhere near or below that $600 mark.[12]

Thus the first stage of the social filter was very severe—few candidates came from the bottom stratum of society. Yet those who declared for office owned quite varied amounts of property. Within each subperiod, the means are two or three times larger than the medians; the standard deviations are considerably greater than the means; and the range extends from zero to several hundred thousands of dollars.[13] Even so, the property distributions for the three city contests differed from each other. Aspirants for the more prestigious at-large positions of mayor and alderman generally seem to have had a higher economic standing than most councilmanic candidates.[14]

For each office, the wide range of property values among contestants *within* each subperiod outweighed distinctions in average property-holdings *between* subperiods. Nonetheless, some changes are noteworthy. After 1884 more mayoral candidates were men with little property. Likewise, a smaller proportion of persons with very great wealth aspired to the office after that year. From the time the aldermanic position was created in 1873 until 1883, contestants for that office were cast from the same financial mold as candidates for mayor. After 1884, when the number of aldermanic positions increased from three to seven, the general economic standing of aldermanic candidates was somewhat lower, even though the extremely wealthy also increased their participation in these contests. In councilmanic races, the mean (and standard deviation) increased while the median property-holdings decreased through time. These figures suggest a moderate but growing polarization by wealth among councilmanic and aldermanic candidates in Atlanta. Given these findings, the success of the citizens' reform movement, which promised an increased political participation of wealthier citizens, appears mixed. Clearly the inception of this movement in 1884 did not mark a watershed on the other side of which men with higher financial status dominated the ranks of office-seekers.

As table 3 indicates, businessmen who sought city office generally were far more prosperous than professional men, but candidates of wide ranges

TABLE 3

Median Property-Holdings of Vocational Groups within Contests for Each Office

	Mayor	Alderman	Councilman	All Contests
Professional	$ 8,590	$ 5,675	$ 4,068	$ 4,624
	(32)	(15)	(120)	(167)
Proprietor	24,513	16,575	10,201	11,176
	(21)	(67)	(394)	(482)
Clerical	[600]	4,037	3,000	3,002
	(1)	(14)	(70)	(85)
Blue Collar	[2,200]	[2,250]	2,021	2,100
	(3)	(6)	(76)	(85)

Note: The property distributions for professionals and particularly the proprietors were extremely skewed to the right within contests for each office; in this situation the median is a better measure of typicality than the mean.

of wealth came from both groups.[15] Among the businessmen were included some of the city's largest capitalists as well as middle-range merchants and proprietors of modest concerns such as grocery stores and saloons. Among the professionals, most physicians were men with modest amounts of property, although some were more substantial citizens. The lawyers ranged from one with no property to one whose property was assessed at over $63,000. Over 20 percent of the professional men had $600 or less in property, but only 3 percent of the businessmen were this poor. On the other hand, 37 percent of the businessmen but only 11 percent of the professional men held more than $16,000. Thus although both groups of candidates were fairly prosperous, a larger proportion of professionals than businessmen were men on the make rather than those already at the top.

Predictably, most candidates with other occupations were noticeably poorer than either businessmen or professional men. The median property-holdings for clerical and blue-collar candidates were approximately $3,300 and $2,000 respectively, compared with $11,000 for businessmen and $4,600 for professionals. Clerical and blue-collar contestants were relatively homogeneous in terms of property-holdings: 80 percent of the former and 88 percent of the latter had less than $6,750 in property.[16] The general differences between white- and blue-collar workers can be seen in the proportion of each—44 Percent and 63 percent respectively— who has less than $2,500 in property. But although both of these groups of office-seekers generally came from lower economic levels than most proprietors or professionals, they obviously ranked far above the general economic status of the great majority of white- and blue-collar workers in the city. In fact, an economic elite of Atlanta's workers, rather than representatives of the bottom stratum of the city, carried the banner of the working classes in municipal elections.

The rhetoric of Atlanta's political contenders and commentators after the Civil War often suggested a battle between rich and poor. The evidence on the economic situations of contestants reveals a weakness in this argument, since not many of the genuinely poor ventured into open combat. Those who campaigned for city office, however, did include those with "no stake" in the community as well as some of Atlanta's wealthiest citizens, and the wide distribution of property reflects contemporary recognition of pronounced differences in wealth among candidates. The above analysis clearly shows that contestants for all offices came from a wide range of socioeconomic situations, although access to at-large positions appeared more restricted. Above all, however, the average property-holdings of contestants, including even clerical and manual workers, indicated that candidates were highly unrepresentative of Atlanta's eligible voters.

Other qualities of candidates also received a good deal of attention in Atlanta politics. Among these attributes were ethno-cultural factors— race, ethnic background, and region of birth—that have long been a major concern of both social and political historians.

RACE

Afro-Americans (who comprised approximately 40 percent of Atlanta's population during this period) were an active and sometimes organized political force that demanded direct representation in municipal government. Despite this emphasis, only twenty-two black citizens campaigned for city office within this period. Black candidates appeared only when whites were seriously divided and willing to compete with each other for the black vote. For example, seven black candidates ran for office on the Republican tickets in 1870 and 1871, five more competed from 1878 to

1880, four in 1887, and nine on the all-black Anti-Primary Ticket in 1890. Even when such black political aspirations surfaced, however, they were quickly beaten down.[17]

Twenty of the black candidates campaigned in only one election— an indication that a single experience was sufficient to convince them of the hopelessness of their cause. Two men ran subsequent campaigns. Mitchell Cargile, after losing his bid for council in 1871, placed second in a similar contest in 1879. William Finch, after his initial victory for City Council in 1870, was defeated in races for councilman in 1871 and for alderman in 1879. Only two other black Atlantans, I. P. Moyer and Willis Murphey, ran for alderman and only one, Jake McKinley, was a candidate for mayor, all in 1890.

Black office-seekers, with the major exception of their occupations, were more homogeneous than were white contestants. All of the blacks came from the South, including eighteen from Georgia. They also were relatively young men; two-thirds were younger than forty with one-third under the age of thirty-five. None of the black office-seekers had lived in Atlanta before the Civil War, and only 52 percent, compared with 75 percent of the whites, had lived in the city for at least ten years previous to running for city office. In the 1870s and 1880s most black candidates resided in areas of black concentration, such as Summer Hill, Shermantown, or Buttermilk Bottom, and thus campaigned from areas adjacent to, but not within, the city's center.[18] None of the Afro-Americans who tried for elective positions had any prior experience in appointive office, although several were prominent in Republican party politics, holding party positions and patronage jobs. Interestingly enough, many black politicians active in party posts and ward organizations, such as W. A. Pledger and H. A. Rucker, refrained from competition for city office.[19]

Overall, three black candidates were professional men, ten were proprietors, and nine were workers—five skilled, one semiskilled, and three unskilled. Some significant differences occurred over time in the occupations of black candidates. Five of seven blacks who sought office in the early 1870s were members of the working class and owned an average of $500 in city property. Black candidates in the late 1870s included four small businessmen and pastor of a Baptist church who averaged about $700 worth of property. The four black men who campaigned in 1887 owned an average of about $200 in property, and except for Alonzo Burnett, editor of the *Weekly Defiance,* held modest occupations. The

1890 Anti-Primary Ticket, however, contained a number of prominent black Atlantans with average property holdings valued at $3,800. Included on this slate were a skilled cotton sampler, a well-to-do drayman, four owners of groceries, an undertaker, a publisher-editor, and a rock contractor who employed one hundred and fifty black workers and white workers.

Despite the wealth of the black candidates in 1890, compared with whites they were significantly poorer on the average. All but Jake McKinley were below the median property level for all candidates, and thirteen of the twenty-two were in the bottom decile of property-holdings. Yet more than likely, at least some and perhaps most of these men represented the upper level of society within the black community. This was true, no doubt, even for men like R. J. Henry, a hotel porter.[20] But no matter what the social characteristics or class standing of black office-seekers, whether in the black community or the total population, their shared attribute of race was by far the most significant.

REGION OF BIRTH

The regional self-consciousness of a post-Civil War southern city requires examination of white candidates who might have been considered outsiders because of their birth in areas other than Georgia or the South. Immigrants, the focus of several other studies, were sometimes victims of this attitude even though they formed fewer than 10 percent of the candidates for Atlanta city office. Only from 1865 to 1883 was the difference between proportions of foreign-born among contestants and that in the general population—7 percent—noteworthy, but it was still far from dramatic. Unlike northern cities such as New Haven or Chicago, Atlanta did not have an even moderately sizeable ethnic base upon which candidates with similar backgrounds could build a political following. Perhaps for this reason, no "ethnic" sought the mayoralty in Atlanta during this time span.[21]

The proportion of immigrants among candidates decreased slightly from 12 percent to 6 percent by the end of the period. Although it is difficult to generalize about the decline in candidacies because of the small number of foreign-born office-seekers, the slight drop might have been related to the exclusion of blacks from the political arena. If, as Richard Hopkins

TABLE 4

Region of Birth of Candidates by Office and by Subperiod

Region of Birth	Mayor			Alderman			Councilman		
	I	II	M	I	II	A	I	II	C
Georgia	56.8%	79.2%	66.1%	50.0%	59.2%	56.9%	41.0%	68.0%	51.5%
Other South[a]	25.0	16.7	21.4	19.2	17.1	17.6	27.8	18.4	24.2
North[b]	18.2	4.2	12.5	15.4	14.5	14.7	18.7	8.2	14.6
Foreign	––	––	––	15.4	9.2	10.8	12.5	5.3	9.7
100% =	32	24	56	26	76	102	385	244	629
Cramer's V =		0.26			0.10			0.27	

Cramer's V (Office) = 0.08

	All Candidates		
	I	II	Overall
Georgia	42.7%	66.9%	53.2%
Other South	27.1	18.0	23.1
North	18.5	9.3	14.5
Foreign	11.7	5.8	9.1
100% =	443	334	787
Cramer's V =		0.24	

[a] Other South includes all candidates born in the ten states of the Confederacy other than Georgia.

[b] North includes those office-seekers born elsewhere than the ten states of the Confederacy. All in fact came from states north of the Ohio River.

suggests, blacks were "surrogate immigrants" in Atlanta society, frozen at the bottom of the economic ladder while whites, including the foreign-born, advanced upward, such may have been the case in politics before the 1890s as well. Moreover, attempts to encourage immigration to the city had ceased by the 1880s, and nativist attitudes were at their peak in Atlanta during the 1890s.

Further explanation of the slight decline may lie in the changing demography of the city. Immigrants increased numerically from 1870 to 1900, but their proportion of the population slightly decreased—from almost 5 percent in 1870 to less than 3 percent by 1900. More important, the numbers of Irish, who had furnished nearly two-thirds of the foreign-born candidates early in the era, dwindled so precipitously that by the turn of the century the newly arrived Russian immigrants outnumbered them.[23] After 1884 most foreign-born contenders were German or English-Canadian. In addition, most immigrant candidates, regardless of nationality, had arrived in Atlanta before the war and took an early interest in politics. Although a few antebellum immigrant settlers remained in the political arena until the turn of the century, a much smaller group of foreign-born office-seekers who had arrived after the war outnumbered them. Immigrants arriving later in Atlanta were too few in number to sustain the political role played by foreign-born early migrants to Atlanta.

Although immigrant candidates may have been outsiders in terms of region of birth, most were insiders according to the length of their connection to the city. In fact, a much larger proportion of foreign-born than native contestants had resided in Atlanta before the Civil War, and almost 90 percent of the immigrant contenders had come to the city before 1871. Foreign-born office-seekers were also more likely than other contestants to have lived in the city at least ten years before seeking city office, regardless of period of arrival. Moreover, fewer than 8 percent of the foreign-born, compared with slightly more than 25 percent of the natives, had less than $2,500 in property. One explanation for so few foreign-born candidates may be that immigrants near the bottom of the economic ladder and without long ties to Atlanta felt less free to seek elective office than native Americans in similar circumstances.

In politics, as in other areas of Atlanta community life, individuals with an identifiable ethnic background apparently were well assimilated into society. Such people did not appear markedly motivated to seek public positions. Although candidates for city office, especially in the early era, did include a larger percent of immigrants than might be expected from their proportion of the city's population, the differences were far from substantial. Atlanta may demonstrate, like Nashville, that political aspirants with ethnic backgrounds appear in politics in significant numbers only after their social base in a city is substantial. The small numbers of immigrant office-seekers in Atlanta, the general similarity between foreign-born and native-born candidates with respect to most attributes, and the strong identification of many immigrants with the early period of Atlanta's growth might explain the low level of visible ethnic antagonism that existed in Atlanta municipal politics.[24]

Examination of the regional differences among native born office-seekers, also shown in table 4, reveals a dominance of southern-born candidates. Just over half of the contestants were native Georgians, and another fourth were from other areas of the South. But perhaps most interesting at first glance was the fairly strong representation of non-Southerners.

Based on the difference between the percentage of candidates from each group and that groups' percentage of the general Atlanta population, native Georgians were severely underrepresented in the city's political contests, and all other regional groups, especially transplanted North-- erners, were overrepresented.[25] However, one must remember that the political system was not really open to black Atlantans, the majority of whom were native Georgians. Therefore, other regional groups were not so overrepresented among candidates as first appeared. The size of their representation is nevertheless considerable.

These regional proportions underwent significant changes through time. From the first to the second subperiod, native Georgians increased from slightly more than two-fifths to two-thirds of all candidates (in spite of the exclusion of blacks from the political arena), while office-seekers born elsewhere decreased in number. The most significant shifts took place in the contests for mayor and councilman. No immigrant ever sought the mayoralty, but candidates born in the North formed 18 percent of these political hopefuls before 1884. After that year only one of twenty-four mayoral candidates was northern-born, and birth in Georgia became almost a prerequisite for mayoral contestants. Candidates born outside the South comprised over 30 percent of the candidates in other contests before 1884, but only 15 percent after that year. Thus, even as Atlanta grew from a small, war-devastated town to a regional metropolis, the origins of its candidates for political office demonstrated an increased parochialism.

The decline in political activism by transplanted Northerners apparently occurred for some of the same reasons as for the foreign-born. Like the immigrant office-seekers, most of the northern-born office-seekers had resided in Atlanta before the Civil War. In contrast, fewer than two-fifths of the native Georgians and fewer than one-third of those born in other southern states had this long prior identification with the city. Furthermore, only 38 percent of the Northerners arrived in Atlanta in the 1860s, fewer than any other group, and an even smaller number came to the city after 1880. Those candidates born in the North who had resided in Atlanta for a long time began to fade out of the political picture later in the period, and sufficient northern-born newcomers did not arrive to take their places.

Despite contemporary concern over carpetbaggers, only a few of the northern-born candidates who arrived immediately after the Civil War became prominent within the Republican party on the local level. A more important base for Atlanta Republicans was formed by several Northerners who had come to the city before the war. A few northern-born Atlantans who voted Republican in national elections sought city office as independents and did not appear to be involved in local party efforts. The national party affiliation of most transplanted northern aspirants was not publicized. In fact, only one-fifth of the Northerners who campaigned from 1865 to 1873, when Republicans were an organized force, ran on Republican tickets. Of the twenty-nine white candidates who ran on Republican tickets in that period, ten were Northerners, nine were native Georgians, six were from other southern states, and four were immigrants. One historian of Atlanta has suggested that the white rank-and-file of the Republican party was primarily northern-born and secondarily foreign-born. Although this may have been true of the party's supporters, only a small fraction of the transplanted Northerners who sought city office had strong ties to that party.[26]

Some interesting distinctions existed between northern-born and native southern office-seekers. A greater proportion of the former not only campaigned four or more times, but also had served previously in appointive offices and on political committees. Thus, candidates born in the North appeared to have larger and more diversified political appetites than other office-seekers. Northerners also were older and usually owned more property than southern-born contestants. In addition, few transplanted Northerners worked at manual trades, sought city office before living at least ten years in Atlanta, or lived in the city's outskirts.

In general, with regard to these characteristics, northern-born candidates resembled foreign-born contestants. Similarly, although some differences existed between native Georgians and other Southerners who migrated to Atlanta, particularly regarding property-holding, these contestants were close to each other in terms of social and political characteristics. Examination of this stage of the social filter indicates that a larger proportion of non-Southerners than natives of Dixie who sought city office possessed qualities considered desirable according to contemporary political comment. A relatively select group of non-Southerners sought public position in Atlanta; northern- or foreign-born younger men who were recent arrivals, members of the working class, or without substantial property-holdings did not enter the political arena in the same proportions as Southerners with similar handicaps. Thus few of Atlanta's "outside" candidates truly deserved that label; when it came to their social characteristics, they were more accurately "insiders."

AREA OF RESIDENCE

Although candidates born outside the South were a noticeable feature in Atlanta municipal politics, the extent of political participation by native Georgians (even though lower than could be expected on the basis of their proportion of the city population) and by migrants from other states of the Confederacy, clearly revealed that Atlanta was a city of the South. Although basically homogeneous with respect to race, national origin, and region of birth, Atlanta's political aspirants were a diverse group in other ways. One striking variation can be seen in the residential patterns of Atlanta's office-seekers.

Data presented in table 5 answer, in part, some of the questions raised in the preceding chapter concerning the residence of office-seekers during the period from 1865 to 1903. Over three-quarters of the candidates before 1884 lived within three-quarters of a mile, easy walking distance, from the Union Depot. This concentration is understandable, since the overwhelming majority of Atlantans also resided within this area. By the end of the era, however, fewer than two-fifths of the contestants lived in the same area. The magnitude of movement is indicated by the substantial value of gamma (0.60), which would have been zero if the proportion of inner and outer city dwellers had been equal in the two time frames, and would have reached one if all candidates had come from the center before 1884 and all had resided in the ring after that year. The pronounced pattern of dispersion of office-seekers over time towards the city limits mirrored the geographical mobility of Atlanta's rapidly expanding population.[27] This pattern also suggests that residents of the outskirts early in the period and citizens living in the center towards the turn of the century had good reason to complain about their lack of representation in local politics.

TABLE 5

Residence Areas of Candidates by Office and by Subperiod

	Mayor			Alderman			Councilman		
	I	II	M	I	II	A	I	II	C
City Center[a]	81.8%	41.7%	64.9%	92.3%	44.2%	56.3%	76.3%	36.8%	60.6%
	(33)	(24)	(57)	(26)	(77)	(103)	(397)	(261)	(658)
Cramer's V =		0.42			0.42			0.40	
Gamma[b] =		0.73			0.88			0.69	

Cramer's V (Office) = 0.11

	All Candidates		
	I	II	Overall
I[a]	11.0%	1.7%	6.8%
II[a]	32.0	13.8	24.0
III[a]	34.6	23.2	29.6
IV	15.6	22.9	18.8
V	4.4	17.7	10.3
VI	2.4	8.8	5.3
VII[c]	0.0	11.9	5.3
100% =	456	362	818
Cramer's V =		0.46	
Gamma =		0.60	

[a]In this study the *center of town* was defined as an area three-quarters of a mile in radius from the center of town—Union Depot. The smaller residence areas shown in the display for all candidates considered together were determined by drawing concentric circles, one-quarter of a mile in radius from the Union Depot. Thus area I defines the very heart of the city, and area VII is the closest to the city limits.

[b]The relationship between ordinal variables such as residence, measured by distance from the center, and time, measured in categories "earlier" and "later," can be captured by gamma. This measure of association ranges from minus one to plus one—perfect negative to perfect positive association—with a value of zero indicating no relationship in the ranked order of variables. See Hubert Blalock, *Social Statistics* (New York, 1972), 298, 424-26. In this case, the value of 0.60 for all candidates indicates a substantial shift of office-seekers to areas more distant from the city's center later in the period.

[c]Candidates could campaign from the seventh circle only after this area was annexed in the early 1880s. Moreover, the West End, an exclusive suburb on the southwest side of Atlanta, was absorbed as the Seventh Ward in 1893. All candidates from this ward—less than one-fourth of the contestants who resided within the seventh circle—necessarily resided in an area farthest from the center. All of the other wards in the city resembled irregular slices of pie carved from the center to the limits.

The dramatic shift in the residential distribution of candidates through time raises the question of whether this change introduced new and different kinds of candidates to Atlanta city politics. At first glance, the answer appears positive with regard to period of arrival and, to a lesser extent, region of birth and political persistence. Overall, fewer than 40 percent of those candidates coming to Atlanta after 1870 resided within the inner belt, but 70 percent of those arriving before 1871 and more than 75 percent of those coming before the war lived there. About 75 percent of the foreign-born and over 67 percent of the Northerners resided in the city's core, compared with about 55 percent of the Southerners. Over 70 percent of the candidates who campaigned three or more times for city office but less than 58 percent of those competing for the first or second time came from the center of town. Yet here it is important to recognize that the relationships so far described were largely the consequence of simultaneous changes among all four characteristics through time. The early settlers, non-Southerners, and political repeaters were a larger proportion among the candidates before 1884, when most office-seekers lived in the city's center. Their place was preempted by the recent arrivals, Southerners (especially native Georgians), and political newcomers after 1884, when the majority of contestants lived in the outskirts. In analyzing these differences between candidates from the core and ring within each subperiod, however, only a few minor distinctions existed between candidates differentiated by area of residence, no matter what the office sought.

It is of particular interest that residential distinctions did not correspond to class differences among the candidates. As noted in chapter three, another historian of Atlanta at least indirectly suggested that such was the case. James Russell, in his discussion of environmental differences between the central city and outlying areas, claimed these differences formed the basis of class conflict in Atlanta's political system, particularly before 1874. According to his interpretation, poorer citizens residing near the outskirts, aggravated by the city government's relentless channeling of public monies to the commercial district, took political action.[28] If Russell were right, class backgrounds, as indicated by occupation and property, should differ between candidates from the inner and outer belts. However, such disparities did not exist. From 1865 to 1873, almost the same proportion of blue-collar candidates as contestants with other occupations lived in the center of town. Moreover, variations in property among candidates within both broad residential areas far outweighed the relatively slight distinctions in average property-holding between them. Since, contrary to Russell's suggestion, both broad areas examined here contained lower- and upper-class groups of citizens before and after 1884, the appearance of diverse groups of office-seekers from both areas could be anticipated. Blue-collar candidates, however, did have a slightly greater propensity to live in the center after 1884—a situation, of course, that Russell could not have predicted. This did not result from a shift in the kinds of skilled trades blue-collar candidates engaged in or a change in location of key industries. Rather, certain political arrangements appeared most significant. Various aspects of campaigning, political meetings, and elections took place in the center of town. Candidates with white-collar occupations would likely have worked in this area and probably had opportunities to escape the confines of their jobs. Therefore it would have been less important for such people to reside in the center than for contestants who were manual workers. Workers' political organizations were the most vocal critics of the monopoly on political activity held by those in the city's core and of the resulting inconvenience to blue-collar candidates and voters.[29]

PERIOD OF ARRIVAL

Although the residence of contestants was not associated strongly with other factors in races for any of the three offices, the overall shift in the residential base of Atlanta's candidates did coincide with another fundamental alteration in the social bases of political aspiration: the disappearance of the early settlers and the rise of recent arrivals.

Other historians of Atlanta have pointed to a surprising degree of continuity in the social and economic life of the city before and after the Civil War.[30] That more than half of the candidates before 1884 (and about two-thirds before the mid-1870s) had resided in Atlanta before the war offers further evidence of this continuity. On the other hand, only 10 percent of the office-seekers at this time had begun their political careers before Sherman's invasion. In other words, more than 90 percent of the contestants in the postwar period were new to the municipal political arena.[31]

TABLE 6
Period of Arrival in Atlanta of Candidates by Office and by Subperiod

Period of Arrival	Mayor			Alderman			Councilman		
	I	II	M	I	II	A	I	II	C
Before 1861	69.7%	29.2%	52.6%	46.2%	19.5%	26.2%	57.4%	12.2%	40.0%
	(33)	(24)	(57)	(26)	(77)	(103)	(403)	(261)	(664)
Cramer's V =		0.40			0.26			0.45	
Gamma =		−0.70			−0.56			−0.81	
Before 1871	100%	54.2%	80.7%	80.8%	49.4%	57.3%	91.3%	38.6%	71.0%
	(33)	(24)	(57)	(26)	(77)	(103)	(403)	(261)	(664)
Cramer's V =		0.57			0.28			0.57	
Gamma =		−1.00			−0.62			−0.87	

Before 1861—Cramer's V (Office) = 0.12
Before 1871—Cramer's V (Office) = 0.12

All Candidates

	I	II	Overall
Before 1851	14.7%	4.7%	10.3%
1851-1860	41.6	9.7	27.5
1861-1870	33.3	26.0	30.1
1871-1880	10.4	35.9	21.6
1881-1903	0.0	23.8	10.4
100% =	462	362	824
Cramer's V =		0.57	
Gamma =		−0.74	

Moreover, contestants who had lived in antebellum Atlanta did not monopolize city politics before 1884; they faced formidable challenges from candidates who came to the city in the aftermath of war and destruction. These later office-seekers then comprised 33 percent of the field before 1884 and 26 percent after that year, when the proportion of the earliest settlers among the candidates shrank to less than 15 percent. From the mid-1890s to the turn of the century, a newer group of political aspirants muscled its way into the political arena: 60 percent of the candidates in this period had arrived in Atlanta after 1870. This succession occurred among contestants for all three municipal offices, although the earliest settlers tended to dominate the mayoral races.

This candidate succession mirrored fundamental changes in the city's population. Although no exact figures are available, the tremendous increase in Atlanta's population during the last third of the nineteenth century was largely due to substantial and continuous migration into the city. As early as 1868 the *Constitution* estimated that half of the population had not lived in Atlanta before the war.[32] If anything, this was an underestimation. Atlanta's population increased from approximately 9,000 in 1860 to nearly 22,000 in 1870, 37,000 in 1880, 65,000 in 1890, and 89,000 in 1900; that this scale of growth could have occurred only by substantial inmigration is strongly supported by evidence of an extensive migration out of the city during this time.[33] In the immediate postwar period, when the extremely large migration to Atlanta gave recent arrivals a substantial base in the city, many newcomers did not wait to seek public position; by the mid-1870s the most numerous among the contestants were those who had arrived in the late 1860s. A "lag" effect was more pronounced for candidates who came to the city later. Individuals arriving during the 1870s were less than one-tenth of the contestants in that same period; they were over one-third of the office-seekers in both the 1880s and 1890s. Similarly, those who migrated to Atlanta in the 1880s were less than one-tenth of the contestants at that time, but constituted slightly more than one-third of the office-seekers in the 1890s.

TEN YEARS' RESIDENCE

That a long identification with Atlanta became more and more important over time is shown in table 7. Before 1884 only about 66 percent of the contestants had lived in Atlanta for at least ten years, but after that year over 85 percent could make that claim. When Atlanta was rising from the ashes, and contained a large number of citizens newly arrived in the city, political doors were more open to newcomers. The struggle between representatives of the new migrants to the city and those returning to Atlanta after their momentary evacuation in the face of Sherman's forces may have formed at least part of the roots of instability and conflict characteristic of Atlanta politics in the immediate postwar period. But as the city matured, contestants had to wait their turns. By the turn of the century even the great majority of post-1870 arrivals had lived at least ten years in the city before seeking elective office.

TABLE 7
Ten Years' Length of Residence in Atlanta of Candidates by Office and by Subperiod

Length of Residence	Mayor			Alderman			Councilman		
	I	II	M	I	II	A	I	II	C
Ten Years' Residence	87.9%	100%	93.0%	73.1%	96.1%	90.3%	66.5%	84.3%	73.5%
	(33)	(24)	(57)	(26)	(77)	(103)	(403)	(261)	(664)
Cramer's V =		0.23			0.34			0.20	
Gamma =		1.00			0.80			0.46	

Cramer's V (Office) = 0.17

	All Candidates		
	I	II	Overall
Ten Years' Residence	68.4%	87.8%	76.3%
100% =	462	362	824
Cramer's V =		0.23	
Gamma =		0.54	

Although citizens who had resided fewer than ten years in the city
clearly were not barred, in law or practice, from political participation,
they largely limited their political goals to councilmanic seats. One-third
of the candidates for council before 1884 and one-sixth after that year
were newcomers. To contest at-large positions, especially after 1884,
a longer stay in the city was required.

Newcomers to a city are an interesting group in politics. Those without long attachment to the city may be more likely to advocate change
or to forsake tradition, if only in the kinds of people who should rule.
Their presence in a political system may signal a challenge to the governing elite, which has deeper roots in the city. A political system that wit-
nesses a transition in leadership cadre from older settlers to recent arrivals
or a constant battle between more established citizens and the relative
newcomers poses an interesting question for the student of politics: does
such a change coincide with other alterations in the system? In Atlanta
this would seem to be true, since the passing of the old guard coincided
with the demise of partisan politics and the emergence of a citizens' re-

form movement and also with the rise of "New South" rhetoric. However, despite the rise of new city politicians after 1884, the idea of "changing the guard" in this sense did not capture the imagination of political pundits and candidates of the period. Throughout the late nineteenth century a long identification with the city remained a valued attribute for office-seekers in contemporary opinion.

It seems reasonable that long-time residents would disappear from politics through time. Certainly this would be the case within a broader sweep of history and also for older men among earlier settlers who sought Atlanta office in the postwar period. Yet even though the average age of earlier settlers was greater than that of more recent arrivals before 1884, both groups contained men young enough to continue political careers beyond that year. Moreover, the fact that by the turn of the century those few candidates who had lived in Atlanta before the war averaged about sixty years of age suggests a lack of aspiration for city office among men born in Atlanta before the war but who reached maturity after 1884.

Robert Dahl, in his study of New Haven, noted the passing of the "patricians"—legally trained men of property from well-established families—from city politics by the early 1840s.[34] Atlanta, a much younger city than New Haven, did not have an established elite in the same sense as evolved in New England. Moreover, a visible proportion of the early settlers who campaigned after the Civil War were blue-collar workers, and little difference in property-holding existed between antebellum arrivals and candidates who came later to Atlanta. Thus a patrician group who enjoyed high socioeconomic position and the more amorphous prestige of a long identification with the city did not materialize in Atlanta.

Indeed, age was the only significant social difference between candidates who came early or late to the city. Earlier settlers generally could be distinguished from recent arrivals by their greater ages in all but mayoral contests, where even newcomers were older men. In part these age distinctions between early and recent arrivals were due to differences in the proportions of each who had lived at least ten years in the city, for newcomers tended to be much younger than more established citizens.

The length of a candidate's identification with the city was also connected to political variables. Predictably, few candidates living less than ten years in Atlanta sought office more than once, and only a handful campaigned as many as four times within their first ten years in the city. Those individuals who initiated shortly after coming to Atlanta what were to be sustained political careers generally had resided in the city at least ten years at the time of their subsequent campaigns.[35] Likewise, only a very few newcomers had previous service either on political committees or in appointive office. Thus without much previous political experience in Atlanta, a group of younger men made a challenge for positions in city government.[36]

AGE

Rather predictably, Atlanta's candidates for city offices in the late nineteenth century were not a representative group in terms of age, although no age group was unrepresented among them. Although the central tendency was towards the middle-age level—50 percent of the candidates ranged in age from thirty-five to forty-eight years—the overall range extended from twenty-one to seventy-five. Ten percent were under thirty; another 10 percent were over fifty-five. Mayoral candidates tended to be somewhat older than those running for alderman, and an even greater age gap lay between both mayoral and aldermanic contestants and those running for City Council, particularly after 1884. Atlantans probably felt that the more prestigious and important at-large positions should be reserved for the more mature. Atlantans sometimes expressed such notions openly, as when the *Constitution* reported some anxiety concerning the maturity of W. H. Hulsey, a thirty-year-old lawyer seeking the mayoralty in 1868.[37]

Table 8 indicates that candidates tended to be older after 1884, especially those seeking aldermanic and councilmanic seats. The average age of forty for contestants before 1884 is substantially lower than the later average of forty-five. The comparison of cutoff points for the lower and upper quartiles of candidates for each of the three offices further indicates the shift in emphasis away from youth at the end of the era. Nonetheless, both young and old could be found among office-seekers for all elective positions throughout the entire period, though clearly not proportional to their strength among Atlanta's male population.

The increase in average age among contestants paralleled a similar increase among all Atlanta males over the age of 21, from 34.2 in 1870 to 37.3 in 1900. These figures also suggest that the average age of office-seekers, particularly in at-large races, was significantly higher than that

TABLE 8

Age of Candidates by Office and by Subperiod

Age	Mayor			Alderman			Councilman			All Candidates		
	I	II	M	I	II	A	I	II	C	I	II	Overall
Median	45.5	47.5	46.5	41.5	46.0	44.4	38.6	42.8	39.8	39.1	44.2	41.3
Mean	46.7	47.9	47.2	40.6	46.2	44.8	39.8	44.1	41.5	40.4	44.8	42.3
Standard Deviation	10.4	9.2	9.8	8.5	8.2	8.6	8.9	10.2	9.6	9.1	9.8	9.7
Coefficient of Variability	0.22	0.19	0.21	0.21	0.18	0.19	0.22	0.23	0.23	0.23	0.22	0.23
Minimum	30	32	30	29	26	26	21	23	21	21	23	21
Maximum	71	71	71	63	67	67	68	75	75	71	75	75
Q_1	39.5	41.0	40.0	33.0	40.0	38.5	32.5	36.0	33.5	33.0	37.0	35.0
Q_3	51.0	51.5	52.0	45.0	51.5	50.5	44.5	52.0	47.0	45.0	52.0	49.0
N	32	24	56	26	76	102	384	243	627	442	343	785
$F =$		0.21(1/54 d.f.)			8.97(1/100 d.f.)			30.99(1/625 d.f.)			43.94(1/783 d.f.)	
$Eta^2 =$		0.06			0.29			0.22			0.23	

F (Office) = 13.28(2/782 d.f.)
Eta^2 (Office) = 0.18

of Atlanta's voters during both subperiods. Examination of other elements of the age distribution delineates this difference. Even using 1900 (when the average age of Atlanta's adult males was highest) as the base year to compare the age of the general population with that of all office-seekers after 1884, the contrast is clear. At the turn of the century, over half of Atlanta's potential office-seekers but less than 16 percent of its actual contenders were younger than 35. During this same period, over 17 percent of the candidates but only about 12 percent of the male citizens were 55 or older. Thus younger males, not unexpectedly, were severely underrepresented among candidates, and older citizens were only slightly overrepresented. The middle-age group of Atlanta's citizens, especially those from 45 to 54, had the most disproportionate number seeking city office.[38]

Age differences among candidates for the three positions and between groups of contestants campaigning early or late in the period were in part reflections of other social distinctions already examined. In particular, age variation through time was related to differences in the proportions of candidates before and after 1884 who had lived ten years in the city. The generally older ten-year residents and earlier settlers had a stronger representation in at-large contests than less-than-ten-year residents and recent arrivals, although in mayoral contests even recent arrivals tended to be older men.

Age distinctions among candidates also were related partly to political longevity.[39] Most contestants younger than thirty-five were competing for the first time, and fewer than 10 percent of these younger men were engaged in their fourth or more campaign. Atlantans with sustained political careers tended to be much older than the average citizen, and a substantially greater proportion of older compared to younger office-seekers had served on political committees or in appointive office. Complaints regarding the political activities of older citizens, as noted in the third chapter, can be understood in this context. Those Atlantans, especially younger office-seekers, who attacked older candidates for their monopoly of city politics appear to have been accurate observers as well as polemicists.

The growing preponderance of older candidates through time cannot be attributed to the link between age and other characteristics. Several groups of candidates that tended to be associated with older age—earlier settlers, non-Southerners, blue-collar workers (and political repeaters)—

comprised a smaller proportion of the office-seekers after 1884 than before; yet throughout the period, the average age of Atlanta's political
hopefuls increased. Two observations, more properly offered as explanations only in comparative analysis, appear pertinent to Atlanta's situation and useful as hypotheses elsewhere: the change from generally younger to older candidates paralleled a growth in the age of a new city (in
particular, an increase in average age among Atlanta's adult males) and
also Atlanta's transition from unstable to settled political conditions.

MINOR CITY OFFICEHOLDING

One possible avenue into campaigns for elective office, and one indicator of a wide interest in local politics, is previous service in appointive office. As table 9 demonstrates, however, such experience does not appear
as an important apprenticeship for campaigning in Atlanta except in the
mayoral contests. A sizeable proportion of mayoral candidates, especially
after 1884, had this background. Most had served on administrative
boards, like E. W. Martin, who had served on the Board of Police Commissioners, and D. C. O'Keefe, who had served on the Board of Health,
although a few, such as City Attorney John Goodwin, had filled other
positions. In contrast, 28 percent of the aldermanic aspirants and 18 percent of the councilmanic contestants had such experience. Some candidates had served five or more terms in appointive office, but in general
there was not a considerable circulation among city offices by local politicos (at least in this order of sequence).[40] Because of the modest number
of candidates who attempted to advance from such positions to major
elective offices, prior performance in minor political offices rarely became a major issue during campaigns.

Certain types of candidates were more likely than others to have had
such formal political experience. This clearly was true in the case of vocational groups. Almost 16 percent of the proprietors and white-collar workers and about 36 percent of the professional men but only 7 percent of
the skilled artisans (none after 1884) had this background. Thus this potential path of recruitment to elective positions seemed closed to manual
workers, while broader political activity was characteristic of professional
men who ran for city office. Although many appointive positions obviously called for skills associated with white-collar occupations, no such pre-

TABLE 9

Previous Minor Officeholding of Candidates
by Office and by Subperiod

	Mayor			Alderman			Councilman		
	I	II	M	I	II	A	I	II	C
Appointive Office Holders	39.4%	50.0%	43.9%	30.8%	27.3%	28.2%	18.1%	18.0%	18.2%
	(33)	(24)	(57)	(26)	(77)	(103)	(403)	(261)	(664)
Cramer's V =		0.11			0.03			0.001	
Gamma =		0.21			−0.08			−0.003	

Cramer's V (Office) = 0.17

	All Candidates		
	I	II	Overall
Appointive Office Holders	20.3%	22.1%	21.1%
	(462)	(362)	(824)
Cramer's V =		0.02	
Gamma =		0.05	

requisite would have been necessary to serve on bodies such as the Board of Police Commissioners. Atlanta laboring men did not seem concerned with representation in appointive offices; at least no workers' organizations or blue-collar candidates publicly called for direct representation on such bodies. Transplanted Northerners were much more likely than immigrants or native Southerners to have served in appointive office before their campaigns. For example, six of the seven northern-born candidates for mayor, compared with two-fifths of the other mayoral contestants, had this experience. Men with early roots in Atlanta had broader political experience than newcomers; partly as a result of this, contestants with previous service in appointive office generally were older than other office-seekers.

Experience on political committees, service in appointive offices, and repeated candidacies were interrelated. In councilmanic contests, candidates who tended to be repeaters in municipal campaigns also had accumulated considerably more political experience in other ways than those who were political novices. In all three races candidates with prior service

TABLE 10

**Previous Membership on Political Committees
of Candidates by Office and by Subperiod**

	Mayor			Alderman			Councilman		
	I	II	M	I	II	A	I	II	C
Committee Service	36.4%	83.3%	56.1%	46.2%	63.6%	59.2%	19.6%	42.9%	28.8%
	(33)	(24)	(57)	(26)	(77)	(103)	(403)	(261)	(664)
Cramer's V =		0.47			0.15			0.25	
Gamma =		0.79			0.34			0.51	

Cramer's V (Office) = 0.24

	All Candidates		
	I	II	Overall
Committee Service	22.3%	50.0%	34.5%
	(462)	(362)	(824)
Cramer's V =		0.29	
Gamma =		0.55	

in appointive office were much more likely than those without that background to have served previously on political committees.

POLITICAL COMMITTEE MEMBERSHIP

Less than one-quarter of the candidates before 1884—only slightly more than the proportion of contestants who had served in minor offices— had been members of political committees. After that year, as shown in table 10, such political experience was a major stepping-stone to campaigning for elective offices. Over four-fifths of the mayoral candidates, nearly two-thirds of the aldermanic contestants, and slightly more than two-fifths of the councilmanic contenders had this kind of previous political exposure. Before 1884 distinctions according to office had been pronounced: 36 percent of the mayoral hopefuls and 46 percent of the aldermanic aspirants but less than 20 percent of the councilmanic contestants had this background.

The increased proportion of candidates who campaigned for major city office after first serving on important political bodies reflected the emergence of the citizen's reform movement. Before 1884 such activity was divided between membership on either the Republican or Democratic executive committees (mainly the latter) and service on partisan nominating bodies. After 1884 this experience entailed either service on one of the nominating committees created by the citizens' reform movement or on the non-partisan City Executive Committee, which emerged at the end of the 1880s.[41] Before 1884 partisan committees were generally small, providing a numerically weak base from which office-seekers could emerge. On the other hand, citizens' committees after 1884 ranged in membership from eighteen to one hundred, and even the City Executive Committee in the second subperiod generally consisted of more people than the earlier partisan committees had.[42] Yet the increased size of committees did not necessarily mean an increase in the proportion of candidates with such service. The expansion through time in the number of appointive offices, for example, did not produce a corresponding increase in the number of candidates with such political background. In this sense, the role of the citizens' reform movement in political advancement transcended the sheer size of the committees it created.

The appearance of substantial numbers of candidates from such a political base is not surprising. Citizens who contributed their services to such committees already were committed to political activity. Persons already interested in competing for office also could see the advantage of taking part in deliberations that sought the formation of a unified ticket and set the rules for nominations and campaigns. The accusations of contemporary critics that the function of such political organizations was to promote the candidacies of their members had some basis in fact, whether or not this was the result of conspiracy. Whatever the motivations of candidates who had served on such committees before running, the establishment of such bodies, in at least one way, considerably narrowed the base of political recruitment. After 1884, when such a large proportion of candidates followed this path to city campaigns, citizens without such service seemed relatively removed from political consideration, particularly in at-large contests.

Channeling large numbers of candidates through this political filter did not cause the changes that occurred in the social characteristics of candidates after 1884. Certain kinds of candidates, however, were more likely to have served in appointive office or on political committees. Long-time residents and older men in general were more likely to have had such prior service than newcomers or younger men. Non-Southerners and blue-collar workers also were more inclined than other political aspirants after 1884 to have this background; at the same time, candidates for City Council with white-collar occupations who had served on political committees before their campaigns generally had more property than those without that experience. Other political factors were much more important correlates of such service than were social attributes. There was a substantial overlap between prior membership in appointive offices and on political committees, and in all but mayoral contests, candidates who had been members of political committees were much more likely than contestants without this experience to have been political repeaters.

POLITICAL PERSISTENCE

The most important measure of political interest is the number of times a candidate campaigned for elective city office. This variable distinguishes between novices—candidates competing for the first, and perhaps only, time—and political repeaters. Individuals who competed for city office four or more times, called *perennial politicians* in this study, can also be differentiated from those whose political careers were more ephemeral. Comparison of the social characteristics of candidates divided in this manner suggests some significant elements of the social bases of Atlanta's politics.[43]

Table 11 reveals a constant influx of new political aspirants into the Atlanta political system throughout the era. Only in the period before 1884 were the political novices less than a majority of the candidates. Moreover, nearly 30 percent of all office-seekers were political transients who ran only once for elective office—an indication of the high degree of fluidity in Atlanta politics. The remaining novices went on to campaign on other occasions, but fewer than 30 percent of Atlanta's political hopefuls competed more than twice. Only a handful of candidates, such as D. A. Beattie, William H. Brotherton, Frank P. Rice, and James G. Woodward, had herculean political appetites; a bare 14 percent of the office-seekers reached the stage where they might be called perennials.

TABLE 11

Political Persistence of Candidates
by Office and by Subperiod

No. of Campaigns	Mayor			Alderman			Councilman		
	I	II	M	I	II	A	I	II	C
First	30.3%	29.2%	29.8%	34.6%	32.5%	33.0%	49.6%	67.8%	56.8%
Second	21.2	29.2	24.6	7.7	39.0	31.1	22.8	16.5	20.3
Third	18.2	16.7	17.5	26.9	11.7	15.5	12.9	7.7	10.8
Fourth or more	30.3	25.0	28.1	30.8	16.9	20.4	14.6	8.0	12.0
100% =	33	24	57	26	77	103	403	261	664
Cramer's V =		0.10			0.33			0.18	
Gamma =		−0.06			−0.22			−0.32	

Cramer's V (Office) = 0.15

	All Candidates		
	I	II	Overall
First	47.6%	57.7%	51.9%
Second	21.6	22.1	22.0
Third	14.1	9.1	11.9
Fourth or more	16.7	11.0	14.2
100% =	462	362	824
Cramer's V =		0.12	
Gamma =		−0.20	

The structure of city government strongly influenced these patterns. In the immediate postwar period, from 1865 to 1873, when the proportion of political newcomers was at its lowest point and that of political repeaters was at its highest, elections were held annually and incumbents were permitted to campaign for office.[44] The 1874 city charter, however, proscribed elected officials from succeeding themselves—a situation that promoted political opportunity for individuals previously uninvolved in municipal contests—and established elections every two years. Less formal sanctions also may have increased opportunities for beginners. Two goals of the citizens' reform movement were to induce individuals who had not sullied their hands in politics to seek city office and to discourage the ambitions of some candidates who had.[45] Since nearly two-thirds of the office-seekers from 1884 to 1893 (the high point of the citizens' movement) were political novices, and only one-tenth were perennials, this movement apparently enjoyed some amount of immediate success.[46]

In spite of the large numbers of political newcomers, greater political experience was still important in campaigns for Atlanta's higher offices. Before and after 1884 less than 33 percent of the candidates seeking-at-large positions were making their first try for city office. The proportion of aldermanic aspirants who were perennial politicians declined from 31 percent before 1884 to 17 percent afterwards, but the proportion of perennial politicians among councilmanic candidates had not exceeded 17 percent even before 1884. With little change through time, almost as many contestants for mayor were perennials as were novices.

As previously noted, other indicators of prior political experience were associated with the political persistence of candidates. Only 14 percent of the novices, compared with 40 percent of the perennials, had previously served in minor offices; less than 25 percent of the former but 60 percent of the latter had been members of political committees. Two factors produced this relationship. First, those candidates with broader political interests were more likely to continue than others; second, contestants who sought city office more than once also tended to accumulate political experience in other ways. One-time candidates had less experience in other political endeavors than novices who continued to campaign; the latter generally had considerably less experience than those campaigning for the second time, and so on. In Atlanta politics, therefore, one correlate of political longevity was a diversified political activism.

Experienced politicians tended to share social attributes different from those of novices. The only two mayoral contestants from lower occupational strata, Woodward and Howell, had both competed for other elective positions several times before running for mayor. Over three-fourths of the beginners had professional occupations, but businessmen predominated narrowly among perennial politicians seeking the mayoralty. Differences in political persistence among members of vocational groups were minor in contests for other offices, although few clerical employees had sustained political careers. Among candidates with white-collar occupations, political novices, especially transients, generally had less property than more practiced contestants; perennials were the wealthiest group of office-seekers. Transplanted Northerners and, to a lesser extent, immigrant contestants generally were more likely than native Southerners to have been political repeaters. Political persistence also was related to long identification with Atlanta. Age had an independent connection with sustained political careers: no matter when candidates arrived in Atlanta, those who were political repeaters, particularly perennials, were generally older than novices.

SUMMARY

Aspirants for mayor were a distinct group among the contestants. Only one black Atlantan and no foreign-born citizen ran for mayor; likewise, only one blue-collar worker and one white-collar employee ever sought this position. The professional men and businessmen who dominated the mayoral campaigns generally owned considerably more property than contestants for other positions. Except for four newcomers to the city who ran in the postwar period, all mayoral candidates had lived in Atlanta at least ten years, and a strong proportion could be counted among Atlanta's early settlers. People seeking the city's highest office also tended to be older than individuals vying for other positions. Finally, candidates for the mayoralty were more likely than other political hopefuls to have had prior political experience—both in appointive office and on political committees—and to be seeking this position after previous attempts for city offices, especially those running before 1884.

Candidates for alderman formed an intermediate group between contestants for mayor and those for councilman in a social as well as political sense. Aldermanic aspirants were less likely than mayoral candidates, but more likely than councilmanic contenders to have been earlier settlers, ten-year residents, older, and wealthier men. Likewise, candidates for alderman had more previous political experience than contestants for council but less than the group of mayoral hopefuls. Only blue-collar workers with considerable political muscle sought aldermanic positions, and only the economic elite among the non-Southerners—in contrast to a relatively more sizeable subgroup of Southerners with modest holdings—attempted these races.

The contests for City Council appeared more open than the at-large races. Certainly candidates for this position were more heterogeneous than aspirants for at-large offices. The larger size of City Council and the greater number of candidates seeking these positions undoubtedly contributed to this relative diversity. Moreover, the at-large positions, and especially the mayor's office, carried greater social and political prestige in Atlanta; clearly the campaigns for these offices received much more extensive press coverage. Thus it is not unexpected that councilmanic contests included greater proportions of recent arrivals and newcomers, blue-collar workers, younger and poorer men, political novices and people without previous political experience in other ways, than the aldermanic and mayoral races. Concentration only on the office of mayor, common in the works of political scientists and sociologists for other cities, would thus have revealed a different picture of the social bases of politics in Atlanta than has been presented in this chapter.

Even given these relative differences among candidates divided by office, Atlanta's office-seekers as a whole were a homogeneous group with regard to occupation, race, region of birth, and length of residence in the city, albeit important exceptions existed. On the other hand, they had diverse ages, times of arrival, locations of residence in the city, political experience, and especially property-holdings. The young and the old, the poor and the very wealthy, sought city office, although most contestants fell between extremes. Earlier settlers and more recent arrivals, individuals from the center and the outskirts of the city, and experienced politicians and novices battled for public position.

There were some significant differences in the types of people who entered political contests before and after 1884. The gradual replacement of the early settlers by the relative newcomers to Atlanta was a fundamental alteration. Only a few of the latecomers, for example, had diverse, multidimensional political backgrounds or inclinations, and few could be considered perennial politicians. Similarly, early in the period when Atlanta was rebuilding and its politics were unsettled and particularly rancorous, citizens residing in the city a relatively brief time sought office in considerably greater numbers than later in the era. The average age of contestants also increased from the beginning to the end of the period, providing another example of maturation in municipal politics.

The residence areas of candidates supplied an additional striking example of change through time (from the core to the ring of the city); less noticeable was the decline in candidacies of the transplanted Northerners and the foreign-born. These two trends, in particular, seemed tied to the changing demography of the city. Demographic changes in Atlanta, however, could not account for other differences through time; the slight decline in the number of blue-collar candidates; the subtle shift, in councilmanic contests at least, towards a greater participation of men with more substantial property-holdings; and a lesser presence of political repeaters, particularly perennials. In these instances, it seemed that the citizens' reform movement conceived in 1884 achieved some of its goals. An unspoken desire to oust other types of politicians—the early settlers, younger men, and less-established citizens—may have contributed to the citizens' movement. Although not an explicit goal of the reformers, the dramatic increase in the number of candidates who had served on political committees also resulted from the citizens' movement.

Perhaps the most important finding from this analysis, however, relates to the nature of what may be called the first stage of the social filter. Both before and after 1884, and in the contests for all three offices (but especially the at-large races), Atlanta's candidates were highly unrepresentative of the citizenry in many ways. This particularly was the case with regard to occupation, property, race, age, and, to a somewhat lesser extent, length of residence in the city. Blue-collar workers (especially semiskilled and unskilled workers), the poor, blacks, young men, and newcomers to the city simply did not appear among the citizens contesting city office in numbers even approaching their strength among the population. Non-Southerners—both transplanted Northerners and immigrants—although a minority among the candidates, were an even smaller proportion of the population. The overrepresentation in city campaigns of these citizens, and of Atlantans born in Southern states other than Georgia, meant a corresponding and surprisingly strong underrepresentation for native Georgians, who remained nonetheless, the largest group among the office-seekers. In terms of geography alone, large areas of the city, depending upon the subperiod, also were poorly represented in campaigns for elective office.

But this marks the operation of the social filter only upon the decision of individuals to seek office and the ability of various political groups to screen potential candidates. Conventional sources provided few hints of systematic social bias at either stage in the emergence of candidates, except for exclusion of blacks, inclusion of only a few manual workers on public slates, and late in the period, a stated preference among Atlantans engaged in nominations for businessmen and professional men with substantial property-holdings. The quantitative analysis used in this chapter brought to the surface several intriguing patterns in the shifting social bases of Atlanta politics from 1865 to 1903. The following chapter assesses the degree to which the social filter was related to whether candidates succeeded or failed in winning the offices to which they aspired.

NOTES

1. Information in this chapter is based on findings from multivariate analysis rather than all apparent (zero-order) associations of one attribute with the others. All percentages reported in the text have been rounded to the nearest whole number, and figures have been approximated where necessary, for example, 82 percent changed to "slightly more than four-fifths." Likewise, references to property-holdings are rounded to the nearest $100 and age to the nearest year. Considerations of economy proscribe publication of all tables that should ideally accompany the discussion, and examination of relatively minor details on interconnections among attributes. Thus the presentation sacrifices some advantages of quantification in the interest of readability. Any interested scholar, however, can obtain the data file on which this analysis rests.

2. I initially examined possible distinctions within four smaller subperiods: 1865-1873, 1874-1883, 1884-1893, 1894-1903. See Eugene J. Watts, "Characteristics of Candidates in City Politics: Atlanta, 1865-1903" (unpublished Ph.D. dissertation, Emory, 1969). But subsequent analysis revealed that the most significant differences distinguished the years 1865-1883 and 1884-1903, with relatively minor distinctions *within* the two subperiods of each era. This suggests that the rise of the citizens' reform movement beginning in 1884 affected the social characteristics of Atlanta office-seekers more than either the new City Charter of 1874 or the establishment of the white citizens' primary in the 1890s.

3. According to Richard Hopkins' analysis of social mobility in Atlanta, 5 percent of the city's white native males who were between the ages of twenty and twenty-nine in 1870 were professionals; 15 percent were businessmen; 28 percent were white-collar employees; and 49 percent were manual workers (occupations could not be identified for 4 percent). The respective proportions for 1880 were 5 percent, 13 percent, 36 percent, and 41 percent, with 2 percent unknown. Richard J. Hopkins, "Patterns of Persistence and Occupational Mobility in a Southern City: Atlanta, 1870-1920" (unpublished Ph.D. dissertation, Emory, 1973), 85. (This is an age group in which upper occupational groups may be underrepresented). Census data permit rough approximations for 1890 and 1900. I calculated that in 1890, 5 percent of Atlanta's males (aged ten and over) were professional men, 18 percent were businessmen, 17 percent were white-collar workers, and 60 percent followed manual trades (most, of course, were not skilled workers). In 1900 the respective estimated percentages were 6 percent, 10 percent, 20 percent, and 64 percent. U. S. Census Office, *Report on the Population of the United States at the Eleventh Census,* part II (Washington, 1897), 634; and U. S. Census Office, *Twelfth Census of the United States, Taken in the Year 1900,* vol. II, part II (Washington, 1902), 55. Clearly proprietors and then professional men

were most overrepresented among office-seekers; blue-collar workers, as well as clerical employees, were underrepresented, although among the former skilled workers fared far better than semiskilled and unskilled workers. Whether the proportions of professional men and businessmen among candidates were unusually small or large requires information from other cities that is not presently available.

4. For examples of similar climates of opinion in other cities during this period, see Robert Dahl, *Who Governs* (New Haven, 1961), 1-86; and Robert C. Schulze, "The Role of Economic Dominants in Community Power Structure,"*American Sociological Review,* XXIII (1958), 3-9. For a discussion of the concern of the business and professional communities for city services, and their frequent lack of unity on these issues, see James M. Russell, "Atlanta, Gate City of the South, 1847-1885" (unpublished Ph.D. dissertation, Princeton, 1973), 332, 342.

5. The only attempt by unskilled workers to organize themselves politically during these years—the Workingman's Union in 1869—was an unqualified failure. Atlanta *Constitution,* November 16, 1869; and Atlanta *Journal,* November 23, 1883.

6. Although one-quarter of all white office-seekers on Republican tickets (and six of seven black G. O. P. candidates) had blue-collar occupations, one must not exaggerate the Republican appeal to the white working class as one historian of Atlanta has. Grigsby H. Wooten, Jr., "New City of the South: Atlanta, 1843-1873" (unpublished Ph.D. dissertation, Johns Hopkins, 1973), 354. Over three-quarters of the white blue-collar candidates from 1865 to 1873 whose party affiliation could be identified were Democrats.

7. The Atlanta *Constitution* in 1868 editorialized on the ideal composition of a Democratic ticket: "Every interest in the city should be fairly represented in the council. Commerce, real estate, railroad, mechanics, the legal and medical fraternities, all should have a showing." Atlanta *Constitution,* November 11, 1868. Also see Atlanta *Daily News,* November 8, 1874. The Atlanta *Journal* fretted over the "serious breach" in the citizens' reform movement in 1884 because laboring men were not "adequately represented" on the slate. Atlanta *Journal,* November 8, 1884.

8. The *Constitution* referred to this practice in 1884: "We fail to see in what way the ticket is a workingman's ticket. It is made up of many men who are not working men." Atlanta *Constitution,* November 3, 1884. The citizens' movement of 1889 avoided the kind of ruptures that occurred in 1884, 1886, and 1888 by placing two blue-collar workers on the slate. Atlanta *Journal,* November 5, 1886; and Atlanta *Constitution,* October 23, 1888; November 17, 1889.

9. Dahl discusses an increased participation by manual workers in city *office-holding* towards the turn of the century. Dahl, *Who Governs,* 37. In Atlanta, however, the overall proportion of working-class candidates in councilmanic races decreased slightly. Ward nominations and elections, more common early in the period, may have contributed to a greater say in politics for workingmen. For support on this point, see Russell, "Atlanta, Gate City of the South," 273-74. Michael Frisch noted an increase in political representation by businessmen and professional men and a corresponding decrease among artisans and workingmen at the end of his period. Michael H. Frisch, *Town Into City: Springfield, Massachusetts and The Meaning of Community 1840-1880* (Cambridge, 1972), 242-44.

10. That variations by office were not pronounced can be seen in the low value of Cramer's V (0.18), which ranges from zero for no variation to one (1.0) if each office had been the private preserve of a different vocational group. See Hubert M. Blalock, *Social Statistics* (New York, 1972), 297.

11. Atlanta *Daily Herald,* October 8, 1873.

12. By dividing the total population (males and females of all ages) into the total amount of assessed real and personal property (including all businesses) for each census year, one finds that the per capita assessed wealth in Atlanta for 1870, 1880, 1890, and 1900 was $910, $536, $703, and $564 respectively (figures rounded to the nearest dollar). Property totals from the Fulton County Tax Digest are presented in George E. Manners, "Finances of Fulton County, Georgia, 1853-1945: A History and Partial Appraisal" (unpublished MBA thesis, Univeristy of Georgia, 1946), table IV, 27a, 27b.

13. It is difficult to imagine a more diverse group of office-seekers with respect to property-holdings. Pearson's measure of skewness for the overall distribution was an extremely high 6.6, compared with the normal range of ± 3. Given this distribution, the median is a better measure of typicality than the mean, although both must be interpreted in light of the distribution's shape. Blalock, *Social Statistics,* 88-89, 55-72.

14. It is debatable whether differences in the average amount of property among groups of candidates competing for the three offices are "significant," given such extreme variation in property. One-way analysis of variance is not totally satisfactory with distributions deviating so much from the "normal" pattern. The squared value of eta indicates the proportion of the total variation in property accounted for by differences between offices was a negligible 0.02. Eta-squared would have been 1.0 only if there had been no variation in property-holdings among contestants for the same office but a difference between the mean of their property-holdings and those of candidates for other offices. It would have been zero only if there was no difference in the mean property-holdings of candidates for all offices. In this case, there are large differences in mean values, but these are outweighed by the tremendous dispersion in property values among candidates within each contest. In this situation, one must also examine other features of the distribution, in particular the quartiles. Comparison of the first and third quartiles for the three groups shows the largest values of both for mayoral contestants, followed by aspirants for alderman and councilman. A multiple range test, based on the Scheffe procedure, clearly distinguished between councilmanic contestants and those who ran for at-large offices on the basis of property-holdings. See Fred N. Kerlinger, *Foundations of Behavioral Research* (New York, 1965), 187-256, for a good introduction to analysis of variance.

15. Distinctions in mean property values among vocational groups were very large, but so were the variations within groups of businessmen and professional men. $(F = 19.0, 5/813 \text{ d.f.}, Eta^2 = 0.07)$

16. Those few candidates with either clerical or manual occupations who had sizeable property-holdings—ten such people had more than $10,000 in city property—may have been incorrectly identified in contemporary sources.

17. See Eugene J. Watts, "Black Political Progress in Atlanta, 1868-1895," *The Journal of Negro History* (July, 1974), 268-86, for a detailed discussion of blacks in Atlanta politics. Six black candidates also appeared as last-minute entrants in 1872, but they received so few votes that they were not recognized by the Atlanta *New Era* or *Constitution*. Atlanta *Daily Sun,* December 5, 1872. Victorious black candidates were more numerous and competed much later in some other Southern cities. See Howard N. Rabinowitz, "From Reconstruction to Redemption in the Urban South," *Journal of Urban History* (February, 1976), 169-94.

18. Howard N. Rabinowitz, "Continuity and Change: Southern Urban Development, 1860-1900," in Blaine A. Brownell and David R. Goldfield, eds., *The City in Southern History: The Growth of Urban Civilization in the South* (Port Washington, 1977), 100.

19. For a capsule biography of Pledger and Rucker, see August Meier, *Negro Thought in America, 1880-1915* (Ann Arbor, 1968), 250-51.

20. For a pertinent discussion of black class structure, see August Meier and David Lewis, "History of the Negro Upper Class in Atlanta, Georgia, 1890-1958," *The Journal of Negro Education,* 28 (Spring, 1959), 128-39. Although the authors maintained anonymity for the people they studied, August Meier later identified several black office-seekers as definitely those listed as upper class by his informants and stated that in his opinion all or most of the men on the 1890 ticket would have to be counted as in that group. Letter from August Meier to the author, November 24, 1974. Most black candidates were included in the brief vignettes of prominent black Atlantans by Rev. E. R. Carter, *The Black Side—A Partial History of the Business, Religious and Educational Side of the Negro in Atlanta* (Atlanta, 1894).

21. By 1900, when an Irish-Catholic lawyer won New Haven's mayoralty, ethnic politics was the "stuff" of that city's political system; no such opportunity existed in Atlanta. See Dahl, *Who Governs,* 37-38.

22. Hopkins, "Patterns of Persistence," 153-55; and Russell, "Atlanta, Gate City of the South," 167-68.

23. Census figures for Atlanta's immigrants are summarized in Hopkins, "Patterns of Persistence," 9. For a history of the Irish in Atlanta, see Carol Louise Hagglund, "Irish Immigrants in Atlanta, 1850-1896" (unpublished M. A. thesis, Emory, 1968); for recognition of immigrant participation in other southern cities see Rabinowitz, "Continuity and Change," 116.

24. Other historians of Atlanta have also concluded that the foreign-born were well assimilated into Atlanta society. See Hopkins, "Patterns of Persistence," 153-56; and Ann Mebane, "Immigrant Patterns in Atlanta, 1880 and 1896" (unpublished M. A. thesis, Emory, 1967). The Atlanta and Nashville experiences can be seen as confirmations of an hypothesis as stated above. Mayer N. Zald and Thomas A. Anderson, "Secular Trends and Historical Contingencies in the Recruitment of Mayors: Nashville as Compared to New Haven and Chicago," *Urban Affairs Quarterly* (1968), 56.

25. Native Georgians formed approximately 80 percent of Atlanta's inhabitants

in the late nineteenth century, and the proportion of the city's population that had migrated from other southern states fluctuated between 12 and 16 percent during the same period. The figures for the foreign-born decreased from nearly 5 percent in 1870 to under 3 percent in 1900, while the transplanted Northerners were fewer than 5 percent in 1870 and approximately 5 to 6 percent in later years. All percentages were calculated from Department of the Interior, *A Compendium of the Ninth Census, 1870* (Washington, 1872), 405; Department of the Interior, *A Compendium of the Tenth Census, 1880* (Washington, 1888), part I, 542-45; U. S. Census Office, *Report on the Population of the United States at the Eleventh Census: 1890,* vol. 1 (Washington, 1897), 580-83; and U. S. Census Office, *Twelfth Census of the United States: 1900,* vol. 1 (Washington, 1902), 706-09.

26. C. Vann Woodward, *Origins of the New South, 1877-1913* (Baton Rouge, 1951), 16; Rabinowitz, "Continuity and Change," 101; and Wooten, "New City of the South," 352, 365.

27. In this discussion several terms are used interchangeably: the center, core, and inner belt refer to the same area, and the outskirts, ring, and outer belt describe the other area. This pattern of dispersion held within each of Atlanta's roughly pie-shaped wards, although it was somewhat stronger in the Third and Fourth wards and weaker in the First and Fifth wards. Thus residential differences need not be discussed on a ward-by-ward basis. The actual mapping of candidates according to their specific addresses does not reveal any strong recognizable neighborhood pattern, with the previously mentioned exception of black office-seekers. As explained in chapter three, the residence areas chosen for analysis here did not conform to any contemporary division in the city; they were designed to measure possible change in the geographical base of political participation, to examine the empirical basis for the contemporary discussion regarding relative representation of certain broad areas, and to provide a mechanism to test the general hypothesis that social and political differences among office-seekers might have followed residential lines. For a discussion of gamma, see Blalock, *Social Statistics,* 298, 424-26.

28. Russell, "Atlanta, Gate City of the South," 270-88.

29. For example, workers' groups opposed periodic "reform" proposals to ban carriages from hauling voters to the polls—which always were located in the city's center—on the grounds that the change would seriously inconvenience working-class voters living and working outside the center. See Atlanta *Constitution,* July 22, 1890.

30. See Arthur Reed Taylor, "From the Ashes: Atlanta During Reconstruction, 1865-1876" (unpublished Ph.D. dissertation, Emory, 1973), 109, 312; and Rabinowitz, "Continuity and Change," 92.

31. Since it was impossible to identify unsuccessful candidates before 1865, the figure of 10 percent may underrepresent the proportion of contestants with political aspirations before this year.

32. Atlanta *Constitution,* November 14, 1868.

33. A comparison of the number of males between the ages of twenty and

twenty-nine in 1870—1,667—and the number of males in 1880 between the ages
of thirty and thirty-nine—2,905—shows the importance of the in-migration, especially since the persistence rate for the 1870 cohort was only 47 percent. Thus
2,122 of the 2,905 (73 percent) males in 1880 between the ages of thirty and
thirty-nine were newcomers. A similar comparison from 1880 to 1890 is compli-
cated by the nature of the age boundaries used for the 1890 census; to estimate
the number of males between the ages of thirty and thirty-nine in the latter year
I divided the number of males between the ages of thirty-five and forty-four in
half and added this to the number of males between the ages of thirty and thirty-
four, arriving at a total estimate of 4,330. There were, by comparison, 3,386 males
in 1880 between the ages of twenty and twenty-nine, and the persistence rate
for this group was only 43 percent. There were 5,691 males in 1890 between the
ages of twenty-five and thirty-four and 5,397 males in 1900 between the ages of
thirty-five and forty-four (similar results can be obtained by using higher age
brackets); persistence rates are unknown, but we can reasonably conclude that the
out-migration more than offset the slight decrease in these cases. Calculations for
1870 and 1880 were made from data supplied by Richard Hopkins; age compari-
sons for 1890 and 1900 were taken from U. S. Census Office, *Report on the Population of the United States at the Eleventh Census: 1890,* Vol. 1 (Washington, 1897),
114; and U. S. Census Office, *Twelfth Census of the United States: 1900,* vol. I
(Washington, 1902), 122.

    34. Dahl, *Who Governs,* 11-24.

    35. D. A. Beattie provides an extreme example. Arriving in Atlanta in the 1860s,
he campaigned five times for city office within the first ten years of his residence
in the city and six more times afterwards; his political career spanned the period
from 1871 to 1898. At the time of his last six campaigns, of course, he could not be
considered a newcomer to the city as defined in this study.

    36. Even controlling for ten years' length of residence, earlier settlers often could
be distinguished from more recent arrivals by their greater political persistence and,
to a lesser degree, previous experience in appointive office and on political committees.

    37. Atlanta *Constitution,* November 14, 1868.

    38. The average age of 34.2 for 1870 was calculated from a sample of 255 males
over age 21 drawn from a population of all Atlanta males 16 years of age and older
that was extracted from the federal census by Richard Hopkins. The means and
standard deviations for 1890—36.8 and 13.0—and for 1900—37.3 and 13.2—were
calculated from the grouped data presented in *Report on the Population of the
United States at the Eleventh Census: 1890,* 114; and *Twelfth Census of the United
States: 1900,* 122. One standard deviation around the mean age of all contestants
after 1884 provides brackets from 35.0 to 54.6, which encompass approximately
67 percent of all candidates; the same age limits in 1900 included only 37 percent
of Atlanta's males. Richard Alcorn, analyzing "leadership" in Paris, Illinois at mid-
nineteenth century, concluded that among his group (which included political
leaders), men under 30 were the most underrepresented, those in their 30s and
40s were only slightly overrepresented, but individuals over 50 were the most

overrepresented. Richard S. Alcorn, "Leadership and Stability in Mid-Nineteenth Century America: A Case Study of an Illinois Town," *Journal of American History,* LXI (December, 1974), 696-97.

39. A positive relationship between age and repetitive campaigning is to be expected, since those candidates competing for the second time, third time, and so on naturally were older than when they first sought city office. The strength of this association, however, is not based on a prime facie case. It was at least possible that many of the people competing for the first time would be older than perennial campaigners who had begun their political careers at a young age.

40. Although only 20 percent of the candidates had this experience before their campaigns, 44 percent held one of these positions at some time in their political careers. Two recognized behind-the-scenes political manipulators at the end of the era provide extreme examples: James W. English and William Brotherton had ended their quests for elective offices in the early 1880s, before their extended service as police commissioners. It also is interesting to examine the relationship between appointive office and campaigns for elective positions from the other vantage point. The number of possible appointive positions increased from ten in 1865 to thirty in 1870 and to sixty-five by the end of the era, for a total of nearly nine hundred positions (filled by less than two hundred men). Of this total, 46 percent ran for elective office sometime (not necessarily subsequently) during this period.

41. Although disparate in some ways, these committees appeared basically similar in terms of prestige and political power. Some politicos, including such notables as Walter Brown, John B. Goodwin, and Evan P. Howell, had served on five or more of these political bodies before at least some of their campaigns. As was the case for appointive officeholding, the proportion of political activists who served on committees was greater than the proportion of those who ran for office only after serving on committees. Altogether, nearly 57 percent of the candidates served on one or more political committees sometime during their political careers.

42. A noticeable percentage of the people who comprised these committees sought city office, but many did so before their committee membership. Of the 1384 possible openings on all executive and nominating committees from 1865 to 1902, 38 percent of the committeemen campaigned for elective office sometime during this same period.

43. This variable also was included to weigh the political impact, in terms of victory or defeat, of previous campaigning, and thus greater or lesser experience and exposure, in the political arena. As noted in chapter three, Atlantans sometimes asserted the benefits or disadvantages of electing individuals with greater experience. Robert Dahl, among others, has observed that virtually all pluralistic political systems produce a small band of professionals within the political stratum. Dahl, *Who Governs,* 306. Since few Atlantans with long political careers, with the exception of Woodward in later years, depended on politics for a living, I prefer to use the word "perennials." Any demarcation point used to define such perennials would be arbitrary, but it seems reasonable to assert that people who

campaign for public position four or more times had made an important com-
mitment to politics.

44. Almost one-fifth of the office-seekers in the pre-1873 period had held
city office before 1865, and thus could not be considered novices. Since 275
candidates competed for city office from 1865 through 1873, but no more than
187 individuals ran in any comparably long time period after 1873, the new
charter clearly had an impact.

45. Atlanta *Journal,* November 27, 1884.

46. Moreover, approximately two-thirds of the newcomers running for mayor
or alderman competed only once for city office, and thus were not using their
campaigns, at least in retrospect, to initiate political careers. The division between
transients and other novices was fairly even in races for council.

5

Victory and Defeat

The voters of Atlanta made the final decision upon contestants' qualifications and suitability to govern the city. Although there are many possible explanations for the outcome of individual contests, if the attributes of office-seekers consistently influenced voters' choices, then patterns of political preference for certain groups of candidates—that is, evidence of a "social filter" in elections—should emerge from analysis of large numbers of electoral contests. Several urban analysts studying other cities have at least implied that such a social filter operated in municipal politics. However, by focusing on the attibutes of office-holders and neglecting the characteristics of losing candidates, these scholars substituted inference for a systematic evaluation of the social basis of past politics. They cannot answer whether the frequently noted domination of city government by businessmen was simply the result of their preponderance among contestants or the result of the voters' conscious rejection of other candidates, which in turn reflected a deeper conviction that businessmen should rule. To answer such questions, this chapter (1) examines the characteristics of winners *and* losers and (2) separates those that had a significant impact upon political fortunes from those that did not.[1]

When black and white candidates competed against one another, racial attributes clearly outweighed all other characteristics. Black contestants, who always ran against whites, received an average vote of 12.7 percent with a very tight dispersion around that mean (S. D. = 8.3 percent). This slight variation in the vote was not due to the attributes of either black office-seekers or their white opponents. Inclusion of blacks, therefore, would add unnecessary steps to the analysis throughout this chapter by forcing repeated statistical controls for race. For example, since all black candidates were native Southerners, their poor performance would initially mask distinctions in political success between southern and nonsouthern whites. In comparison to whites, black office-seekers also were poor, young, politically inexperienced, recent arrivals, and residents of the outskirts. These qualities had no bearing upon the outcomes of black candidates' campaigns. Several were important, however, for those of whites even though no group of white contestants in Atlanta enjoyed a clear path to victory or defeat. Thus, this chapter includes only white political hopefuls.[2]

OCCUPATION

As shown in table 12, the occupation of office-seekers was no sure predictor of election results. This in itself is an important discovery. The press and many participants in the political process frequently reiterated that the upper occupational class ought to control city government. If the voters had accepted this notion, Atlanta's politics would have paralleled trends reported for New Haven, Chicago, Nashville, and other cities during most of this period.[3] Yet this analysis shows that occupation generally was not an important factor in Atlanta's elections, although there were some interesting variations in the success rate of candidates with different vocations.

In general, Atlanta politics pitted members of dissimilar vocational groups against each other in municipal campaigns. Only one direct confrontation between two blue-collar workers occurred, and in only three contests did two white-collar employees seek the same office. White- and blue-collar workers also rarely faced each other. Two mayoral contests featured only professional men, but no professionals competed solely against each other in aldermanic races. Professionals running for City Council had other professionals as opponents only one-sixth of the time. Proprietors formed such a large majority among office-seekers that two-fifths of them—33 percent in councilmanic contests, 50 percent in mayoral races, and 55 percent in aldermanic battles—campaigned exclusively against each other. Yet even in these cases the general practice was to oppose men of different occupations. Thus the various success rates displayed in table 12 are not the consequence of intragroup competition.

TABLE 12

Percentage of Victorious Candidates within
Vocational Groups by Office and by Subperiod

Occupation	Mayors			Aldermen		
	1865-1883	1884-1903	1865-1903	1865-1883	1884-1903	1865-1903
Professional	38.1% (21)	54.5% (11)	43.8% (32)	[50.0%] (2)	61.5% (13)	60.0% (15)
Proprietor	66.7 (12)	[50.0] (8)	60.0 (20)	63.2 (19)	60.0 (45)	60.9 (64)
White Collar	— (—)	[0.0] (1)	[0.0] (1)	[33.3] (3)	54.5 (11)	50.0 (14)
Blue Collar	— (—)	[33.3] (3)	[33.3] (3)	[0.0] (1)	[80.0] (5)	[66.7] (6)
Cramer's V =	0.28	0.25	0.21	0.30	0.11	0.08

Occupation	Councilmen			All Candidates		
	1865-1883	1884-1903	1865-1903	1865-1883	1884-1903	1865-1903
Professional	50.0% (58)	52.5% (59)	51.3% (117)	46.9% (81)	54.2% (83)	50.6% (164)
Proprietor	56.0 (241)	58.3 (144)	56.9 (385)	57.0 (272)	58.4 (197)	57.6 (469)
White Collar	28.9 (45)	36.0 (25)	31.4 (70)	29.2 (48)	40.5 (37)	34.1 (85)
Blue Collar	59.6 (47)	60.0 (20)	59.7 (67)	58.3 (48)	60.7 (28)	59.2 (76)
Cramer's V =	0.20	0.12	0.16	0.18	0.11	0.15

Note: Readers must examine the percentages for mayoral and aldermanic contests in this and subsequent tables with care. The small size of certain subgroups among at-large contestants within the two subperiods provides a very small base for percentages, and thus the situation where a difference in victory or defeat for only a few people could change the overall impression. This situation, of course, was considered in the writing of this chapter.

Although blue-collar workers were a small proportion of Atlanta's political hopefuls, a working-class identification did not condemn a candidate to defeat. The few semiskilled (and black unskilled) workers who ran did lose their bids for City Council, but skilled tradesmen, the least likely of the major white occupational groups to furnish contestants for city office, had a slightly larger proportion of winners than any other group. The commonly expressed notion, particularly by organized workingmen's groups, that some members of city government should directly represent workers undoubtedly helped blue-collar candidates, especially when only a few competed in elections. Such a situation maximized the likelihood that working-class voters would rally to the support of their men.[4] This desire for representation, however, did not appear to apply to at-large positions until late in the period. Only the ambition and ability of one individual, James G. Woodward, prevented the exclusion of the working class from the office of mayor. Successful in five of nine campaigns for city office during this time, Woodward captured the mayoralty in 1898 after losing once before. His victory coincided with the rise of the "ex-plebes" to political power noted by Robert Dahl in New Haven. Woodward also won election to the Board of Alderman in each of his three attempts. Only one other blue-collar worker gained admittance to that body; two others tried but met defeat. As a rule, skilled tradesmen were limited to positions on City Council.[5]

White-collar workers, who had no well defined or organized base on which to support their campaigns and no express sense of social station or class, had the hardest time winning elections. Unlike that of manual workers, the occupational status of clerical employees never appeared as an issue in Atlanta's municipal campaigns, nor were such people purposefully placed on "balanced" tickets. Even though they competed in slightly greater numbers than blue-collar workers, they won fewer offices. Most clerical employees competed for City Council, and here voters elected them less than one-third of the time. White-collar workers did enjoy relatively greater success in aldermanic races than in councilmanic contests, but this can be explained by the circumstances involved in specific cases. Albert Howell, the only white-collar worker to seek the mayoralty, was able to win aldermanic office twice—once as an uncontested candidate. A member of one of Atlanta's most prestigious families, Howell maintained close contact with the working-class organizations and was perceived as representing them rather than white-collar workers.

According to the press, he was a member of the American Protective
Association and maintained close ties to one of Atlanta's bosses, William
H. Brotherton, who strongly supported him. Two additional white-collar
workers won aldermanic positions by defeating other white-collar workers, and another victor, M. M. Welch in 1900, was a reputed member of
the Brotherton machine. On the whole, men from lower white-collar
backgrounds—low in prestige and bereft of organized support—seemed
to face the greatest handicaps in municipal politics of the four vocational
groups.

Professional men broke almost exactly even in their contests for city
office, with their relatively poor performance in mayoral races early in
the era the only deviation. In part, this can be explained by other qualities of professional men and businessmen seeking the mayoralty. The
latter group usually owned larger amounts of property and had more
previous campaign experience than the former. Since these characteristics
correlated more significantly than occupation with political success, businessmen enjoyed a built-in advantage in the period before 1884. In both
subperiods, however, the occupation of mayoral contenders was far from
an overriding matter in elections. Constituting a majority among mayoral
contestants overall, mayors with professional occupations thus narrowly
outnumbered mayors with business backgrounds.

Contestants from the business community performed most consistently in their races and had approximately the same ratio of victories to defeats regardless of the office sought or period of campaign. Atlanta's
voters did not evince any consistent preference for such candidates when
others opposed them, but the overwhelming majority of businessmen
among office-seekers guaranteed their dominance in city government as
long as they continued to win more contests than they lost.[6]

Before 1884 representatives of the business community captured nearly two-thirds of the elected offices, including half of the mayoral positions
and all but two aldermanic seats. Professionals gained one-sixth of the
offices—half of the mayoral, one aldermanic, and 14 percent of the councilmanic posts. No blue-collar workers filled at-large positions early in the
era, but they earned 14 percent of the councilmanic offices. In contrast,
only 6 percent of the latter positions and one aldermanic seat were held
by clerical employees. The pattern of the 1885-1903 years deviated only
slightly from that of the preceding years. Businessmen won three-fifths
of the posts in aldermanic and councilmanic races, and four of eleven

mayoral positions. As a result of their greater participation, professionals held close to one-quarter of the elected offices, including six mayoral and 18 percent of the aldermanic chairs. White-collar and blue-collar workers constituted 13 percent and 9 percent, respectively, of the Board of Aldermen; the former were 7 percent and the latter were 9 percent of the men who sat on City Council.[7]

Of all the candidate characteristics considered in this study, only size of property-holdings had a consistent differential effect upon the ability of vocational groups to win elections. Regardless of occupation, contestants with greater amounts of property generally were more successful than those with less stake in the community, although blue- and white-collar workers with substantial holdings were few in number. Eight of ten aspirants who clearly identified with blue-collar occupations but had more than $6,750 in property won their races; fewer than one-sixth of the clerical employees with $2,500 or less but almost two-fifths of those with more property were victorious. Variations were much more striking for professionals and proprietors, however, Overall, two-thirds of the businessmen owning more than $16,000 in property and three-quarters of the most substantial lawyers and physicians won their races, whereas only one-third of the small shopkeepers and slightly less than one-third of the lesser professionals—men with $2,500 or less in property-succeeded in winning office. Moreover, among the lowest quartile group of candidates according to property-holdings only the blue-collar contestants had a favorable ratio of victories to defeats. Clearly then, greater amounts of property were not as politically important for skilled tradesmen as they were for professional men, businessmen, and clerical workers.

PROPERTY

Thus between the two indicators of class positions—occupation and property-holdings—the latter exerted a more important influence in Atlanta's municipal elections than the former. Table 13 presents distinctions in average amount of property between winners and losers, organized according to elective office and period of campaigning. There were economic differences between winning and losing candidates for all three positions, but property apparently increased the likelihood of victory more in at-large races than in contests among candidates from individual

TABLE 13

Average Property-Holdings of Winning and Losing Candidates by Office and by Subperiod

Mayors

	1865-1883		1884-1903		1865-1903	
	Winners	Losers	Winners	Losers	Winners	Losers
Median	$ 12,985	$ 7,575	$ 27,800	$ 8,472	$ 24,450	$ 8,000
Mean	45,454	28,145	50,412	10,845	47,475	20,987
Standard Deviation	69,309	44,870	54,940	14,173	62,757	36,119
Coefficient of Variability	1.52	1.59	1.09	1.31	1.32	1.72
Minimum	0	528	750	0	0	0
Maximum	215,000	175,000	154,608	52,461	215,000	175,000
N =	16	17	11	12	27	29
F =	0.73, 1/30 d.f.		5.8, 1/21 d.f.		3.81, 1/54 d.f.	

Aldermen

	1865-1883		1884-1903		1865-1903	
	Winners	Losers	Winners	Losers	Winners	Losers
Median	$ 26,320	$ 10,340	$ 13,400	$ 7,552	$ 16,284	$ 7,640
Mean	40,366	18,035	31,764	10,282	33,805	12,362
Standard Deviation	42,640	20,888	75,583	9,260	68,956	13,541
Coefficient of Variability	1.06	1.16	2.38	0.90	2.04	1.10
Minimum	1,050	2,350	500	505	500	505
Maximum	156,875	64,973	495,512	36,700	495,512	64,973
N =	14	11	45	30	59	41
F =	2.52, 1/22 d.f.		2.39, 1/73 d.f.		3.85, 1/98 d.f.	

Councilmen

	1865-1883		1884-1903		1865-1903	
	Winners	Losers	Winners	Losers	Winners	Losers
Median	$ 8,580	$ 5,503	$ 9,004	$ 3,510	$ 8,676	$ 4,720
Mean	13,798	12,691	25,158	9,067	18,315	11,306
Standard Deviation	19,151	23,082	51,731	15,715	36,207	20,628
Coefficient of Variability	1.39	1.82	2.06	1.73	1.98	1.82
Minimum	0	0	0	0	0	0
Maximum	132,187	143,575	408,855	107,400	408,855	143,575
N =	206	186	136	115	342	301
F =	0.27, 1/390 d.f.		10.32, 1/249 d.f.		8.8, 1/641 d.f.	

All Candidates

	1865-1883		1884-1903		1865-1903	
	Winners	Losers	Winners	Losers	Winners	Losers
Median	$ 9,155	$ 6,202	$ 10,128	$ 4,545	$ 9,271	$ 5,300
Mean	17,520	14,193	28,153	9,435	22,290	12,180
Standard Deviation	23,697	25,549	58,340	14,525	44,762	21,685
Coefficient of Variability	1.35	1.80	2.07	1.54	2.01	1.78
Minimum	0	0	0	0	0	0
Maximum	215,000	175,000	495,512	107,400	495,512	175,000
N =	236	214	192	157	428	371
F =	1.67, 1/448 d.f.		15.37, 1/347 d.f.		15.72, 1/797 d.f.	

wards. Comparison of the means of property owned by winners and losers shows that the former were nearly twice as prosperous as the latter, although the size of the standard deviations indicates the extremes of wealth, particularly at the higher end, were represented in both categories.[8]

Property distinctions were least significant before 1884, when class conflict was so frequently discussed. Attacks against "kid gloves" and "aristocratic" candidates and tickets apparently offset some of the advantages of wealth. Wealthy and poor men could be found among both winners and losers particularly in mayoral and councilmanic races before 1884, when differences in average property-holdings *between* victors and vanquished were outweighed by the tremendous dispersion *within* the ranks of each. Although in 1873 "reformers" from the city elite pushed through a series of changes in city government, comparison of the relationship between property and election outcome between 1865-73 and 1874-83 reveals no significant difference. The one exception occurred within races for the newly created Board of Alderman. Wealthier contenders were more successful in gaining access to this board, which controlled the city budget, than they were in capturing other city offices.

After 1884 candidates with "greater stake" in the community generally were more successful in their campaigns. The inception of the citizens' reform movement, with its emphasis on electing the "best people," appears to have substantially increased the impact of property in city campaigns. The large discrepancies in average property-holdings of winners and losers present a powerful argument for the political importance of property in Atlanta elections after 1884, and analysis of the difference in property between victorious and defeated candidates in *direct competition* supplies supporting evidence.[9] The average gap in property between victors and vanquished generally was much less before than after 1884 except in campaigns for alderman. Initially winners had less property than losers in two-fifths of the councilmanic contests, nine of sixteen mayoral races, and four of ten aldermanic campaigns. After 1884 winners were poorer than losers in less than one-fourth of the councilmanic battles, only two of twelve mayoral contests, and ten of twenty-six aldermanic races. Overall, the average of the differences, both positive and negative, were much greater in at-large races than in councilmanic contests. In 60 percent of Atlanta's elections contestants were separated by more than $6,000, and in only 108 of 311 total confrontations did victorious candidates hold less property than those who were

defeated. The median and mean differences in those contests were
—$7,184 and —$19,312 respectively. Median and mean differences for
the elections in which the victor was wealthier than the loser were
$10,459 and $26,024.

Although the amount of property held by political hopefuls was not
a certain predictor of the outcome of elections, table 14 underscores
important differences in political success for candidates in four strata
of property-holdings. The disparity in political success between the rich-
est and poorest candidates was most dramatic. Less than one-sixth of the
office-seekers with $600 or less in property but nearly two-thirds of those
with more than $40,000 were triumphant. Furthermore, of the twenty-
five men with no property at all who sought city office, only four succeeded.

The relationship between property levels and the outcome of elections
was particularly strong in at-large races. Only three of twelve mayoral candidates with $2,500 or less in property were successful. But the deviation
of aldermanic races after 1884 from this overall monotonic pattern between property and political performance is striking. In these contests
those at opposite ends of the property-holding spectrum were most successful in winning. But one must remember that a social filter had already
had its effect: few men of little property were candidates in mayoral and
aldermanic contests. Men with $2,500 or less in property comprised only
18 percent of the candidates in at-large elections, and the group with over
$16,000 supplied 40 percent of them. Inevitably, the rich supplied more
winners than any other group, no matter how well the few poor candidates ran. The combination of greater success for wealthier office-seekers
and the domination of city campaigns by a relatively elite group of Atlantans led to a city government firmly in the hands of propertied citizens. The median property-holdings for mayors, aldermen, and councilmen during the entire period were $24,450, $16,284, and $8,651 re-
spectively.[10] Except for aldermen, officeholders after 1884 were much
wealthier than those in similar positions before then.

Even so, certain factors modified the basic equation between property
and political success.[11] Prominent politicians who ran often for city office and whose political power was widely recognized could win mayoral
elections despite modest property-holdings. Among the seven mayoral
candidates worth only $2,500 to $6,700, the four winners were all well-
known politicos, as were the nine successful aldermanic candidates from

TABLE 14

Percentage of Victorious Candidates within Each Quartile of the Property Distribution by Office and by Subperiod

	Mayors			Aldermen		
	1865-1883	1884-1903	1865-1903	1865-1883	1884-1903	1865-1903
$0-2,500	16.7% (6)	33.3% (6)	25.0% (12)	50.0% (2)	78.6% (14)	75.0% (16)
$2,501-6,750	66.7 (6)	0.0 (1)	57.1 (7)	50.0 (2)	47.4 (19)	47.6 (21)
$6,751-16,000	37.5 (8)	16.7 (6)	28.6 (14)	12.5 (8)	31.3 (16)	25.0 (24)
$16,001-	61.5 (13)	80.0 (10)	69.6 (23)	84.6 (13)	76.9 (26)	79.5 (39)
Cramer's V =	0.37	0.59	0.40	0.64	0.39	0.46
Gamma =	0.34	0.65	0.47	0.66	0.09	0.21

	Councilmen			All Candidates		
	1865-1883	1884-1903	1865-1903	1865-1883	1884-1903	1865-1903
$0-2,500	41.8% (91)	33.8% (71)	38.3% (162)	40.4% (99)	40.7% (91)	40.5% (190)
$2,501-6,750	51.5 (103)	50.7 (67)	51.2 (170)	52.3 (111)	49.4 (87)	51.0 (198)
$6,751-16,000	58.0 (119)	65.3 (49)	60.1 (168)	54.1 (135)	53.5 (71)	53.9 (206)
$16,000-	58.2 (79)	71.9 (64)	64.3 (143)	61.9 (105)	74.0 (100)	67.8 (205)
Cramer's V =	0.13	0.30	0.20	0.15	0.26	0.19
Gamma =	0.18	0.43	0.29	0.21	0.36	0.28

the bottom property quartile. On the other hand, prior appointive office-holding was a characteristic associated with defeat in mayoral contests, and large property-holdings did help here. The only successful mayoral candidates who had held minor municipal posts owned property worth more than $16,000.

Although there were persistent candidates of modest means, property and political success were related to repetitive campaigning. *Perennial politicians*—those who competed four or more times—generally were wealthier and more successful than political novices. Before 1884 substantial property-holdings only aided those competing the first or second time. Among more practiced politicians property contributed very little to political success. After 1884, however, larger amounts of property improved the chances of candidates regardless of their status as beginners or repeaters.

Throughout the period the political impact of property-holdings varied according to candidates' time of arrival in Atlanta. Earlier settlers generally fared better at the polls than those who came later, except for men with more than $16,000 in property; at this level of wealth, early or late arrival made virtually no difference as to victory. Among recent arrivals to the city, larger property-holdings were more strongly associated with political success. Thus it appears that large property-holdings may have compensated for the political handicap of recent arrival to the city, and an early connection with Atlanta proved a definite political asset to candidates with small holdings.

REGION OF BIRTH

Although property was an important factor in political performance in Atlanta, nativity generally was not. As previously discussed, antiforeign and antinorthern sentiment usually was not a significant feature of Atlanta politics. Men born outside the South certainly did not abjure political participation; in fact, they were overrepresented in municipal campaigns in relation to the proportion of non-Southerners among the general population. Table 15 confirms that non-Southerners generally were not treated as outsiders by Atlanta's electorate, and that those native to the South, even native Georgians, were not especially favored.[12] Mayoral contests seem to have been the sole exception: Nedon L. Angier, a wealthy, early

TABLE 15

Percentage of Victorious Candidates
by Region of Birth, by Office, and by Subperiod

	Mayors			Aldermen		
	1865-1883	1884-1903	1865-1903	1865-1883	1884-1903	1865-1903
Georgia	61.1% (18)	50.0% (18)	55.6% (36)	66.7% (12)	61.4% (44)	62.5% (56)
Other South	50.0 (8)	50.0 (4)	50.0 (12)	40.0 (5)	58.3 (12)	52.9 (17)
North	16.7 (6)	0.0 (1)	14.3 (7)	50.0 (4)	72.7 (11)	66.7 (15)
Foreign	—	—	—	50.0 (4)	42.9 (7)	45.5 (11)
Cramer's V =	0.33	0.20	0.27	0.22	0.15	0.13

	Councilmen			All Candidates		
	1865-1883	1884-1903	1865-1903	1865-1883	1884-1903	1865-1903
Georgia	58.1% (148)	56.1% (157)	57.0% (305)	59.0% (178)	56.6% (219)	57.7% (397)
Other South	49.1 (106)	60.0 (45)	52.3 (151)	48.7 (119)	59.0 (61)	52.2 (180)
North	59.7 (72)	45.0 (20)	56.5 (92)	56.1 (82)	53.1 (32)	55.3 (114)
Foreign	45.8 (48)	46.2 (13)	45.9 (61)	46.2 (52)	45.0 (20)	45.8 (72)
Cramer's V =	0.11	0.09	0.07	0.10	0.06	0.07

settler in Atlanta, who was unopposed in his second mayoral candidacy in 1876, was the sole Northerner to capture this position.

Aside from the pointed failure of six of seven Northerners to win mayoral contests (no immigrant sought this position), nativity subgroups performed almost equally well in Atlanta elections. This was not the result of candidates with similar regional backgrounds facing each other. Atlanta's campaigns generally featured opponents differentiated by nativity; and each subgroup of office-seekers, as defined by place of birth, had roughly the same proportion of uncontested elections.[13]

In some ways this is surprising. Despite the lack of publicized anti-northern or anti-immigrant sentiment and the presence of some positive evidence that early in the era Atlanta welcomed northern capital and migrants and encouraged immigration, the bitterness of the Civil War would have explained a determination to keep Southerners in control of the city. Yet non-Southerners, for the most part running against natives, were able to win office from Reconstruction to the turn of the century when, according to C. Vann Woodward, Southerners began referring to "the lost cause" and emphasizing the superiority of their heritage.[14]

Still, the success of nonsouthern candidates was not due entirely to their warmhearted acceptance. Successful northern- and foreign-born contestants possessed other desirable characteristics that outweighed possible distaste for their origins. For example, most non-Southerners were early settlers, a group that generally enjoyed greater political success than latecomers no matter where they were born. Even among postwar arrivals, however, Northerners did not encounter any particular liability; in contrast, immigrants who were newcomers had a difficult time winning elections in the early era. The general success initially enjoyed by the foreign-born, therefore, appeared due to their long identification with Atlanta. The greater wealth of immigrants and Northerners compared to southern-born office-seekers also helps to explain the lack of association between birthplace and political success. This was particularly true in aldermanic contests, in which only five of fourteen non-Southerners with less than $16,000 in property but ten of twelve with more than that were victorious, suggesting that large property-holdings may have compensated for nonsouthern identification.

The fact that most nonsouthern candidates had a long identification with the city and were fairly wealthy men seemed to mean more than their birthplace in Atlanta politics and contributed to their surprising success in all but mayoral races. Even though all northern candidates for mayor were substantial businessmen and professional men and all but one were relatively old, antebellum settlers, they were not success-ful.[15] Atlanta's mayors not only had to be from the South, but preferably from Georgia. Candidates native to the state were the most numerous and successful of mayoral contestants.

AREA OF RESIDENCE

Over time, the proportion of candidates from the center of the city declined, and the representation of residents from the outskirts among candidates increased. Table 16 shows, however, that this change was not accompanied by any consistent, pronounced preference of the electorate, before or after 1884, for candidates from either the core or ring of the city.[16] This might be explained by the propensity of candidates living in the same general area to compete against each other. About one-half of the contestants directly opposed in mayoral and councilmanic elections resided within the same general area of Atlanta, and in aldermanic races almost two-thirds of the competitors lived in the same broad division of the city. But even in elections in which men from different sections of the city competed, there still was no particular advantage for one group over the other. In fact, residence appears to have been an important polit-ical consideration in only a few cases.

When other variables in candidates' social profiles are held constant, area of residence may have been significant after 1884 for some groups of councilmanic contenders. Businessmen who were inner-city dwellers had greater political success than those who were not, and professional men who resided in the ring did much better than those who lived in the core. Almost all defeated inner-city professional men held less than $6,750 in property; wealthier professionals from both areas of the city did about equally well. In Atlanta, therefore, a visible identification with the down-town area may have been helpful for members of the business community, regardless of their property-holdings, but was a liability for professional men with relatively small amounts of property. It may have been that this latter group was made up of less prestigious professionals who were attempting to advance rapidly through local politics and consequently were rejected by voters, but such notions were not reported in the con-

TABLE 16

Percentage of Victorious Candidates
within the Center and Outskirts of Atlanta by Office and by Subperiod

	Mayors			Aldermen		
	1865-1883	1884-1903	1865-1903	1865-1883	1884-1903	1865-1903
Center	48.1%	40.0%	45.9%	54.2%	67.6%	62.2%
	(27)	(10)	(37)	(24)	(34)	(58)
Outskirts	50.0	53.9	52.6	[100.0]	53.7	54.8
	(6)	(13)	(19)	(1)	(41)	(42)
Cramer's V =	0.01	0.14	0.06	0.18	0.14	0.07
Gamma =	0.04	0.27	0.13	—	−0.29	−0.15

	Councilmen			All Candidates		
	1865-1883	1884-1903	1865-1903	1865-1883	1884-1903	1865-1903
Center	54.8%	58.2%	55.6%	54.3%	59.3%	55.7%
	(299)	(91)	(390)	(350)	(135)	(485)
Outskirts	46.1	51.9	49.8	46.9	52.3	50.6
	(89)	(160)	(249)	(96)	(214)	(310)
Cramer's V =	0.07	0.06	0.06	0.06	0.07	0.05
Gamma =	−0.17	−0.13	−0.12	−0.15	−0.14	−0.10

temporary sources.[17] Residence in the outskirts also seemed helpful to recently arrived and younger councilmanic candidates after 1884, but there was little significant variation in victory or defeat between inner- and outer-city dwellers among men older than forty-eight and contestants with at least a ten-year attachment to the city. Although residence in more populous areas close to the city limits appeared advantageous for latecomers and young men, possibly because younger newcomers set- tled there, there is no indication in contemporary sources that these candidates made an issue of where they lived.

After holding other attributes constant, residence in the center also appeared significant for some groups of aldermanic aspirants after 1884. Among those candidates with at least $6,750 in property, residents of the ring fared poorly compared to center-city dwellers. Although among aldermanic candidates with less property, men from the outskirts had about the same success rate as those from the center. Moreover, core- based candidates did much better than those from the ring among political novices; among more practiced politicians, residents of the outskirts and the center fared equally well. Still, these distinctions in councilmanic and aldermanic races do not seriously alter the basic finding that gen- erally the residence of contestants was not a discriminatory factor in Atlanta elections. As a result, officeholders as well as office-seekers re- flected general population patterns in Atlanta in their areas of residence.

PERIOD OF ARRIVAL

Another significant change through time in the social basis of Atlanta politics involved the decline in numbers of the earlier settlers and the rise of relatively recent arrivals among office-seekers. But this increased political participation by newer arrivals was partially offset by the grow- ing rates of success for early settlers, reflecting one of the constant re- frains of Atlanta campaigns—the value of a long identification with the city. Results displayed in table 17 suggest an almost unbroken preference for earlier settlers among Atlanta's electorate, especially in comparing pre- and post-1870 arrivals. Men who arrived in the 1860s generally per- formed the same as antebellum settlers throughout the entire period, including the Reconstruction era. Those who came after 1870 were not as successful as the earlier arrivals. This remained valid even near the end of the period when they constituted a majority among the candidates.

Before 1884, when nearly two-thirds of the pre-1870 arrivals battled exclusively among themselves, over one-half of them were victorious. In contrast, only one-fourth of the later arrivals—almost all of whom faced earlier settlers—could muster a victory. After 1884, when over half of the contested elections matched men who had arrived before and after 1870 in direct competition, 65 percent of the oldtimers and almost 50 percent of the post-1870 arrivals were victorious. Thus the ratio of victories to defeats among early settlers was higher after 1884 mainly because they no longer competed as frequently against each other.

The period of arrival of uncontested candidates before and after 1884 underscores the changes that took place in Atlanta politics. In the first subperiod, only one of the post-1870 migrants was unchallenged for office, and thirty-one of forty-one uncontested candidates had come to the city before the war. In the second subperiod, the latecomers held a majority of twenty-six to seventeen among uncontested candidates, approximately proportional to their numbers among all office-seekers.

An early connection to the city was especially important for certain groups of office-seekers in councilmanic campaigns and in pre-1884 aldermanic contests.[18] Period of arrival generally made the greatest political difference among the least wealthy 50 percent of the contestants; only among political hopefuls with $16,000 in property did recent arrivals perform as well as old-timers. An early tie to Atlanta also seemed especially significant before 1884 for blue- and white-collar workers, political novices, and immigrants. Throughout the years an early identification with Atlanta was more important for younger office-seekers in winning office than it was for older contestants.

Preference for long-time residents of Atlanta did not prevent the slow transfer of the reins of city government to the latecomers, but it took place more slowly than their increasing proportion among all office-seekers promised. Three-fourths of Atlanta's mayors before 1884 and three of eleven after that year were antebellum settlers; only four post-1870 arrivals won this position. Five of twelve winners of aldermanic races before 1884 had come to the city after the war; after 1884 nearly half of the aldermen were pre-1870 settlers and over one-fifth had prewar connections to the city. The recent arrivals made their greatest inroads in the City Council, because of their larger proportions of councilmanic candidates rather then greater likelihood of success. Thirty-seven percent of the councilmen before 1884 were postwar settlers, although less than 4 percent had arrived after 1870. During the second half of the

TABLE 17

Percentage of Victorious Candidates by Period of Arrival, by Office, and by Subperiod

	Mayors			Aldermen		
	1865-1883	1884-1903	1865-1903	1865-1883	1884-1903	1865-1903
Before 1861	52.2%	42.9%	50.0%	66.7%	66.7%	66.7%
	(23)	(7)	(30)	(12)	(15)	(27)
After 1860	40.0	50.0	46.2	46.2	58.3	56.2
	(10)	(16)	(26)	(13)	(60)	(73)
Cramer's V =	0.11	0.07	0.04	0.21	0.07	0.10
Gamma =	0.24	−0.14	0.08	0.40	0.18	0.22
Before 1871	45.5%	58.3%	51.1%	65.0%	63.2%	63.8%
	(33)	(12)	(45)	(20)	(38)	(58)
After 1870	—	36.4	36.4	20.0	56.8	52.4
		(11)	(11)	(5)	(37)	(42)
Cramer's V =	—	0.22	0.12	0.36	0.07	0.11
Gamma =	—	0.42	0.29	0.76	0.13	0.23

	Councilmen			All Candidates		
	1865-1883	1884-1903	1865-1903	1865-1883	1884-1903	1865-1903
Before 1861	57.3%	70.0%	58.8%	57.3%	65.4%	58.7%
	(225)	(30)	(255)	(260)	(52)	(312)
After 1860	47.4	53.1	50.7	46.9	54.1	51.3
	(156)	(207)	(363)	(179)	(283)	(462)
Cramer's V =	0.10	0.11	0.08	0.10	0.08	0.08
Gamma =	0.20	0.35	0.16	0.21	0.23	0.17
Before 1871	55.6%	66.3%	57.8%	55.4%	64.8%	57.8%
	(351)	(92)	(443)	(404)	(142)	(546)
After 1870	26.7	48.3	44.6	25.7	49.2	44.2
	(30)	(145)	(175)	(35)	(193)	(228)
Cramer's V =	0.16	0.18	0.12	0.16	0.15	0.13
Gamma =	0.55	0.37	0.26	0.56	0.31	0.27

period, the post-1870 arrivals held only a slight majority in the City Council even though they had comprised over three-fifths of the contestants. Men identified with prewar Atlanta still held one-sixth of the Council seats. An early connection to the city did seem to count in Atlanta elections, but not nearly enough to resist the challenges of time.

TEN YEARS' RESIDENCE

Just as pre-1870 migrants to Atlanta fared better politically than those who had arrived later, men who had lived at least ten years in the city before seeking office fared better than those who did not wait as long, especially after 1884 (see table 18). Ten years' residence was most important for post-1870 arrivals. Among this group who ran for office after 1884, one-half of those living in Atlanta at least ten years were winners, compared with only one-third of those who had resided in the city for a shorter time. But even these post-1870 settlers who had spent ten years in Atlanta did not succeed in winning office in the same proportions as earlier settlers. Nearly two-thirds of the latter triumphed.

Initially, about 67 percent of Atlanta's contested elections pitted candidates who could be distinguished by length of residence; after 1884 only 30 percent of the contests could match such opponents. Before and after 1884, almost all newcomers faced more established citizens. About 33 percent of the unopposed councilmanic contestants before 1884 and just 6 percent after that year had lived less than ten years in Atlanta. The large proportion of newcomers uncontested in these races before 1884 emphasizes the lack of severe liability for a brief residence; the small proportion after that year suggests a change in attitude among Atlantans regarding the acceptability of the newly arrived. Few *arrivistes* sought at-large positions, and none of the five uncontested mayoral candidates and only one of twelve unchallenged aldermanic aspirants lived such a short time in the city. However, those few newcomers who did compete in contested at-large elections were surprisingly successful: two of four mayoral candidates and seven of ten aldermanic aspirants new to the city triumphed. That the 1872 mayoral race included only two such recent arrivals in Atlanta—T. Stobo Farrow and Samuel B. Spencer, and that Spencer defeated a respected early settler in the next year, may have helped pull the trigger on the "reformers'" successful push for a new city charter in 1873 as much as the more publicized reason of class conflict. That almost

TABLE 18

Percentage of Victorious Candidates by Length of Residence, by Office, and by Subperiod

	Mayors			Aldermen		
	1865-1883	1884-1903	1865-1903	1865-1883	1884-1903	1865-1903
Ten Years or more	48.3%	47.8%	48.1%	50.0%	59.7%	57.8%
	(29)	(23)	(52)	(18)	(72)	(90)
Not ten years	50.0	---	50.0	71.4	66.7	70.0
	(4)	---	(4)	(7)	(3)	(10)
Cramer's V =	0.01	---	0.01	0.19	0.03	0.07
Gamma =	-0.03	---	-0.04	-0.43	-0.15	-0.26

	Councilmen			All Candidates		
	1865-1883	1884-1903	1865-1903	1865-1883	1884-1903	1865-1903
Ten Years or more	54.7%	58.7%	56.5%	53.8%	58.1%	56.2%
	(267)	(213)	(480)	(314)	(308)	(622)
Not ten years	48.0	28.9	43.6	49.3	31.7	44.5
	(125)	(38)	(163)	(136)	(41)	(177)
Cramer's V =	0.06	0.21	0.11	0.04	0.17	0.10
Gamma =	0.13	0.55	0.25	0.09	0.50	0.23

all citizens identified with the 1873 reform movement were early settlers certainly seems as notable as the fact that almost all of them were
substantial citizens, especially since many newcomers engaged in politics,
such as Spencer, also were substantial property-holders.

After 1884 social status affected the chances for success of newcomers
more than it did for candidates better established in the community. Neither property or occupation compensated sufficiently for a very short stay
in Atlanta, and the combination of lower prestige vocations and small
amounts of property with less than ten years' residence was a serious handicap. Only 5 percent of newcomers but 46 percent of the ten-year residents with $2,500 or less in property won their races; 50 percent of the
former but 70 percent of the latter with more than $16,000 gained city
office. A short stay in the city penalized contestants from all occupational
backgrounds, but none of the few skilled tradesmen and clerical employees in such a situation could win.

AGE

Aspirants for at-large positions generally tended to be older than councilmanic contenders, and candidates before 1884 on the average were
younger than those who sought elective office after that year. This suggests that youth may have been a more valuable attribute early in the
era, and generally more important for councilmanic than at-large candidates. Distinctions in average age between winners and losers displayed
in table 19 partly support these suggestions. Youth does appear as a positive factor, particularly in councilmanic campaigns, from 1865 to 1883.
Greater maturity appears significant to some degree among mayoral contestants after 1884, but even in these cases the age dispersion within ranks
of winners and losers outweigh average distinctions.

From 1865 to 1903 over 70 percent of Atlanta's contested elections
matched competitors with at least six years difference between them.
Examination of the distribution of disparities in age among candidates in
direct competition verifies the greater importance of youth early in the
era and older age in the latter part of the period. Before 1884, when the
average (mean, sign ignored) difference between contestants was over ten
years, 58 percent of the councilmanic contests, eight of eleven aldermanic
races, and half of the mayoral campaigns were won by younger men. After
1884, when the average difference in age was nearly twelve years, 55 per-

cent of the councilmanic and aldermanic races and ten of twelve mayoral contests were won by older men. On the basis of this evidence, older age appears as a more important factor in mayoral races than in other campaigns, especially after 1884, and youth counted more in aldermanic and councilmanic races before 1884.

Information supplied by table 20 rounds out the picture of the association between age and the outcome of Atlanta's elections. Among candidates divided into four age strata, younger groups generally fared better at the polls before 1884; the importance of older age in post-1884 mayoral contests is underlined by the fact that none of the four men younger than forty-two was able to win. Moreover, over one-third of the uncontested candidates from 1865 to 1883 were younger than thirty-six, and three-fifths were under forty-one. After 1884 two-fifths of the men without opposition were forty-nine or older and only one-ninth were thirty-five or younger. The greater acceptance by the electorate of youth in councilmanic campaigns, and the relatively younger ages of contestants for these positions, led to a lower average age for councilmen compared with at-large office-holders. The age of Atlanta's public officials in all three major offices generally was greater after 1884 than before that year, an alteration that paralleled the maturation of city politics. Campaigns became more orderly and less raucous as the age of candidates and officials increased.[19]

Several other attributes—period of arrival, political persistence, and property-holdings—were related with age to the outcome of aldermanic and councilmanic elections. Simultaneous examination of these factors sharpens the picture of the political impact of age. In general, younger contenders enjoyed a considerable edge over older office-seekers only among poorer political novices who arrived in the city before 1870—a sizeable group. Otherwise, little difference in winning or losing existed between younger and older contestants.

MINOR CITY OFFICEHOLDING

Previous service in minor appointive office provided one avenue into municipal elective positions; in Atlanta, about 20 percent of the candidates had such experience before their campaigns. In virtually all of the elections in which former appointive officeholders competed, they were

TABLE 19

Age of Winning and Losing Candidates by Office and by Subperiod

Mayors

	1865-1883		1884-1903		1865-1903	
	Winners	Losers	Winners	Losers	Winners	Losers
Median	42.5	46.5	48.0	44.5	47.6	46.0
Mean	46.9	46.4	50.3	45.5	48.3	46.0
Standard Deviation	11.9	8.9	9.1	9.5	10.8	9.0
Coefficient of Variability	0.25	0.19	0.18	0.21	0.22	0.20
Minimum	30	32	42	32	30	32
Maximum	71	59	71	62	71	62
N =	16	16	11	12	27	28
F =	0.01, 1/30 d.f.		1.51, 1/21 d.f.		0.69, 1/53 d.f.	

Aldermen

	1865-1883		1884-1903		1865-1903	
	Winners	Losers	Winners	Losers	Winners	Losers
Median	40.5	41.2	45.8	48.0	44.4	44.5
Mean	39.9	40.9	46.2	46.7	44.7	45.1
Standard Deviation	10.7	5.2	7.4	9.6	8.6	8.9
Coefficient of Variability	0.27	0.13	0.16	0.21	0.19	0.20
Minimum	29	32	26	31	26	31
Maximum	63	48	60	67	63	67
N =	14	11	45	29	59	40
F =	0.08, 1/23 d.f.		0.07, 1/72 d.f.		0.05, 1/97 d.f.	

Councilmen

	1865-1883		1884-1903		1865-1903	
	Winners	Losers	Winners	Losers	Winners	Losers
Median	37.2	40.6	42.8	44.0	38.9	41.6
Mean	38.4	41.7	44.1	44.7	40.6	42.9
Standard Deviation	8.1	9.4	9.7	10.9	9.2	10.1
Coefficient of Variability	0.21	0.23	0.22	0.24	0.23	0.24
Minimum	23	21	24	23	23	21
Maximum	61	68	69	75	69	75
N =	202	171	129	105	331	276
F	13.47, 1/371 d.f.		0.21, 1/232 d.f.		8.2, 1/605 d.f.	

All Candidates

	1865-1883		1884-1903		1865-1903	
	Winners	Losers	Winners	Losers	Winners	Losers
Median	37.9	41.0	44.0	44.8	40.4	42.2
Mean	39.1	42.0	45.0	45.2	41.7	43.3
Standard Deviation	8.8	9.3	9.3	10.5	9.4	9.9
Coefficient of Variability	0.23	0.22	0.21	0.23	0.23	0.23
Minimum	23	21	24	23	23	21
Maximum	71	68	71	75	71	75
N =	232	198	185	146	417	344
F =	11.73, 1/428 d.f.		.03, 1/329 d.f.		5.8, 1/760 d.f.	

TABLE 20

Percentage of Victorious Candidates within Each Quartile of the Age Distribution of Candidates by Office and by Subperiod

	Mayors			Aldermen		
	1865-1883	1884-1903	1865-1903	1865-1883	1884-1903	1865-1903
21-34	50.0% (4)	0.0% (2)	33.3% (6)	85.7% (7)	20.0% (5)	58.3% (12)
35-41	62.5 (8)	0.0 (2)	50.0 (10)	16.7 (6)	68.7 (16)	54.5 (22)
42-48	50.0 (8)	63.6 (11)	57.9 (19)	50.0 (10)	70.0 (20)	63.3 (30)
49-75	41.2 (12)	50.0 (8)	45.0 (20)	100.0 (2)	57.6 (33)	60.0 (35)
Cramer's V =	0.16	0.46	0.16	0.57	0.25	0.06
Gamma =	-0.19	0.36	0.02	-0.10	0.02	0.05

	Councilmen			All Candidates		
	1865-1883	1884-1903	1865-1903	1865-1883	1884-1903	1865-1903
21-34	64.7% (116)	56.8% (44)	62.5% (160)	65.4% (127)	51.0% (51)	61.2% (178)
35-41	55.6 (117)	54.5 (55)	55.2 (172)	54.2 (131)	56.2 (73)	54.9 (204)
42-48	46.8 (77)	54.5 (55)	50.0 (132)	47.4 (95)	59.3 (86)	53.0 (181)
49-75	41.3 (63)	55.7 (79)	49.3 (142)	42.9 (77)	55.8 (120)	50.5 (197)
Cramer's V =	0.17	0.02	0.11	0.17	0.05	0.08
Gamma =	-0.26	-0.01	-0.15	-0.25	0.03	-0.11

TABLE 21

Percentage of Victorious Candidates with and without Previous Minor Officeholding by Office and by Subperiod

	Mayors			Aldermen		
	1865-1883	1884-1903	1865-1903	1865-1883	1884-1903	1865-1903
No Appointive Office	60.0% (20)	63.6% (11)	61.3% (31)	58.8% (17)	59.3% (54)	59.2% (71)
Appointive Office	30.8 (13)	33.3 (12)	32.0 (25)	50.0 (8)	61.9 (21)	58.6 (29)
Cramer's V =	0.29	0.30	0.29	0.08	0.02	0.01
Gamma =	0.54	−0.56	−0.54	−0.18	0.06	−0.01

	Councilmen			All Candidates		
	1865-1883	1884-1903	1865-1903	1865-1883	1884-1903	1865-1903
No Appointive Office	51.1% (319)	54.9% (204)	52.6% (523)	52.0% (356)	56.1% (269)	53.8% (625)
Appointive Office	58.9 (73)	51.1 (47)	55.8 (120)	54.3 (94)	51.3 (80)	52.9 (174)
Cramer's V =	0.06	0.03	0.03	0.02	0.04	0.01
Gamma =	0.16	−0.08	0.06	0.05	−0.10	.02

matched against individuals without this experience. Thus ample opportunity existed for this factor to emerge as significant. But table 21 shows
that previous appointive political experience was not important in aldermanic and councilmanic elections; men with and without such backgrounds did about equally well throughout the period. Moreover, roughly
the same proportions of both groups as existed among all candidates ran unchallenged for these offices. As a result, among aldermen and councilmen former minor officeholders were represented in about the same proportion as they had been among the candidates.

Mayoral candidates, on the other hand, were seriously handicapped by
prior appointive officeholding in contested elections, and only one of five
unopposed mayoral candidates tried to use his appointive as an automatic
springboard to that office. Atlantans apparently did not often favor men
who attempted to advance to the highest public position in the city from
such positions as city attorney or comptroller. Small property-holdings
increased this negative effect of prior appointive officeholding in mayoral
races. None of the twelve mayoral candidates with previous appointive
service who owned less than $16,000 in property won; eight of eighteen
less wealthy mayoral candidates without this experience did. Distinctions
were minor among contestants with $16,000 or more in property: eight
of thirteen who had held appointive office and ten of thirteen who
had not were successful. Moreover, in post-1884 councilmanic races
candidates with prior appointive officeholding experience managed to
win largely because they owned greater amounts of property and had
an earlier connection to the city; controlling for these two characteristics
reveals that minor officeholders generally did worse at the polls than
those without such experience, suggesting that the citizens' reform movement was at least partly successful in preventing the victory of "politicians."[20]

MEMBERSHIP ON POLITICAL COMMITTEES

From 1865 to 1883, membership on political committees—partisan or
non-partisan executive committees or nominating groups—launched a few
candidates' careers and had no effect on subsequent victory or defeat.
After 1884, however, such service was a major stepping stone into campaigns for all three elective positions, especially at-large offices. Men

TABLE 22

Percentage of Victorious Candidates with and without Previous Membership on Political Committees by Office and by Subperiod

	Mayors			Aldermen		
	1865-1883	1884-1903	1865-1903	1865-1883	1884-1903	1865-1903
No Political Committee	47.6%	75.0%	52.0%	53.8%	57.7%	56.4%
	(21)	(4)	(25)	(13)	(26)	(39)
Political Committee	50.0	42.1	45.2	58.3	61.2	60.7
	(12)	(19)	(31)	(12)	(49)	(61)
Cramer's V =	0.02	0.25	0.07	0.05	0.03	0.04
Gamma =	0.05	−0.61	0.14	0.09	0.07	0.09

	Councilmen			All Candidates		
	1865-1883	1884-1903	1865-1903	1865-1883	1884-1903	1865-1903
No Political Committee	52.4%	49.0%	51.3%	52.2%	50.9%	51.7%
	(313)	(143)	(456)	(347)	(173)	(520)
Political Committee	53.2	61.1	57.8	53.4	59.1	57.0
	(79)	(108)	(187)	(103)	(176)	(279)
Cramer's V =	0.01	0.12	0.06	0.01	0.08	0.05
Gamma =	0.02	0.24	0.13	0.02	0.17	0.11

with and without this political identification appeared in direct competition in approximately half of Atlanta's contested elections for all three offices, thus offering a good test of political significance for this factor. Yet table 22 indicates that despite the connection between this kind of political activism and nomination to office, there was only a slight relationship between such experience and the outcome of elections. Nor was any large benefit from previous service on political committees reflected in the more subtle process of eliminating competition through uncontested elections. Although ten of twelve unchallenged aldermanic aspirants had served on such committees, only one-fourth of the unopposed councilmanic candidates and none of the five uncontested mayoral contestants had done the same.

Only a few groups of candidates gained from this kind of experience and exposure. Nearly two-thirds of the blue-collar workers who had been members of these committees were victorious but only one-third without this service won. This factor also appeared helpful for contestants with small amounts of property, regardless of their occupation; for those with $2,500 or less in property, one-half with this background and about one-fifth without it won. The insignificance of prior membership on these committees for other groups of contestants in Atlanta elections is surprising. These political bodies had high visibility and considerable political muscle. Moreover, membership often was elective and thus demonstrated vote-getting appeal. One also would expect membership, even on nonelective committees, to have signified a good deal of political prestige and clout in the city. If so, this was not reflected in a favorable election return. Still, service on such committees provided a wide avenue into the campaigns themselves with the inception of the citizens' reform movement. Thus after 1884 a clear majority of mayors and aldermen and nearly half of the councilmen had begun their political careers in such a capacity. Even though the electorate evinced no favortism toward such men, previous political experience clearly led indirectly to elective positions.

POLITICAL PERSISTENCE

A third measure of political experience—the number of previous campaigns for elective office—was more important in municipal elections before 1884 than afterwards (see table 23). The decline in significance of prior political exposure in winning elections paralleled an increase in

TABLE 23

Percentage of Victorious Candidates within Categories of the Number of a Candidate's Campaign by Office and by Subperiod

	Mayors			Aldermen		
	1865-1883	1884-1903	1865-1903	1865-1883	1884-1903	1865-1903
First	30.0% (10)	50.0% (6)	37.5% (16)	55.6% (9)	65.2% (23)	62.5% (32)
Second	14.3 (7)	42.9 (7)	28.6 (14)	100.0 (2)	46.7 (30)	50.0 (32)
Third	66.7 (6)	50.0 (4)	60.0 (10)	66.7 (6)	66.7 (9)	66.7 (15)
Fourth or more	80.0 (10)	50.0 (6)	68.8 (16)	37.5 (8)	76.9 (13)	61.9 (21)
Cramer's V =	0.53	0.07	0.33	0.34	0.24	0.13
Gamma =	0.62	0.02	0.40	-0.24	0.10	0.02

	Councilmen			All Candidates		
	1865-1883	1884-1903	1865-1903	1865-1883	1884-1903	1865-1903
First	44.0% (191)	55.7% (167)	49.4% (358)	43.8% (210)	56.6% (196)	50.0% (406)
Second	60.0 (90)	55.8 (43)	58.6 (133)	57.6 (99)	51.3 (80)	54.7 (179)
Third	59.6 (52)	60.0 (20)	59.7 (72)	60.9 (64)	60.6 (33)	60.8 (97)
Fourth or more	62.7 (59)	33.3 (21)	55.0 (80)	62.3 (77)	50.0 (40)	58.1 (117)
Cramer's V =	0.17	0.13	0.09	0.16	0.07	0.08
Gamma =	0.26	-0.11	0.13	0.25	-0.06	0.13

the number of novices seeking political office after 1884. This shift was caused by many factors: the charter change of 1874, which prevented incumbents from seeking reelection as it extended the terms of mayors and councilmen; the apparent success of the citizens' reform movement begun in 1884, which discouraged professionalism in politics and encouraged newcomers to compete for public position; and the gradual disappearance of certain groups of individuals, especially early settlers, who were more likely to campaign several times.

Previous experience in campaigning for elective office was a particular advantage before 1874, when two-thirds of the perennials, many of whom were incumbents, and only one-third of the novices were victorious. After the 1874 charter change, this pattern began to alter, and after the growth of the 1884 citizens' reform movement, novices were more likely to win and perennials were more likely to lose. Moreover, a larger proportion of novices than perennials won councilmanic elections after 1884.[21] One exception to this pattern of change occurred in contests for the Board of Alderman. These already were won more often by relative political newcomers than by more established political figures before 1884. However, after that year persistent politicians were more likely to run unopposed, offsetting the disadvantage they faced when directly challenged by novices. Therefore there was a slight positive relationship between political persistence and performance in post-1884 aldermanic races. In general, well-established politicians were more able than novices to eliminate competition in at-large races: all uncontested aldermanic aspirants before 1884 and all but one unchallenged mayoral contestant were well-known campaigners. In contrast, about one-half of the councilmen without opposition before 1884 and nearly three-fourths after that year were newcomers to city elections.

Atlanta's contested elections almost always matched men with varying campaign experience. Virtually all of the more practiced politicians, particularly perennials, faced opponents with less campaign experience. Conversely, in nearly all at-large races and in over three-fifths of the councilmanic contests in which novices competed, they met opponents who previously had campaigned for elective office. Thus the variation in political success between novices and seasoned campaigners frequently was the result of head-to-head competition.

As with membership on political committees, prior campaign experience aided certain kinds of candidates but was of little importance for other groups. Before 1884 it was a major asset for blue-collar workers and less substantial businessmen and professional men in councilmanic races, but was not very significant for merchants and professional men with more than $6,750 in property. Likewise, in mayoral races before 1884, only the high visibility afforded by earlier political campaigns compensated for lack of property. After 1884, however, property assumed paramount importance and previous campaigns were no longer a factor in mayoral races. Political persistence also helped newcomers to the city in campaigns before 1884. At this time recent arrivals fared poorly in their initial tries for office, but on subsequent campaigns they performed even better than antebellum settlers. After 1884 political persistence could not offset the handicap of recent arrival in Atlanta and even hurt the chances of long-time Atlanta residents.

Because political persistence was only moderately associated with victory or defeat in aldermanic and councilmanic elections, the proportion of men in these positions with previous political experience reflected the proportions of such people among the candidates. In contrast, the relatively strong relationship between this kind of experience and success in winning the mayoralty before 1884 meant that the highest office in Atlanta was more often held by practiced politicians. In fact, two-fifths of Atlanta's mayors could be called perennial politicians and only one-fifth were new to city elections. Overall, however, because of the frequency with which novices sought office, those who governed Atlanta were to a surprising degree men new to elective office. Even before 1884, two-fifths of the office-holders were novices, and after that year, nearly three-fifths were newcomers. The proportion of perennials in the governing councils of the city dropped from one-fifth to one-tenth during this period. Thus the constant influx of new political aspirants into Atlanta's political system ultimately led to a high degree of fluidity in city government, which clearly showed that only a few of the men who governed Atlanta considered politics their profession.[22]

SUMMARY

Of all the characteristics investigated in this study, only four—nativity, political persistence, prior service in appointive office, and occupation—played a significant role in determining political success among men who sought Atlanta's mayoralty from 1865 to 1883 (see table 24). The degree

TABLE 24
Summary Results of a Multiple Discriminant Analysis for Mayoral Candidates with Won-Lost as the Dependent Variable by Subperiod

Variable	F Ratio	Wilk's Lambda	Standardized Discriminant Functions	Actual Result (Row)	Predicted Result (Column) Lost	Won
1865-1883						
Nativity	3.43	0.90	0.40	Lost	12	4
Political Persistence	3.78	0.79	0.61	Won	4	12
Minor Officeholding	3.33	0.71	−0.56		$Phi^2 = 0.50$	
Occupation[a]	1.03	0.68	0.29		P (percent cases correctly classified) = 0.75	
N = 32 C (canonical correlation) = 0.55						
1884-1903						
Property	4.66	0.78	0.0062	Lost	8	1
Minor Officeholding	9.86	0.49	−0.0044	Won	1	9
Occupation	2.53	0.42	−0.0037		$Phi^2 = 0.79$	
Age	2.82	0.35	0.0027		P = 0.89	
N = 19 C = 0.81						
1865-1903						
Minor Officeholding	6.10	0.89	−0.0046	Lost	19	6
Property	3.54	0.83	0.0052	Won	8	18
Nativity	3.98	0.76	0.0066		$Phi^2 = 0.45$	
Political Persistence	2.88	0.72	0.0039		P = 0.73	
Age	1.54	0.69	0.0031			
N = 51 C = 0.55						

[a]Only proprietors and professionals are included for mayoral races.

to which these four factors discriminated between winners and losers can be determined through *multiple discriminant analysis.* This technique enables the researcher to assess the relationship between each attribute and political success while adjusting for all other attributes and to rank the characteristics in the order of their greatest to least contribution towards the outcome of Atlanta's elections.[23] The standard discriminant function coefficients represent the contribution of each attribute to the discriminant function derived from the analysis. Through Wilk's Lambda and the canonical correlation (C), the impact of all important characteristics upon political success—that is, a quantitative measure of the social filter in elections—can be found. Finally, the degree to which candidates' characteristics were associated with success or failure can be measured empirically by comparing the actual political performance with the political outcome predicted by the discriminant function.[24]

In pre-1884 mayoral contests, as seen from the relative sizes of the standard discriminant function coefficients, political factors were most important, followed by place of birth and occupation. Men who had previously campaigned for elective office, individuals who were *not* trying to advance from appointive positions, Southerners, and businessmen were most successful in winning the mayoralty. These results confirm in a more precise fashion the findings previously discussed. The value of 0.68 for Lambda indicates a strong, but not overwhelming, discrimination between winners and losers of early mayoral races according to these attributes. If those who won and those who lost had been completely polarized according to these factors (that is, if all native Southerners had won elections and all non-Southerners had lost, for example), Lambda would have been zero.[25] Moreover, the value of C would have been 1.0, and one could have correctly predicted the political performance of every candidate $(P = 100$ percent). As it is, the function generated by these four attributes accounts for 30 percent of the variation in political success, and one can correctly "predict" three-quarters of the men who won and who lost knowing their nativity, political persistence, service or nonservice on appointive office, and occupation.

After 1884 the social filter in mayoral races was more stringent with the increased significance of other attributes. Property assumed such importance that only a few men with less than $16,000 in property managed to win while 80 percent of the wealthier contestants were successful. Previous service in minor office remained a significant liability, even when lack of property and other negative factors were taken into consideration.

Multiple campaigns were no longer an important factor, and a southern identification became almost mandatory. All but one candidate for mayor was a Southerner and only five contenders were from outside Georgia. Two other attributes—occupation and age—made a slight difference in post-1884 mayoral races after controlling for other characteristics. At this time professional men were somewhat more likely to succeed than businessmen, primarily because they could defeat proprietors when each had roughly equal amounts of property; older office-seekers had an edge on younger competitors among inexperienced campaigners. Lambda's value of 0.35 shows an extremely strong separation between winners and losers according to such factors; the canonical correlation indicates that one can explain 65 percent of the variation in political performance by information about these qualities. Moreover, after the amount of property, service in appointive office, vocation, and age are known, the outcome of mayoral campaigns can be predicted for all but one of the winners and one of the losers.

The mayoralty in Atlanta, therefore, was an exclusive position. Only one blue-collar and one white-collar candidate, and no immigrant, ever sought this position. Only one black Atlantan, Jake McKinley, on the abortive 1890 all-black slate, ever attempted the race. Men who ran for mayor were on the average wealthier and older than contestants for other positions, and they were more likely to have been native Southerners and especially Georgians, earlier settlers and more established citizens according to length of residence, political repeaters and people with prior service in appointive office and on political committees. Even among this elite group, the wealthier and older native Southerners campaigning for their third or more time were more likely to win than other groups of contestants. Previous experience in appointive office, of course, was a liability in these campaigns, but remaining attributes simply were not significant.[26]

Aldermanic contests were a more complex affair. As shown in table 25, from 1874 to 1883 only three factors discriminated between the winners and losers of these races—period of arrival, length of residence, and property-holding. A prewar connection to the city was particularly beneficial in these early aldermanic contests, but somewhat paradoxically, all but one of the victorious more recent arrivals had lived less than ten years in Atlanta. Such findings make assigning particular significance to a long identification with the city difficult. Inclusion of property-holding

TABLE 25

Summary Results of a Multiple Discriminant Analysis for Aldermanic Candidates with Won-Lost as the Dependent Variable by Subperiod

Variable	F Ratio	Wilk's Lambda	Standardized Discriminant Functions	Actual Result (Row)	Predicted Result (Column)	
					Lost	Won
1865-1883						
Period of Arrival	3.48	0.87	0.0043	Lost	9	2
Length of Residence	3.51	0.75	−0.0044	Won	5	9
Property	2.16	0.68	0.0030		Phi^2 = 0.45	
					P = 0.72	
	N = 25	C = 0.57				
1884-1903						
Property	2.38	0.97	0.018	Lost	18	11
Residence	1.06	0.95	−0.012	Won	19	26
					Phi^2 = 0.27	
					P = 0.59	
	N = 74	C = 0.22				
1865-1903						
Property	3.82	0.96	0.017	Lost	20	20
Period of Arrival	1.19	0.95	0.010	Won	21	38
					Phi^2 = 0.14	
					P = 0.59	
	N = 99	C = 0.22				

provides a solution to the problem. The successful very recent arrivals were all men with substantial property. Initially property appeared to be the single most important factor in these races since only three of twelve men with less than $16,000 but eleven of thirteen with greater holdings were triumphant. But most wealthier contestants were either early arrivals or latecomers who had not lived at least ten years in the city; most remaining recent arrivals were among the poorer aldermanic aspirants. Statistically, therefore, the political impact of property appears secondary to that of length of residence; substantively, both wealth and longer residence were politically significant.

Thus a moderate pattern of favoritism existed towards early settlers and the very substantial property-holders in early aldermanic contests. The values for Lambda and the canonical correlation fall between strong and weak association, and knowledge of the candidates' relative positions on these three attributes permits successful prediction of 72 percent of the actual outcome of these races—nine of eleven losers and nine of fourteen winners. Wealthy candidates and early arrivals did not have a sure path to victory; sufficient numbers of candidates without such qualities were able to win so the results of seven contests involving such men were predicted erroneously.

It appears from table 25 that after 1884 no social filter really existed in aldermanic races. Only two factors—property and area of residence—were associated with political success. Wealthier contestants and those residing in the center were more successful than relatively poorer candidates and those living in the outskirts, but the distinctions in performance were so small that we can explain only 5 percent of the variation in victory or defeat and predict correctly the outcome of only 59 percent of the contests. One could have had almost equal predictive success by flipping a coin. Such findings reflect the greater accessibility of the Board of Alderman for various groups of contenders after 1884. This branch of the city legislature was originally intended as an elite position, with only three members who were elected at large and for a longer period than other officeholders and who had direct control over the city's budget. The size of the board was expanded beginning in 1883 and by the turn of the century it had seven members. A more diversified group of people sought this position after 1884, when the prestige of the aldermanic position clearly declined. By 1904 aldermen were no longer elected at-large, but like councilmen, represented particular wards.

TABLE 26
Summary Results of a Multiple Discriminant Analysis for Councilmanic Candidates with Won-Lost as the Dependent Variable by Subperiod

Variable	F Ratio	Wilk's Lambda	Standardized Discriminant Functions	Actual Result (Row)	Predicted Result (Column)	
					Lost	Won
1865-1883						
Age	13.47	0.96	−0.46	Lost	101	70
Political Persistence	14.49	0.93	0.32	Won	64	138
Period of Arrival	4.86	0.92	0.20		$Phi^2 = 0.27$	
Minor Officeholding	2.04	0.91	0.14		P = 0.64	
		N = 373	C = 0.30			
1884-1903						
Length of Residence	8.89	0.96	0.0060	Lost	67	39
Property	7.76	0.93	0.0065	Won	53	78
Political Persistence	3.51	0.92	−0.0058		$Phi^2 = 0.22$	
Period of Arrival	4.25	0.90	0.0048		P = 0.61	
Political Committee	1.29	0.89	0.0028			
		N = 237	C = 0.32			
1865-1903						
Age	7.82	0.99	−0.019	Lost	163	112
Property	10.25	0.97	0.014	Won	139	196
Period of Arrival	7.74	0.96	0.012		$Phi^2 = 0.16$	
Length of Residence	4.96	0.95	0.010		P = 0.59	
		N = 610	C = 0.22			

This change simply recognized the de facto situation since the late 1880s in which different wards took turns in electing aldermen.[27]

Candidates for City Council were considerably more numerous and heterogeneous than contestants for at-large positions in Atlanta. Perhaps partly as a result of this, so many different kinds of councilmanic contenders were able to win city office before and after 1884 that no strong pattern of political preference emerges from the analysis displayed in table 26. Initially, younger men, political repeaters, early settlers, and minor municipal officials can be viewed as relatively more successful after other attributes are taken into consideration. Yet, as discussed earlier, such distinctions were not pronounced. After 1884, when age was no longer a factor and political persistence was not as significant as in the pre-1884 period (although perennial politicians did not perform as well as men new to electoral battles in the latter time frame), a long connection with the city and large amounts of property appeared as the most important factors in councilmanic campaigns. However, the dispersion in property within both groups of winners and losers was sufficiently strong that no firm predictions of the outcome of elections could be made on the basis of wealth. Moreover, the fact that property to some extent separated early from more recent arrivals in these races explains the relatively lesser importance of wealth in councilmanic contests controlling for period of arrival.

Although these are noteworthy findings, the most significant fact is that no strong social pattern emerges from the careful and controlled study of the relative political performance of various subgroups competing for positions on City Council.[28] Although it may have been true, of course, that certain candidate characteristics had been crucial determinants of political success in individual contests, most councilmanic elections and post-1884 aldermanic races in Atlanta did not hinge to any great extent upon the social or political qualities of contestants.

The finding that only a minute social filter existed in these elections contravenes contemporary opinions that often suggested an almost overriding significance for certain characteristics. The social filter of Atlanta politics was more important at the nominations stage than in the elections. After that initial hurdle had been cleared, councilmanic and later aldermanic campaigns were open affairs in which all sorts of people could expect to win. Analysis of both stages of the social filter clearly reveals that the predominance of certain groups, for example, businessmen, on

the Board of Alderman from 1884 to 1903 and City Council throughout the period was a result of their greater political activism and not any
strong favoritism for such people among the electorate.

In contrast, certain characteristics of candidates carried significant
political importance in Atlanta's mayoral races, the most publicized and
important contests in the city, and in early races for the newly established
office of Alderman, at that time portrayed as an elite body. In these elections, winners and losers could easily be distinguished by several attributes, and thus both stages of the social filter were important. One can never
answer with assurance, of course, what were the motives of that abstract
collectivity called "Atlanta's voters," but the evidence of elections and
contemporary comment upon the value of certain qualities points toward
distinct preference of the body politic for certain kinds of people to fill
the city's most prestigious office.

NOTES

1. In the analysis upon which this chapter is based, I have cross-tabulated
social characteristics of candidates with winning and losing, controlling for other
relevant variables, but I generally have omitted a blow-by-blow description of percentage differences and statistical measures of association to avoid overburdening
readers with a mass of detail. This basic form of multivariate analysis is crucial in
capturing interrelationships that would not clearly emerge from more summary
analysis. To help evaluate the political importance of sociopolitical characteristics,
I also turned to multiple discriminant analysis. This tool enables the researcher to
measure the cumulative political significance of all these characteristics, showing
to what degree the pattern of winning and losing can be connected to characteristics of candidates rather than to other causes. A more detailed discussion of multiple discriminant analysis is presented on page 149.

2. For a full discussion of black candidates and their campaigns, see Eugene
J. Watts, "Black Political Progress in Atlanta, 1868-1895," *The Journal of Negro
History* (July, 1974), 268-86.

3. Exclusive examination of officeholders, as done by Robert Dahl and others,
can lead to mistaken evaluations of the political performance of different vocational
groups. For example, a group may have large numbers of officeholders simply because a larger proportion of candidates belonged to it than others, even though they
lost a disproportionate number of elections. Or a group might have included a very
small number of political hopefuls and therefore few officeholders, who nonetheless enjoyed greater chances for political success than men with other occupations. Or the proportion of some groups among elected officials may have generally

mirrored their representation among office-seekers, as was the case in Atlanta. Only the analysis of the vocational backgrounds of all contestants and then of the relationship between occupation and the outcome of elections allows us to choose among these alternatives.

4. Few working-class organizations or spokesmen advocated the domination of city government by lower classes, if only because such a proposition would have met strong opposition from other groups in the city. Moreover, if members of the working class had been united in support of direct representation, then all blue-collar candidates might have gained city office. Clearly, Atlanta's voters considered factors other than whether contestants shared their own occupational level.

5. The "formula" plan of representation, which openly apportioned nominations to various interest groups, including workers, was discussed in chapter four. No other working-class candidate matched Woodward's charisma, campaign style, and recognition among the electorate. He gained a commanding influence in Atlanta politics during the first two decades of the twentieth century. Lucian Lamar Knight, *History of Fulton County, Georgia* (Atlanta, 1930), 167; and Robert A. Dahl, *Who Governs* (New Haven, 1961), 37.

6. Each vocational group of office-seekers had members unchallenged for city office roughly in proportion to their numbers among all candidates. Eighty-seven men (including all eleven winners of the 1865 election, for whom the identity of opponents, if any, remains unknown) were unopposed for Atlanta city office during this period. Many of these men campaigned on unified slates, including the Democratic ticket of 1868 and most members of that party's slate in 1875 and 1877 and of the Citizens' tickets of 1885, 1886, and 1889.

7. Officeholding by white- and blue-collar workers largely has gone unnoticed. See, for example, Howard N. Rabinowitz, "Continuity and Change: Southern Urban Development, 1860-1900," in Blaine A. Brownell and David R. Goldfield, eds., *The City in Southern History: The Growth of Urban Civilization in the South* (Port Washington, 1977), 109-10.

8. I have discussed the relationship between property and political success in an earlier article, which did not, however, include uncontested candidates in the analysis or consider the important dimension of change through time that is developed here. Moreover, the article focused on the relationship of property to percentage of votes received (using multiple regression analysis) rather than to victory and defeat. Eugene J. Watts, "Property and Politics in Atlanta, 1865-1903," *Journal of Urban History* (May, 1977), 295-322.

9. These differences were calculated by subtracting the property of losers from that of winners in contested elections and analyzing positive and negative differences separately, that is, differences when winners had more property and when they had less property than losers. A full discussion of the differences distribution is given in Watts, "Property and Politics," 303-05.

10. The respective mean property-holdings for mayors, aldermen, and councilmen were $47,474, $33,805, and $18,212. Only three mayors held less than $2,500 in property, but three-fifths held more than $16,000. One-fifth of the aldermen had less than $2,500 in property, but over half had over $16,000. Not quite one-fifth of the councilmen had $2,500 or less, but the very wealthy were not so overrepresented.

11. Relatively minor variations according to other attributes are discussed in Watts, "Property and Politics in Atlanta." Distinctions by vocational groups were mentioned previously.

12. Although a larger proportion of foreign-born than other office-seekers lost their races, the distinction is small.

13. In contested elections, over 90 percent of the candidates born in the South other than Georgia faced opponents born elsewhere. About 65 percent of the native Georgians, who, especially after 1884 were such a large proportion of candidates, met opponents with different regional backgrounds. Only in mayoral races did most native Georgians—about 60 percent—compete against each other. Non-Southerners, when they attempted at-large races, always faced Southerners, and there were only two councilmanic contests in which immigrants battled each other and transplanted Northerners tried for the same position.

14. C. Vann Woodward, *Origins of the New South, 1877-1913* (Baton Rouge, 1951), 155-57. Also see Robert T. Daland, *Dixie City: A Portrait of Political Leadership* (Tuscaloosa, 1956), 6-7.

15. Only one of these Northerners, William Markham in 1869, ran as a Republican and thus was virtually guaranteed defeat because of his party allegiance alone.

16. No significant variations in the relationship between residence and the results of elections occurred within individual wards. Moreover, no recognizable pattern emerged from analyzing a series of seven concentric circles or from studying the specific locations of winning and losing contestants. About 10 percent of the candidates from the center and 12 percent of the office-seekers from the outskirts were uncontested in their campaigns.

17. Chapter four noted that the residences of office-seekers did not follow class lines. Furthermore, simultaneous examination of occupation and property-holdings of candidates with residence and the outcome of elections does not support an interpretation that class conflict was related to residential distinctions.

18. The relative lack of political importance for period of arrival in mayoral and post-1884 aldermanic campaigns can be attributed to several causes: most important, perhaps, recent arrivals compared well to earlier settlers in respect to property-holdings. In mayoral contests, earlier settlers more than recent arrivals also counted among their number appointive office-holders and Northerners—groups more likely to lose than win these elections.

19. From 1865 to 1883 over 67 percent of the councilmen were age forty or younger; afterwards only 40 percent were so young. Moreover, the proportion of councilmen older than forty-eight increased from 13 percent to 34 percent. Seven men under age forty-one won the mayoralty before 1884, but no mayors were this young after that year. Fifty percent of the aldermen from 1874 to 1883 were younger than forty-one; about 25 percent from 1884 to 1903 were this young. Only two aldermen before 1884 were older than forty-eight; after that year over forty percent were at least that old.

20. In councilmanic campaigns before 1884, prior appointive officeholding could make up for lack of previous campaigning but was irrelevant for seasoned campaigners.

21. Analysis of the success rate of individuals who sought city office on only

one occasion—the "transients"—supports an interpretation of major change around 1884. Transients were similar in social background to other novices—those who later continued political careers. They differed in political performance; the former were much more likely to have lost their campaigns, a situation that doubtlessly dissuaded losers from additional attempts. Only 30 percent of the transients won before 1884, but nearly 50 percent were successful after that year. Fourteen of these victorious transients after 1884 were uncontested. Such candidates, when they won and then never offered themselves for elective office subsequently, demonstrated forcefully the extent of amateurism in Atlanta municipal politics after 1884.

22. The absence of large numbers of professional politicians in Atlanta is typical of southern cities at this time; see Rabinowitz, "Continuity and Change," 109-10. Moreover, studies of northern cities have documented the rise of professionals in the twentieth century; see, for example, Bradley and Zald, "From Commercial Elite to Political Administrator." What may have been unusual was that in Atlanta the numbers of perennial politicians decreased rather than increased throughout the period. The lack of professionalism in politics also belied, at least on the surface, the notion that Atlanta was managed by a clique; at least factions in Atlanta were forced to encompass a very large number of members.

23. Property and age are measured on an interval scale, but other attributes are treated as dichotomies or "dummy variables": blue-collar or white-collar (businessmen or professionals in mayoral races); resident of the center or outskirts; non-Southerner or native Southerner; ten-year resident or less than ten-year resident; arrival in Atlanta before or after 1870 (1860 for mayoral races); previous service in appointive office and on political committees or lack of such experience; and first or subsequent campaign for elective city office. These distinctions appear most substantively important and also practically useful (given small numbers of certain other configurations).

24. The interpretation of standardized discriminant function coefficients is analogous to that of beta weights in multiple regression analysis. Wilk's Lambda ranges in value from zero to unity, with values closer to zero indicating greater differences in sociopolitical characteristics between victors and vanquished. The canonical correlation ranges from zero for no relationship to unity for perfect association and, when squared, can be interpreted as the proportion of variance in the discriminant function "explained" by subgroups of the dependent variable. Thus it is analogous to the correlation ratio, Eta, in one-way analysis of variance. Since one would have a 50 percent chance of correctly guessing whether a candidate won or lost by some random method such as tossing a coin, the difference between this percentage and that estimated from the discriminant function indicates how much better one can predict actual performance through knowledge of the characteristics. Refer to William Klecka, "Discriminant Analysis," *Statistical Package for the Social Sciences* (New York, 1975), 434-67, for a more detailed explanation.

25. The nature of the first stage of the social filter prevented any possibility of this kind of perfect relationship to emerge in elections; for example, North-

erners and Southerners did not compete against each other in all mayoral campaigns.

26. There was a substantial degree of social discrimination in mayoral races for the entire period as a whole, although not to the same high degree as in the post-1884 period. The poor chances for success of the transplanted Northerners and small property-holders provided the greatest difference between winners and losers, followed by the difficulty of minor municipal office-holders to advance to the highest position in the city. Property doubtlessly was important before 1884, but was strongly associated with political persistence. The generally greater success of political repeaters, a product of the first subperiod, and of older office-seekers, a factor only after 1884, further distinguished between victors and the vanquished in Atlanta's mayoral contests. Differences in performance between professional and businessmen varied by subperiod and thus cancelled each other out over the long run. Results shown in tables 24 to 26 differ from findings from multiple regression analysis published elsewhere, partly because of differences in the dependent variable and partly because I excluded uncontested candidates in the regression analysis. Watts, "Property and Politics in Atlanta."

27. Over the entire period, only property and period of arrival emerge as noteworthy political factors in aldermanic contests. Still, one could predict only 50 percent of the losers and 64 percent of the winners of these races; the latter difference was due largely to the fact that most uncontested and thus automatically victorious aldermanic aspirants were wealthy, early settlers in the city.

28. Younger and relatively wealthier men, earlier settlers and those living at least ten years in the city, enjoyed a slight advantage in Atlanta's councilmanic contests throughout the period. The positive impact of long political persistence before 1884 largely cancelled out the negative effect after that year, and the small relationship between victory and prior service in appointive office before 1884 was not sustained throughout the entire era.

6

Conclusion

Contemporary accounts of campaigns provided only one perspective on the social bases of Atlanta politics from 1865 to 1903. The claims of candidates and opinions of other observers alone did not reveal how social conflict was resolved or what deeper social issues were implicated. Systematic examination of the characteristics of candidates, and their relationship to political success, helped to decipher the social code contained in contemporary discussion, and also permitted testing of several propositions regarding political recruitment that were not much discussed during those years.

Atlantans in the late nineteenth century frequently stressed social characteristics of candidates during campaigns. Of these attributes, those pertaining to social class appeared most important. Press and public alike almost always identified contestants by their vocation and general economic standing and often asserted the need to choose among them on these bases. Workers, a term very loosely defined in the press, demanded direct representation in municipal government, and businessmen and professional men were equally if not more insistent upon nominating and electing representatives of their own kind. Conflict between classes was often—though vaguely—discussed as the difference between rich and poor contestants. According to many participants and political commentators, property—presumably the more the better—was a desirable possession for political hopefuls although some contemporaries expressed contrary opinions. Statistical analysis of candidate characteristics and the association between these factors and the outcome of elections revealed which of these views was accurate.

Although workers were a majority among the general population, they were a distinct minority among candidates. With few exceptions, semi-skilled and unskilled laborers did not perceive themselves as viable candidates for city office; nor were they the choices of politicians or working-class organizations for nomination. Skilled tradesmen and clerical employees also were not markedly motivated to enter the political arena (except, perhaps, in comparison with other cities at this time) and thus constituted only one-fifth of the office-seekers. Those blue-collar and white-collar workers who emerged as contestants represented an elite within the working class on the basis of property-holdings, although they stood several levels below most businessmen and professional men. Proprietors, followed by professionals, formed a large majority among Atlanta's office-seekers. But they were quite varied according to financial status and included small shopkeepers and lesser professionals as well as some of the most substantial property-holders in the city. Aspirants for alderman and mayor generally had a higher socioeconomic status than contestants for council, although a few people on the lower rungs of the social ladder (but not the bottom) competed even for the at-large offices.

Occupation, the obvious and visible badge of social position, was not a determinent of victory or defeat. This important point would have gone unrecognized in an exclusive examination of officeholders. Only clerical employees, bereft of specific political organization and a sense of class position, seemed politically disadvantaged. Several possible explanations account for the general insignificance of occupation in Atlanta elections, but the wide acceptance of the formula system of representation for "all interests" upon tickets for city office appears most plausible. Atlanta's elite devised this plan to insure their dominance early in the era, when politics possessed a raucous tone supposedly because of lower class participation, and they resurrected it whenever their preeminence seemed seriously threatened. Manual workers, for their part, appeared willing to accept this formula for limited recognition.

Among candidates with white-collar occupations, property-holdings helped to predict the outcome of elections. Richer contestants according to this criterion were more often successful than their poorer counterparts, especially in at-large races. Such an identifying standard, however, did not guarantee victory or defeat. Some candidates with comparatively small holdings, including a few with no property at all, were successful, while several of the wealthiest men in the city met defeat. Yet frequent distinctions in property between winners and losers signified a municipal government dominated by substantial property-holders.

For the first half of the period under study (1865-1883), these property differences were not as important as qualities such as political experience, age, and period of arrival in the city. During the second half of the period, however, property assumed greater political importance than other attributes of candidates. In most political systems, the structure and process of campaigning provide advantages to wealthier individuals. This is particularly true of nonpartisan systems, which emphasize amateurism and which lack political organizations to support and sustain men of more modest means.[1] By the late 1870s, Atlanta had switched to such a system. Moreover, the citizens' reform movement begun in 1884 deliberately aimed at placing city affairs firmly in control of wealthier businessmen and professional men. Although the greater ability of men of property to mobilize allies and agencies of public information undoubtedly contributed to the pattern described above, equally significant was the message such people conveyed to the public that their property-owning qualified them to exercise power. Choices were available, however, and most voters seemed to select those candidates with such qualifications.

Region of birth did not play as important a role in Atlanta as in northern cities. Immigrants could not appear in Atlanta politics in significant numbers when their social base in the city was so small. Foreign-born contestants did not differ much from native candidates with respect to other qualities, although immigrants were less likely to compete for public position if they were relative newcomers to the city or had small property-holdings. Indeed, foreign-born office-seekers in Atlanta generally were substantial citizens and clearly did not represent a thrust up from the bottom. Immigrants, once nominated, did not face particular handicaps in winning municipal office. Thus it appears that in politics, as in other areas of community life, the foreign-born were well assimilated in Atlanta society and, unlike blacks, were not victims of bigotry and intolerance.

This also seemed true for northern-born migrants to Atlanta, who campaigned with surprising frequency, particularly in the postwar years. Many of these transplanted Northerners, like the immigrants, were antebellum settlers. Few of the Northerners who came after the war were identified with the carpetbagger element of the Republican party, and, after the demise of the Republicans in city campaigns in the early 1870s, even those Northerners who had been connected with that party did not encounter particular problems in municipal elections. Several switched party allegiance and campaigned on Democratic slates. The decline through time in the proportions of Northerners and immigrants among office-seekers reflected the disappearance of early arrivals and the failure of foreign and northern newcomers to replace them. Clearly the spread of northern firms and capital southward did not introduce business representatives and agents into Atlanta municipal politics in noticeable numbers.[2]

Unlike immigrants, Northerners were not reluctant to enter mayoral contests. Yet a northern identification was a severe drawback in these races; all but one transplanted Northerner were denied the highest position in city government. Further analysis also indicated that a non-Southern connection may have had negative connotations for certain groups of candidates—recent arrivals and poorer men—in other contests. Northerners and immigrants who shared these characteristics were not able to win city office as often as native Southerners in similar social circumstances. The long identification with Atlanta and substantial property-holdings of non-Southerners helped to explain their surprising success. Nonetheless, several Northerners and immigrants who were recent arrivals and less substantial citizens were able to win city offices.

As a southern city with a large and politically active black population, Atlanta provides an opportunity to measure black political progress during this period. The heart of the historical debate is whether blacks in the South made advances toward achieving a better position in society until some time when such progress was terminated and, indeed, turned back.[3] This study offers evidence on both sides of the controversy. From 1868 to the early 1890s blacks formed a large proportion of Atlanta's voters and appeared to have gained a limited voice in city affairs. From the 1870s to the late 1880s blacks and whites stood on the same platforms, addressing integrated audiences; black politicians sometimes were referred to as "Mr." or "Captain." During the 1890s, however, blacks were effectively deprived of the franchise by the white primary. White candidates no longer listened to black political requests or consulted black voters in organized public meetings. The numbers of registered black voters declined drastically during the last few years of the century.

Focusing on black office-seekers, and on their chances for success, pro-

vides additional important evidence. Only twenty-two blacks contested
Atlanta city elections from 1870 to 1890, and none did so in the last
decade of the century. The small number of black candidates for city
office is noteworthy, given their sizeable proportion among the Atlanta
electorate. A conscious decision not to participate in city politics but
to concentrate on economic advancement—an attitude epitomized in
the late 1895 "Atlanta Compromise" of Booker T. Washington—surely
contributed to the low number of black office-seekers. Fear of white
retaliation and a realistic recognition of almost certain defeat, primarily
because of the general-ticket system and secondarily because of divisions
among black voters, also undoubtedly kept some potential hopefuls
from running for office. Only two black men managed to win, both in
1870 when the Republican legislature altered electoral rules for their
benefit. All other black candidates suffered crushing defeats, and race
rather than other attributes clearly was the deciding factor. After several
instances of rejection and defeat, some black Atlantans adopted a more
militant position in municipal politics. This new attitude, which surfaced
dramatically during the 1880s with stronger demands by black political
leaders for direct representation, produced a white reaction that eventually
led to the white citizens' primary.

The lesson is clear. Although obvious differences in black political participation existed in Atlanta before and after 1890, at no time did most
whites concede that blacks were equal partners in politics. Black Atlantans could exercise the franchise, and obtain a few benefits, as long
as one or more competing white factions believed they would benefit
from that arrangement. But white voters emphatically proscribed what
had become by the 1880s the principal black demand—direct representation in city government.

Studies of public leadership in other cities have not systematically
analyzed the residences of officeholders. Since this factor was often cast
into the political spotlight in Atlanta during these years, however, one
might hypothesize that residence would have influenced the voting of
many Atlantans. Moreover, the size and shape of Atlanta's wards, which
resembled large pieces of pie sliced out of the circular city, promised
a greater potential significance for this factor in Atlanta than in cities
with smaller political divisions. The residences of candidates did in fact
change dramatically from 1865 to 1903, with the clustering of contestants
in the very center of town gradually giving way to a marked dispersion

in all directions toward the city limits. This shift reflected the general geographical mobility of the population, and also led to complaints of underrepresentation by citizens from the outskirts early in the era and by residents of the central city later on. But the study does not confirm the hypothesis that residence was important in politics. Even after adjusting for other attributes, residence was not significantly associated with victory or defeat, although living in either the core or ring of Atlanta seemed to advance campaigns of some groups. Despite the claims of many contemporary Atlantans, residence appears to have been a minor issue, important only in isolated cases.

Two measures of a long identification with the city—period of arrival and a ten-year interval of residence before campaigning—proved useful in studying Atlanta politics. When Atlanta's office-seekers referred to an early identification with the city they meant either the prewar years or, later on, the period after the war when the city was rebuilt. Candidates who had arrived in Atlanta at least before 1870 could lay claim to being among the city's founders, and often assumed that publication of that fact would aid in their appeal for votes. Even contestants who came after 1870 stressed, when appropriate, the length of their identification with the city as proof of their knowledge of city affairs and problems.

Antebellum settlers, a majority among office-seekers before 1884, clearly provided continuity with the past; men who arrived in the 1860s, many of whom sought city office before living ten years in Atlanta, were the newcomers in the pre-1884 period. Competition between those two groups may have contributed as much to the bitterness characteristic of post-Civil War campaigns as did more publicized matters of race and class. The tumultuous atmosphere early in the era not only encouraged large numbers of very recent arrivals to enter the political fray but also allowed them to win city office with the same facility as earlier settlers. After 1884, prewar residents and men who arrived in the 1860s began to be displaced by more recent arrivals, even though a relatively brief period of residence in the city was a definite political handicap. Thus, as the city matured, candidates who campaigned before living in Atlanta at least ten years had to fight an uphill battle. A longer attachment to the city was more advantageous, since even those candidates who came after 1870 and who had lived at least ten years in the city were less successful than the earlier settlers.[4] Long residence in the city was especially helpful throughout the period for certain groups of contestants, who lacked such desirable qualities as large property-holdings. However, it was never the overriding matter in municipal elections that some participants suggested, and certainly did not provide an unbeatable political advantage in the young, rapidly expanding, forward-looking capitol of the New South.

The age of candidates was another characteristic that changed significantly through time. Atlanta's office-seekers generally were younger before 1884 than contestants after that year. Possibly, the greater age of office-seekers was an important correlate of greater political stability and a natural corollary of the growth of a new city (including the increased average age of Atlanta's population). The aim of the citizens' reform movement to promote the candidacies of more established and successful members of the community also led to the greater participation of relatively older Atlantans in contests for all three offices after 1884. Candidates for mayor and alderman generally were older than councilmanic contestants throughout the years. This suggested that Atlantans expected greater maturity for men holding these more prestigious at-large positions.

The political activity and success of younger men was frequently noted in postwar Atlanta and, according to some contemporaries, contributed to the city's unstable political conditions. The turbulent postwar years may have promoted political opportunities for younger men. Evidence on elections before 1884 partly supported this interpretation, since younger men were more often successful than older contestants, especially in councilmanic campaigns. Even later in the period, many candidates emphasized their youth. But quantitative analysis refuted the idea, advertised in several candidates' campaigns, that youth continued to be a desirable quality after 1884 and also contravened complaints by some youthful contenders that the political process favored older office-seekers, at least in aldermanic and councilmanic elections. Older contestants were favored in mayoral races, but the age of candidates after 1884 did not influence the results of a large number of other elections.

Examination of the association between age and political performance, after adjusting for other attributes, provided important information on the social bases of Atlanta politics. In general, younger contenders enjoyed a noticeable edge over older office-seekers only among poorer political novices who came to Atlanta before 1870. This suggests two matters of importance. First, the rejection of older earlier settlers before 1884 presents clearer evidence of a sharp break with the past than does the success rate of recent arrivals at that time alone. Second, throughout the years, Atlantans may have perceived younger men without substantial property-holdings who were just entering politics as talented men moving up, but were not so generous in evaluating older men in similar circumstances.

In addition to social characteristics of candidates, investigation into the impact of three important indicators of previous political experience and recognizable political status—service in appointive office, membership on political committees, and number of campaigns for elective office—proved instructive. A noticeable number of candidates had previously served in minor municipal posts, but such experience was no guarantee of victory. Indeed, it was a strong drawback in mayoral campaigns; Atlantans apparently did not regard favorably men who attempted to advance to the highest elective office in the city from appointive positions. After holding other qualities of candidates constant, prior service in minor munici-pal posts also appeared as an impediment in post-1884 councilmanic con-tests, providing further evidence that the citizens' reform movement's objective of defeating "politicians" was at least partly successful.[5]

Although partisan committees were extremely important early in the era, surprisingly few candidates had served on them before their cam-paigns. The nominating and executive committees associated with the citizens' reform movement, however, provided a major stepping-stone into campaigns for elective offices after 1884.[6] But such experience was not a general ticket to political success in Atlanta before or after 1884, although it appeared beneficial for skilled tradesmen and other poorer contestants. It undoubtedly helped some of these people become contenders and possibly aided them in winning public positions that otherwise would have been more difficult to obtain. The finding that this type of political experience did not have widespread electoral re-percussions contravened occasional complaints that committee members were too often successful in furthering their own careers and corroborated contemporary accounts of campaigns that rarely mentioned such service.

A substantial number of political novices participated in Atlanta polit-ics throughout this period, particularly after 1884. Conversely, the number of political repeaters, especially perennials, declined through the years. Analysis revealed that repetitive campaigning was especially politically advantageous before 1874 and was helpful to a lesser extent between 1874 and 1883. After 1883, however, novices were more likely to win than beforehand, but the reverse held for perennials; more important, beginners and repeaters enjoyed similar rates of political success, and the former were more successful than perennials in councilmanic races. The constant influx of new political hopefuls into Atlanta's political system, therefore, ultimately led to a high degree of rotation in city government. This turnover, however, did not lead to equal access into the governing halls for all social groups in Atlanta. In fact, it may have had an opposite effect, since political persistence primarily increased opportunities to win office for blue-collar workers, small property-owners, and recent arrivals.

General conclusions from analysis of these attributes indicate that the first stage of the social filter—self-selection and nomination processes—produced a body of contestants that was not homogeneous but highly unrepresentative of the general population of Atlanta's adult males. Blacks, very young and very old men, and newcomers to the city did not appear among candidates in numbers even approaching their strength among the citizenry. Non-Southerners were a small minority among political hopefuls but still had a larger representation among this group than among all Atlantans. Citizens living in large areas of the city, depending upon the subperiod, also were poorly represented in campaigns for elective office. Most important, perhaps, blue-collar workers and people who owned small amounts of property were severely underrepresented among office-seekers.

Examination of the second stage of the social filter—the relative political performance of social groups in elections that matched opponents with different attributes—revealed that although candidates were highly unrepresentative of the general population, office-holders were often even more so. Voters tended to choose certain social groups over others in mayoral races throughout the period and in aldermanic contests in the early era. Consistent voter preferences were not as noticeable in aldermanic races after 1884 or in councilmanic campaigns throughout the years, but since the "better class" won more than they lost, especially towards the end, they were able to maintain their dominance in municipal government.

This continued dominance in Atlanta politics of the "better class" differs from what occurred in other cities that have been studied. In Robert Dahl's analysis of changes in the social backgrounds of elected officials (especially mayors) in New Haven, he found that *entrepreneurs,* wealthy self-made men of business without high social standing, obtained a virtual monopoly on the mayoralty from 1842 to 1900. Dahl offered as reasons the lack of independent working-class outlook and the wide-spread belief in the peculiar virtues and meritorious attainments of businessmen. These entrepreneurs were overthrown in 1900 after the working class had developed distinctive programs and immigration had transformed society. From 1900 to midcentury, the *ex-plebes*—clerks, manual workers, and middle-range merchants who played the game of ethnic politics and relied on party organizations—dominated New Haven politics.[7]

Other studies pointed out this same theme. Donald Bradley and Mayer Zald used an expanded list of social characteristics of mayors to analyze sociopolitical change in Chicago. Zald and Thomas Anderson later undertook a similar study of Nashville. Both studies reported important variations from Dahl's findings but found similar changes taking place in occupation and wealth backgrounds of mayors.[8] Robert Schulze stated that a *bifurcation of power*—that is, when the economic elite abandoned the municipal political arena to a separate, rising political elite—occurred in 1900 in "Cibola" (Ypsilanti, Michigan). Schulze connected this development to Cibola's change from a self-contained community to one tied directly to the national economy. Local government therefore became less important to economic dominants. Donald Clelland and William Form found a similar pattern in "Wheelsburg" (Lansing, Michigan), even in the absence of the outside economic forces (for example, the introduction of national firms into the city) that seemed instrumental in Cibola.[9]

Samuel Hays, concentrating on councilmen rather than mayors, described a gradual rather than abrupt displacement of the economic elite in urban politics throughout the latter part of the nineteenth century. He also connected change with the new century: "By 1900, the typical ward-elected city councilman was a small businessman . . . a clerk, a skilled artisan, or an unskilled laborer. Professional and large business classes were greatly outnumbered." He attributed this alteration to the system of ward representation more than to broad social trends or to economic developments.[10]

In Atlanta, however, as previously mentioned, such changes did not take place. The numbers of skilled artisans, clerical employees, and small shopkeepers among candidates did not increase through time; nor were such contestants more successful later in the period than they had been before. The period from 1884 to 1903 witnessed an increased rather than decreased political activism by the "better citizens," including dominant economic groups, and Atlantans more often than not chose wealthier citizens to represent them. Thus middle-range merchants, professional men, and the representatives of the upper classes did not slowly surrender the reins of Atlanta city government.[11] Furthermore, bifurcation of power did not occur in Atlanta. Political experience afforded positive advantages in Atlanta municipal elections only early in the era, and few perennial politicians were in evidence at the turn of the century. Prior service in appointive office, if anything, was a handicap, and many candidates with previous service on important political committees also were very substantial citizens.

The above distinctions between Atlanta and other cities were most likely due to obvious demographic and political differences. Ethnic considerations could not be important in southern cities like Atlanta for obvious reasons, and immigrant office-seekers in Atlanta tended to be well-established members of the "better class." Atlanta's large black population and the general southern solution to race relations in politics had an effect. Working-class whites and blacks failed to forge a political alliance, and Atlanta's elite appeared as the special beneficiary of this situation.[12] This provides only partial explanation, however, since wealthy Atlantans continued to be successful even after black influence in municipal politics clearly had ended. Certain political arrangements contributed more than racial conflict to the ability of the city's "better class" to maintain control of municipal government. The 1874 charter proscription against incumbent succession, which considerably reduced political repeating and prevented the bifurcation of power that occurred in other cities, possibly retarded political advancement by lower class citizens. The 1874 charter also enshrined into law the system of city-wide voting favored by Atlanta's elite, effectively curbing the political power of individual wards, and enacted for the first time a voting registration law with a tax-paying provision that was intended to restrict the size of the electorate. This charter had been pushed through the state legislature by a group of elite "reformers" without Atlantans ever having the opportunity to vote on the changes. One decade later, an equally elite group of Atlantans conceived the citizens' reform movement, thereby preventing the return to city politics of partisan organizations that were the most effective means for mass mobilization of voters and a common route of political mobility for men of modest or meagre means. Because the nominating committees connected to this movement generally included a sizeable number of citizens chosen at-large and because these committees voted as a whole, resurgent efforts by citizens within individual wards to circumvent the citywide voting system through ward nomination failed. Partly for these reasons, Atlanta's elite was able to achieve its goals of ending professionalism in politics and of placing city affairs firmly in its own hands. Like the reformers of 1874, the citizens' reform movement also was helped by stricter taxpaying and registration procedures adopted in the early 1880s.

Registration laws were designed to reduce the size and to control the character of the electorate, and thus mainly represented attempts to affect the second stage of the social filter. Maintenance of only one polling place in the center of town within each ward, especially when coupled with the anticarriage "reform" of 1890, further discouraged a large turnout. The general-ticket system of voting affected the second stage of the social filter in a different way—by making grass roots political organization and campaigning more difficult. The rule against incumbent succession and the firm establishment of a nonpartisan system, on the other hand, were intended to place constraints primarily on the first stage of the social filter.

Both stages of the social filter made Atlanta's office-holders highly unrepresentative of the citizenry. Factors in both components of the first stage explain why this occurred there. First, few people of lower occupational status and with little or no property opted to stand for election. Such prosaic reasons as lack of time and money to conduct campaigns doubtlessly were important,[13] but no more so, certainly, than being captives of a political culture that placed a premium on higher socioeconomic status for public officials. Contemporary notions of what types of people should govern also may have deterred some blacks, very young and very old people, and very recent arrivals from running for city office, either because they shared the belief that others should rule or because they recognized the poor odds of winning sufficient votes. Demographic facts appeared more important in the case of white non-Southerners; simply too few immigrants and Northerners resided in Atlanta to form a base from which sizeable numbers of political aspirants could spring.

Second, the nominating process screened out some groups of potential contestants. This clearly was the case for blacks, who never were selected for organized tickets (other than their own) after the demise of the city Republican party. The formula to balance tickets in Atlanta generally gave only limited recognition to workers, non-Southerners (even though larger than their proportion among the population might have warranted), the very young and very old, and newcomers to the city. At the same time it provided disproportionate representation to businessmen and professional men often of substantial property-holdings, men of middle age, and earlier settlers.

Although undeniably severe, especially in at-large contests, the first stage of the social filter nonetheless left some choice for citizens on election day. Several candidates not chosen on organized slates continued campaigns anyway, and competing tickets virtually always existed. Moreover, most social groups rarely competed against each other. This was true for all vocational groups except businessmen, for blacks, for non-Southerners, and for recent arrivals; substantial gaps in property-holding and age (and political experience) also generally existed between candidates in direct competition.

Thus the second stage of the social filter revealed that office-holders were unrepresentative of the general population because some social groups of contestants were more successful at the polls than others. Two reasons exist for the greater success of more substantial property-holders. On a practical basis, their greater ability to finance more expensive campaigns had some effect. Mundane reasons also can be offered to explain the greater success of earlier settlers and of prominent and practiced politicians early in the period, since these people had greater opportunity to make important contacts and to earn citywide recognition. Such explanations, however, cannot account for the success of political novices and younger men during certain periods. Furthermore, practical reasons ignore the second significant reason for certain groups' success—the existence of a political culture that as seen in the rhetoric at ward meetings and mass rallies, speeches on the stump, and paid advertisements and editorials in newspapers, emphasized the desirability of certain qualities among officeholders.

Nevertheless, it is important to note that a distinct preference of Atlanta's voters for certain kinds of people existed only in those offices that carried considerable social and political prestige and that captured the most newspaper coverage—the mayoralty and (early in the period) alderman. In mayoral races, politically experienced Southerners who had not previously held minor appointive offices were favored before 1884; wealthy and older men without prior political experience got the nod after that year. Large property-holders and long-time residents of the city generally were chosen for the Board of Alderman, but the democratization of this position after 1884 led to less sharp differentiation according to these factors. Certain social groups also were more successful than others in councilmanic races throughout the years, but in these contests Atlanta voters did not exhibit strong or consistent preferences for social uniformity. In short, contrary to contemporary suggestions, no significant second stage of the social filter existed in councilmanic campaigns or in post-1884 aldermanic races. Instead, the first stage of the social filter—self-selection among the citizenry and nominations and other combinations into tickets—produced a City Council and, after 1884, a Board of Alderman that was unrepresentative in their social backgrounds of Atlanta's voters, whereas both stages of the social filter made the Board of Alderman initially and the mayoralty throughout the years even more exclusive.

Although this study is a local one, it has more significant ramifications. The findings from Atlanta challenge at several points interpretations based on research in other cities, but existing studies do not permit systematic comparison. Further research in other cities that applies the model used here, or one similar to it, is needed to determine whether Atlanta represented a truly deviant case in urban political history. This strategy might change general conclusions or provide valuable information on the socio-political structure of municipal government. In the final analysis, therefore, exploration of social patterns in Atlanta politics leads to broader questions regarding the systematic, comparative investigation of the social filter concept in urban political systems. For example, were political factors more important than social variables in cities with strong party organizations and a system of ward rather than citywide elections? Did these political arrangements contribute to greater participation and opportunity for political success for working-class citizens? Were more substantial citizens in fact fading out of the political picture, as other writers suggest, or did property-owning become more important through time as in Atlanta? Does an increase in age among political elites reflect growth of a new city or a transition from unstable to settled social and political conditions? Are times of political stress and strain connected to challenges by younger men and newcomers to the city for political power? Does the relative success of certain age groups and of candidates identified as oldtimers or latecomers indicate differences in citizens' expectations and perceptions of the prestige of certain positions?

Comparative analysis of the social bases of urban politics, isolating crucial factors such as size, region, composition of the population, and political arrangements (for example, partisan versus nonpartisan elections, ward versus citywide voting), would give the best chance of answering the above questions. Until such additional studies exist, generalizations must be tentative. The participation of various groups and their relative chances for victory in Atlanta often appeared at odds with results reported from other studies. Likely reasons for distinctions have been suggested, but application of the model used in this study in a number of cities also might reveal which of the two primary factors linked to the findings in Atlanta—elements of the political culture or the political structure and historical situations—were more fundamental.

For example, examination of all office-seekers, and for positions other than the mayoralty, might reveal extensive participation by immigrants in northern cities at a much earlier date than that suggested by other writers. Careful analysis of the relationship of ethnic background with the outcome of elections would supply a more precise picture of which kinds of immigrants became acceptable as city officials, and when. Identification by birth with the state or region may have been as unimportant in other cities in the late nineteenth century as it was in Atlanta, but this cannot be concluded until the evidence is collected and evaluated. If the pattern found in Atlanta occurred elsewhere in the South, one might question present-day interpretations of Reconstruction and the claim that a southern identification became even more important with the passing of time. Such considerations, as seen in both contemporary reporting of campaigns and the statistical analysis of this study, were not foremost in the minds of Atlantans. Moreover, if further research should reveal that region of birth was not politically significant in other southern cities, it would be tempting to conclude that voters in urban areas were not particularly parochial or regionally self-conscious.

This study thus presents a starting point for further investigation. Certain key elements of the research and analytic design need to be repeated. First, candidates for all major municipal elective offices and not simply the mayoralty should be included since the small number of mayoral candidates limits possible findings. Moreover, mayors and mayoral elections may have been as distinctive in other cities as they were in Atlanta. Second, the importance of examining winners and losers cannot be overestimated. Only through analysis of both groups can the underlying mechanics of the social filter be uncovered. Third, a number of group-defining social and political characteristics—not simply occupation, property, and ethnic background—should be analyzed. Fourth, multivariate analysis should be used. Such analysis can, as is true in several instances in this book, correct faulty, first-glance impressions of relationships between characteristics of candidates and outcome of elections.

The model used in this study should be tested by a number of historians, each analyzing one city; this would be practical in terms of time, money, and normal actuarial tables.[14] As long as similar definitions and classifications are used, data can be pooled among scholars for comparative analysis. The model is sufficiently flexible to allow for modifications, such as adding other attributes to the analysis, without affecting the overall effort. This arrangement can be likened to the possibilities inherent in jazz, in which certain themes are universal but in which there is considerable room for improvisation.

NOTES

1. Other writers have stressed the importance of partisan organization for the rise of lower-class office-holders. See Peter H. Rossi, "Power and Community Structure," in Willis D. Hawley and Frederick M. Wirt, eds., *The Search for Community Power* (Englewood Cliffs, 1968), 78-92.

2. Howard N. Rabinowitz, "Continuity and Change: Southern Urban Development, 1860-1890," in Blaine A. Brownell and David R. Goldfield, eds., *The City in Southern History: The Growth of Urban Civilization in the South* (Port Washington, 1977), 97.

3. See C. Vann Woodward, *The Strange Career of Jim Crow* (New York, 1966), 31-65, for the principal discussion of an "interregnum" in race relations before the 1890s. I have commented on his interpretation at greater length in Eugene J. Watts, "Black Political Progress in Atlanta, 1865-1895," *The Journal of Negro History* (July, 1974), 268-86.

4. The fact that period of arrival was more strongly associated with political success than ten years' length of residence may indicate that the ten-year interval selected for this study—a choice largely dictated by availability of sources—is too narrow. Other intervals could be employed in the study of other cities, although a variety of choices would add appreciably to the research. See chapter three, fn. 37.

5. Minor officials who managed to win these races tended to have greater amounts of property and a long period of residence in Atlanta, two desirable qualities that outweighed an otherwise negative association between appointive office-holding and political success.

6. Political party organizations were more important in other cities at this time and did provide a wider path of political recruitment in such cities as Chicago and New Haven. Donald S. Bradley and Mayer N. Zald, "From the Commercial Elite to Political Administrator: The Recruitment of Mayors of Chicago," *The American Journal of Sociology,* LXXI (1965), 153-67; and Robert A. Dahl, *Who Governs* (New Haven, 1961).

7. Dahl, *Who Governs,* especially 1-86. Readers should recall that Dahl and other writers analyzing the social-filter concept did not include all office-seekers or all attributes used in this study.

8. Bradley and Zald, "From the Commercial Elite to Political Administrator," 153-67; and Mayer N. Zald and Thomas A. Anderson, "Secular Trends and Historical Contingencies in the Recruitment of Mayors: Nashville as Compared to New Haven and Chicago," *Urban Affairs Quarterly,* III (1968), 53-68.

9. Robert S. Schulze, "The Role of Economic Dominants in Community Power Structure," *American Sociological Review,* XXIII (1958), 3-9, and "The Bifurcation of Power in a Satellite Community," in Morris Janowitz, ed., *Community Political Systems* (Glencoe, 1961), 19-80; and Donald A. Clelland and William H. Form, "Economic Dominants and Community Power: A Comparative Analysis," in Hawley and Wirt, eds., *The Search for Community Power,* 78-92.

10. Samuel P. Hays, "The Changing Political Structure of the City in Industrial America," *Journal of Urban History,* I (November, 1974), 14. Another historian suggested a contrary pattern for Springfield, Massachusetts, but did not carry his research past 1880, Michael H. Frisch, *Town Into City: Springfield, Massachusetts, and The Meaning of Community, 1840-1880* (Cambridge, 1972), 242-44.

11. Conclusions from this study refute the interpretation that the economic elite withdrew from Atlanta politics by 1874 presented in James A. Russell, "Atlanta, Gate City of the South, 1847-1885" (unpublished Ph.D. dissertation, Princeton, 1972), 179-80, 335-42.

12. Populism of the 1890s provides a familiar example of such a failure on the state, regional, and even national levels. The attempt had been made in Atlanta urban politics even before the mid-1880s but white workers and blacks were firmly opposed to such an alliance by the 1890s. According to one historian, the urban elite rather than the white working class led the fight to disenfranchise blacks in some other southern cities. Rabinowitz, "Continuity and Change," 120.

13. When office-holding is a part-time occupation, paying too low a salary to afford a livelihood, as it was in late nineteenth-century Atlanta, an artisan or clerk who must labor eight or more hours a day, six days a week, ordinarily cannot be an effective candidate or official.

14. This proposal is a natural corrolary to earlier suggestions of Lee Benson in "Quantification, Scientific History, and Scholarly Innovation," *Toward the Scientific Study of History* (New York, 1972), 98-104. For a good discussion of the use of explicit models in historiography, see Lance E. Davis, "'And It Will Never Be Literature'—The New Economic History: A Critique," in Robert P. Swierenga, ed., *Quantification in American History* (New York, 1970), 274-87. I earlier presented a detailed description of my design, "A Quantitative Model for the Study of Urban Politics," at the April 1973 meeting of the Missouri Valley Historical Society.

Bibliographic Essay

Several local histories of Atlanta include a discussion of all or a part of the period under study. The most complete and important of these is Franklin M. Garrett, *Atlanta and Environs: A Chronicle of the People and Events* (3 vols., New York, 1954). Other works useful particularly for their treatment of local politics in the early stages of Atlanta's history are Walter G. Cooper, *Official History of Fulton County* (Atlanta, 1934); Lucian Lamar Knight, *History of Fulton County, Georgia* (Atlanta, 1930); and Wallace P. Reed, *History of Atlanta, Georgia* (Syracuse, 1889). Several other studies provided useful references. The most helpful contemporary studies, products of the booster spirit in Atlanta, are E. Y. Clarke, *Atlanta Illustrated* (Atlanta, 1881); Atlanta City Council and the Atlanta Chamber of Commerce, *Handbook of the City of Atlanta* (Atlanta, 1898); *City of Atlanta, A Description, Historical and Industrial Review of the Gateway City of the South,* World's Fair Series on Great American Cities (Louisville, 1893); Thomas H. Martin, *Atlanta and Its Builders: A Comprehensive History of the Gate City of the South* (2 vols., Atlanta, 1902); and *Pioneer Citizens' History of Atlanta* (Atlanta, 1902). A contemporary study of special interest is E. R. Carter, *The Black Side: A Partial History of Business, Religious and Educational Side of the Negro in Atlanta* (Atlanta, 1894). Also consulted for this study were four works written after the period: *Atlanta Centennial Year Book, 1837-1937* (Atlanta, 1937); John R. Hornady, *Atlanta, Yesterday, Today and Tomorrow* (New York, 1922); Paul W. Miller, ed., *Atlanta, Capitol of the South* (New York, 1949); and Workers of the Writers' Program of the Work Projects Administration in the State of Georgia, comp., *Atlanta: A City of the Modern South* (New York, 1942).

Several recent theses and dissertations offer a more scholarly examination of Atlanta's past. Carole Louise Hagglund, "Irish Immigrants in Atlanta, 1850-1896" (unpublished M. A. thesis, Emory, 1968); and Ann Fonvielle Mebane, "Immigrant Patterns in Atlanta, 1880 and 1896" (unpublished M. A. thesis, Emory, 1967), provided information on Atlanta's foreign-born population. Richard J. Hopkins, "Patterns of Persistence and Occupational Mobility in a Southern City: Atlanta, 1870-1920" (unpublished Ph.D. dissertation, Emory, 1972), ranks as one of the finest examples of systematic analysis of social mobility and is an indispensible source for students of Atlanta's history. Arthur Reed Taylor, "From the Ashes: Atlanta during Reconstruction, 1865-1876" (unpublished Ph.D. dissertation, Emory, 1973); James M. Russell, "Atlanta, Gate City of the South, 1847-1885" (unpublished Ph.D. dissertation, Princeton, 1972); and Grigsby H. Wooten, Jr., "New City of the South: Atlanta, 1843-1873" (unpublished Ph.D. dissertation, Johns Hopkins, 1973), present solid scholarship on Atlanta's social, cultural, and business life. The latter two writers also devote considerable space to city politics, but they ignore important previous work on this subject, basing their interpretations on strongly biased newspaper opinion and a limited examination of elected officials.

Clarence A. Bacote, "The Negro in Georgia Politics, 1880-1908" (unpublished Ph.D. dissertation, University of Chicago, 1955), was a valuable source on black Atlanta politicians, as were two articles authored by him: "The Negro in Atlanta Politics," *Phylon,* XVI (December, 1955), 333-50, and "William Finch, Negro Councilman and Political Activities in Atlanta during Reconstruction," *Journal of Negro History,* XL (October, 1955), 341-64. Two other articles that discuss the role of blacks in Atlanta politics are John Hammond Moore, "The Negro and Prohibition in Atlanta, 1885-1887," *South Atlantic Quarterly,* LXIX (Winter, 1970), 38-57; and Eugene J. Watts, "Black Political Progress in Atlanta, 1868-1895," *Journal of Negro History,* LIX (July, 1974), 268-86. Howard N. Rabinowitz, "From Reconstruction to Redemption in the Urban South," *Journal of Urban History* (February, 1976), 169-95, includes Atlanta in his comparative study of blacks in several southern cities.

Unfortunately, extant personal papers of Atlantans of the period offer no insights into the conduct and character of city politics. Atlanta newspapers, however, provide a rich and colorful account of municipal politics in the late nineteenth century. Newspapers, searched from 1865 to 1915, also were the only complete source for the names of all candidates for city office and their votes and for membership on partisan political committees and on various citizen nominating and executive committees. Furthermore, the press sometimes printed brief biographical sketches of candidates that were helpful in determining their social backgrounds. The most complete collection is the microfilm depository at the Atlanta Public Library; the Atlantic Historical Society possesses several important bound volumes of early Atlanta newspapers. The Atlanta *Constitution,* for which a complete run from 1868 to the present exists, was an indispensible guide for this study. The Atlanta *Journal,* which commenced publication in 1883, also is entirely extant. After 1883 these two newspapers were the only dailies in Atlanta for any extended time until the turn of the century. Several other newspapers were important in the early period. The Atlanta *Daily Intelligencer,* the city's oldest newspaper (1857-1870), vied with the *Constitution* after the Civil War to be the "official organ" of the Democratic party. The Atlanta *New Era,* published from 1866 through 1871, often represented the views of city Republicans. The Atlanta *Daily Herald* conducted a crusade to cleanse city politics during its brief existence from 1872 through 1875. The Atlanta *Daily News* was examined for the years it was published, 1874-75. Another newspaper similar in name, part of the Hearst syndicate, was issued in Atlanta after the opening of the new century. The Atlanta *Daily Sun,* 1870-72, also provided some coverage of local politics, but other newspapers that lasted only a short time were not very helpful. Ruth Feldman, "A Checklist of Atlanta Newspapers, 1846-1948" (M.A. thesis, Emory, 1948), is a useful guide to extant Atlanta newspapers. Of the several black newspapers published in Atlanta during this period, only the Atlanta *Weekly Defiance,* published from 1881 to 1889, was actively involved in politics. Only a few scattered issues of this paper are extant in the New York State Historical Society and in the New York City Public Library. No copies of the Atlanta *Times,* issued from 1891-93, are extant. The Atlanta *News* was published only in 1896, after black political activity on the municipal level had ended. See John Wiley Rozier, "A History of the Negro Press in Atlanta" (unpublished M. A. thesis, Emory, 1947).

The Minutes of the City Council of Atlanta, from 1848 to the present, and the Minutes of the Board of Alderman of Atlanta, dating from 1874, are entirely extant. The Atlanta Historical Society maintains both sets of minutes for the period through 1900; the remainder of these records are on file with the city clerk in Atlanta's City Hall. The manuscript form of the Minutes of City Council contain the annual reports of city government before 1884; beginning that year the Annual Reports of City Officers were published separately and are now available at the Atlanta Historical Society. The annual reports, examined for the period from 1880 to 1915, identify all minor municipal officers and members of administrative boards; the histories of Franklin Garrett and Walter G. Cooper contain the names of these office-holders from the beginning of city government to the early 1880s. Other official records were also extremely helpful. All volumes of the Georgia Laws from 1865 to 1905, housed at the State Library in the Judicial Building in Atlanta, were consulted, as were the 1866, 1869, 1873, 1875, 1891, 1899, and 1909 copies of the Charter and Ordinances of the City of Atlanta, most easily found at the Atlanta Historical Society. These sources gave information on the changing structure of city government and laws pertaining to the conduct of campaigns, registration, and voting.

City directories, published by various authors in 1859, 1867, and 1870 beyond 1903 (none published in 1873), can be found in the Atlanta Public Library and in the Atlanta Historical Society. Directories were used to document the occupation, residence, and length of residence in Atlanta of candidates. Directories for each year commonly were compiled at the end of the preceding year, when campaigns were waged; thus the edition for the year following a campaign, when possible, was used to record information on each candidate's occupation and residence. In those cases in which individuals (or their occupation or residence) were not listed, the directory for the preceding year was used. Directories for the closest year (or the newspapers) were consulted in those few instances (1865, 1869) where this rule could not be followed. The same procedure, but for ten years before the candidacy, was used to measure length of residence. Given gaps in city directories (partially compensated for by the federal censuses), the actual period for this variable is longer than ten years for candidates competing from 1870 to 1872, and shorter than ten years for office-seekers in the periods 1867-68 and 1873-76.

The federal censuses of 1850, 1860, 1870, and 1880, which can be found in the Georgia Department of Archives and History and at the Atlanta Public Library, and a locally taken and handwritten census of Atlanta for 1896, located at the Emory University Library, were used to assemble data on period of arrival (together with directories for the decade

year), race, ethnic identification, birthplace, and age, with newspapers as
a supplementary source. Whenever possible, candidates were located in
more than one census. Information on property, both real and personal,
was taken from the Fulton County Tax Digests, complete from 1854 on
(except for 1865 and 1867), located at the Georgia Department of Archives and History.

Histories of Atlanta, newspapers, sections of city directories, and
various miscellaneous records provided information on the religion, education, membership in fraternal and civic groups, and Civil War experience
of too few candidates, generally the most prominent, to be systematically
analyzed in this study. Membership lists for four prestigious social groups
in Atlanta—the Capitol City Club, Piedmont Driving Club, Pioneer Historical Society, and the Social Register—available at the Atlanta Historical
Society are generally useful for defining a social elite, but were compiled
too late in the period to be applied in the analysis presented in this book.
All information collected for this study, including the above-mentioned
variables not actually used in the analysis, are available to interested scholars on magnetic tape from the Historical Archives of the Inter-University
Consortium for Social and Political Research at the University of Michigan.

Studies of the social bases of municipal politics based on backgrounds
of elected officials generally begin with Robert Dahl's influential work,
Who Governs? (New Haven, 1961), although a much less ambitious analysis by Robert T. Daland, *Dixie City: A Portrait of Political Leadership*
(Tuscaloosa, 1956), preceded Dahl's study by several years. Other social
scientists followed Dahl's lead. Donald S. Bradley and Mayer N. Zald,
"From Commercial Elite to Political Administrator: The Recruitment
of the Mayors of Chicago," *American Journal of Sociology*, LXXI (1965),
153-67, used an expanded list of social attributes to analyze sociopolitical
change in a midwestern city. Zald and Thomas A. Anderson later studied
a southern city in a similar manner: "Secular Trends and Historical Contingencies in the Recruitment of Mayors: Nashville as Compared to New
Haven and Chicago," *Urban Affairs Quarterly*, III (1968), 53-68. Several
sociologists have examined the changing social characteristics of municipal
officials to analyze political power in American cities. Robert P. Schulze,
studying Ypsilanti, Michigan, introduced the concept of "bifurcation" of
power—separation between political and economic elites—in "The Role
of Economic Dominants in Community Power Structure," *American
Sociological Review*, XXIII (1958), 3-9, and expanded his argument in

"The Bifurcation of Power in a Satellite Community," in Morris Janowitz, ed., *Community Political Systems* (Glencoe, 1961), 19-80. Donald A. Clelland and William H. Form, "Economic Dominants and Community Power: A Comparative Analysis," in Willis D. Hawley and Frederick Wirt, eds., *The Search for Community Power* (Englewood Cliffs, 1968), 78-92, replicated Schulze's analysis for Lansing, Michigan. Perhaps the most perceptive summary of the literature on community power is presented by Peter H. Rossi, "Power and Community Structure," in Hawley and Wirt, *The Search for Community Power*, 394-401.

By now the list of prosopographic studies done by historians is too long to be printed here. Allan G. Bogue mentioned a number of such works in "United States: The 'New' Political History," in Robert P. Swierenga, ed., *Quantification in American History* (New York, 1970), 38. For the best recent works on urban political elites see Richard S. Alcorn, "Leadership and Stability in Mid-Nineteenth Century America: A Case Study of an Illinois Town," *Journal of American History,* LXI (December, 1974), 685-702; Michael H. Frisch, *Town Into City: Springfield, Massachusetts, and the Meaning of Community, 1840-1880* (Cambridge, 1972); and Edward Pessen, "Who Governed the Nation's Cities in the 'Era of the Common Man'?" *Political Science Quarterly,* LXXXVII (December, 1972), 591-614. Samuel P. Hays, in "The Changing Political Structure of the City in Industrial America," *Journal of Urban History,* I (November, 1974), 6-38, effectively summarizes previous scholarship on social backgrounds of urban political leaders.

Index

Age: association of, with other attributes, 79, 84, 92, 95-97, 100, 103; association of, with political success, 136-37, 150, 154, 157 n.19, 166-67; association of, with political success and other attributes, 130-31, 137; of candidates, 93-95, 103-05; contemporary mention of, 20, 25, 59-60; measurement of, 60-61, 69 n.41; of population, 95, 111 n.38

Alcorn, Richard, 111 n.38

Alderman. *See* Candidates, social differences among; Officeholders, social differences among; Offices

American Protective Association, 17, 49, 56, 118

American Voter, The, 41 n.35, 66 n.14, 69 n.38

Amorous, Martin F., 59

Analysis of variance, 108 n.14

Anderson, Thomas A., 169

Angier, Nedon L., 22, 55, 125

Announcements for campaigns, 15-16

Anticarriage rule, 35, 171

Anti-Primary Ticket, 30, 79-80, 150

Anti-Ring. *See* Rings

Arnold, Reuben, 27, 74

Asbury, J. W., 28

Atlanta, Georgia, 3-4, 12-15, 21, 55-56, 85, 90, 169-70, 173-74

Atlanta Business Men's League, 19

Atlanta Compromise of 1895, 164

Atlanta *Constitution,* 15-17, 19, 25-27, 31-32, 34-35, 39 n.19, 41 n.35, 50-55, 59-61, 90, 93

Atlanta *Daily Herald,* 19, 52, 60, 64, 74

Atlanta *Daily Intelligencer,* 19

Atlanta *Daily News,* 19, 56

Atlanta *Daily Sun,* 64

Atlanta Federation of Trades, 18, 49

Atlanta *Journal,* 15, 27, 31-32, 36, 61, 64

Atlanta Liquor Dealer's Association, 18, 39 n.17, 62

Atlanta *New Era,* 19, 32, 35, 50

Atlanta Prohibition Club, 18

Atlanta *Weekly Defiance,* 67 n.24, 79

Australian ballot, 34

Baldwin, E. A., 48

Beattie, D. A., 100, 111 n.35

Benson, Lee, 9, 66 n.8, 176 n.14

Berkhofer, Robert F., 66 n.9

Bird, W. H., 54

Blacks: as candidates, 21-22, 30, 78-80, 109, 163-64, 171; coalition of, with white workers, 28-29; eligibility of, as voters, 14; exclusion of, from politics, 24, 29-31; lack of unity among, 21-22, 25; militance of, 21, 164; political role of, 20, 23, 27-28, 42 n.49, 163, 170;

proportion of, among population, 12; proportion of, among voters, 41 n.39, 53. *See also* Race
Board of Aldermen. *See* Offices
Bogue, Allan G., 9
Bradley, Donald S., 55, 169
Brannan, M. M., 34
Brotherton, William H., 17, 51, 64, 100, 112 n.40, 118
Brown, Walter, 35, 52, 112 n.41
Bullock, Governor, 14
Burnett, Alonzo, 79
Business men: candidacies of, 71-73, 103-05, 161, 169-70, 172; contemporary preference for, 26-27, 49-50; domination of, in city politics, 6-7; organizations of, 66 n.13, 107 n.4; political activity of, 18-19, 24, 31, 50, 161; political advantages of, 35; political success of, 118, 128, 150, 154; proportion of, among population, 106 n.3; social characteristics of, 77-78, 96. *See also* Occupation
Button-holing, 32

Candidates: campaigns of, 12, 15-16, 26, 31-36; competition among, in social groups, 115, 122, 127-28, 131, 134, 136-37, 142, 144, 146, 157 n.13, 172; contemporary focus on, 4; numbers of, 6; selection of, 5, 13, 38 n.11; social differences among, by office, 74, 76, 79, 83, 91, 93, 96-98, 102-04, 122-23, 136-37, 161, 166, 168; uncontested, 127, 131, 134, 137, 142, 144, 146, 156 n.6, 157 n.16
Canonical correlation, 149-50, 152, 158 n.24
Capital City Club, 65 n.4
Cargile, Mitchell, 53-54, 79
Carpetbaggers, 55, 84, 162
Carter, E. R., 54, 109 n.20
Censuses, 13, 67 n.25, 69 n.41

Chamber of Commerce, 19, 24, 42 n.48
Chudacoff, Howard, 58
Citizens' nominating committee, 26-31, 62, 99, 167
Citizens Reform Club, 56
Citizens' reform movement, 16, 18, 20-21, 26-29, 71, 76, 91-92, 99, 101, 122, 142, 144, 146, 162, 166-67, 170-71
Citizens' Ticket, 19, 27-31, 33, 51
City Charter of 1874, 13-15, 32, 101, 106 n.2, 113 n.46, 122, 134, 136, 146, 170
City Council. *See* Offices
City Executive Committee, 23-24, 29-31, 35, 42 n.48, 62-63, 99
Citywide voting. *See* General ticket system
Civil War, 13, 22, 46, 79, 82-84, 88
Class conflict, 22-25, 27-29, 49, 52, 134, 160. *See also* Occupation; Property; Workingclass
Clelland, Donald A., 169
Coefficient of variability, 75
Collier, Charles, 43 n.53
Collier, John, 24
Conservative Club, 17
Councilmen. *See* Candidates, social differences among; Officeholders, social differences among; Offices
Cramer's V, 72, 108 n.10

Dahl, Robert A., 55, 59, 92, 107 n.9, 112 n.43, 117, 168-69, 176 n.7
Daland, Robert T., 67 n.26
Democratic party, 14, 18-25, 39 n.19, 62, 73, 99, 163
Directories, city, 13, 68 n.37
Discriminant analysis, 7-8, 10 n.10, 149, 155 n.1, 158 n.24
Dracoes, 18
Dykstra, Robert, 68 n.35

Education, 46

1890 Club, 17, 62
Elections: conduct of, 26, 31-36; eligibility for, 14-15, 37 n.6; expenses for, 33-34, 43 n.56, 52; times for, 35, 43 n.59; violence during, 21
Eligibility. See Elections
English, James W., 17, 112 n.40
Eta, 75, 108 n.14, 158 n.24

Farrow, T. Stobo, 134
Finch, William, 54, 79
Flynn, John H., 56
Foreign-born: assimilation of, 56, 109 n.24; candidacies of, 55, 67 n.25, 80-81, 103-05, 150, 170, 174; classification of, 67 n.25; contemporary comment upon, 55-56; political success of, 127-28, 162; proportion of, among population, 12, 81-82, 171; social characteristics of, 82, 87, 102. See also Nativism; Region of birth
Form, William H., 169
Fraternal affiliation, 46, 65 n.4
F ratio, 75
Fraud, 14, 35
Frisch, Michael, 107 n.9
Fuller, W. A., 58

Gamma, 85-86
Garmany, J. S., 48
General ticket system, 12-13, 21-24, 40 n.22, 164, 170-71, 173-74
Glenn, Tom, 35
Goldsmith, J. W., 61
Goodwin, John B., 30, 51, 60, 96, 112 n.41
Greenback party, 25

Haas, Aaron, 56
Hammock, C. C., 55
Hays, Samuel P., 169
Henry, R. J., 80
Hillyer, George, 27
Hopkins, Richard J., 37 n.1, 56,

66 n.5, 68 n.33, 80, 106 n.3, 109 n.23, 111
Howell, Albert, 43 n.53, 73, 102, 117
Howell, Evan P., 15, 49, 112 n.41
Hulsey, W. H., 93

Immigrants. See Foreign-born
Incumbents, 13, 15, 101, 170-71
Independents, 22-25, 41 n.32
Industrial Union Council, 18, 49, 73
Issues, 3, 32-33, 43 n.55

James, John H., 22
Jones, O. H., 49, 65 n.2

Kimball, H. I., 49
King, Porter, 57
Knights, Peter R., 69 n.41
Knights of Labor, 17-18, 28
"Know-Nothing," 56. See also Nativism
Kontz, A. L., 38 n.8, 51

Labor. See Workingclass
Labor Union No. 1, 18, 49, 107 n.5
Length of residence: association of, with other attributes, 79, 82, 84, 92-93, 95, 100, 102; association of, with political success, 134-36, 150-52, 165-66; association of, with political success and other attributes, 136; of candidates, 90-91, 103-05; contemporary mention of, 20, 25, 58-59; measurement of, 59, 68 n.37, 175 n.4
Lester, J. S., 28
Lewis, Branch, 51
Liberal Club, 18, 60
Longley, B. F., 54
Lost Cause, 67 n.26, 127
Lynch, J. J., 59

McAfee, Jerome, 57
McCullough, D. N., 60
McDuffie, D. A., 48
McKinley, Jake, 79-80, 150

Mapp, David, 53
Markham, William, 157 n.15
Martin, E. W., 96
Mass meetings, 21, 32-33, 63
Mayoralty. See Offices
Mayors. See Candidates, social dif-
ferences among; Officeholders,
social differences among
Mebane, Ann F., 56
Meier, August, 109 n.20
Military service, 46
Miller, Zane, 58
Mims, Livingston, 43 n.55
Minor city office-holding: associa-
tion of, with other attributes, 79,
84, 93, 95, 96-98, 102; association
of, with political success, 137-42,
147-50, 154, 167, 170, 175 n.5;
association of, with political suc-
cess and other attributes, 125,
142; of candidates, 96-97, 103-
05, 112; contemporary mention of,
61-62
Minor city offices, 14, 37 n.5, 61, 69
n.42, 96
Moran, P. J., 56
Moyer, I. P., 79
Multiple discriminant analysis. See Discriminant analysis
Murphey, Willis, 79
Mutual Aid Brotherhood, 17, 28, 49

Nativism, 17, 56, 125
Neal, T. B., 18
Negro Press Association of Georgia, 54
New South, 92, 166
Nominations, 8-9, 19-20, 22-26, 28,
30-31, 62-63, 171. See also Citizens' reform movement; Democratic party; Republican party
Nonpartisanship, 12, 20-21, 26, 28-
29, 42 n.50, 162, 171, 174
Northerners: candidacies of, 82-83,
103-05, 157 n.13, 174; contemporary comment upon, 55; political success of, 125-28, 149-50,

162-63; proportion of, among
population, 83, 171; social characteristics of, 84-85, 87, 97, 102.
See also Region of birth
Novices, political, 63, 97, 100-02, 104,
113, 130, 137, 146-47, 158 n.21,
166-68, 172. See also Political persistence

Occupation: association of, with other
attributes, 76-80, 84, 87-88, 96-
97, 100, 102; association of, with
political success, 115-18, 147-50,
160-61; association of, with political success and other attributes,
119, 128, 131, 136, 144, 147-50; of
candidates, 71-74, 103-05, 170-71;
classification of, 47, 50-51; contemporary mention of, 20, 48-50;
political importance of, 66 n.14,
169; of population, 106 n.3
Officeholders, 5-6, 63, 176 n.13; social
differences among, by office, 118-
19, 123, 128, 130-31, 134, 137,
142, 144, 147-55, 156 n.10, 157
n.19, 159, 168, 172-73
Offices: description of, 13-14; elections
for, 23; eligibility for, 14-15, 38 n.8;
selection of, 5
Office-seekers. See Candidates
O'Keefe, D. C., 96

Patronage, 31-32
Pearson's measure of skewness, 108
n.13
People's Ticket, 19, 27-28
Perennials, 63, 100-03, 105, 112 n.43,
125, 146-47, 154, 158 n.22, 167-
68. See also Political persistence
Period of arrival: association of, with
other attributes, 79, 82-83, 87, 92,
97; association of, with political
success, 130-34, 150-54, 165-66;
association of, with political success
and other attributes, 125, 127, 131,

137, 142, 147; of candidates, 88-90,
103-05; contemporary mention of,
58-59; measurement of, 59; of population, 90, 111 n.33
Piedmont Driving Club, 65 n.4
Piedmont Exposition, 31
Pioneer Historical Society, 65 n.4
Pledger, W. A., 28, 79
Police, 13, 17, 31, 96-97
Political committee membership: association of, with other attributes,
84, 93, 95, 97, 100, 102, 170; association of, with political success, 142-44, 167; association of,
with political success and other attributes, 144; of candidates, 98-99,
103-05, 112; contemporary mention
of, 63
Political committees, 16, 41 n.35, 62,
170. *See also* City Executive Committee; Citizens' nominating committee
Political culture, 8-9, 11 n.12, 45, 60,
171-72, 174
Political parties, 12, 16, 21. *See also*
Democratic party; Republican party
Political persistence: association of,
with other attributes, 79, 84, 87,
92, 95, 97, 102-03; association of,
with political success, 144-50, 166-
68, 170; association of, with political success and other attributes,
123, 125, 130-31, 137, 147; of candidates, 100-05; contemporary mention of, 20, 25, 64-65; measurement
of, 63
Polling places, 10 n.5, 34-35, 171
Poll-workers, 33, 35-36, 44 n.62
Populism, 42 n.50, 176 n.12
Professional men: candidacies of, 71-73,
103-05, 161, 169, 172; contemporary mention of, 26, 49; organizations of, 66 n.13, 107 n.4; political advantage of, 35; political success of, 118, 128, 147, 150; proportion of, among population, 106 n.3;

social characteristics of, 77-78, 96-
97
Progressive Labor League Ticket, 17
Prohibition, 17, 28, 33, 41 n.40
Property: association of, with other
attributes, 79-80, 82, 84, 87-88,
92, 100, 102; association of, with
political success, 119-23, 149-54,
156 n.8, 160-62, 170; association
of, with political success and other
attributes, 123-25, 127-28, 131,
136-37, 142, 144, 147; of candidates, 74-78, 103-05, 172; contemporary mention of, 20, 51-52;
functional importance of, 52; measurement of, 53, 67 n.20; of population, 108 n.12
Prosopography, 4, 8

Quantitative analysis, 3, 6-8, 71, 105,
106 n.1, 155 n.1, 166, 174-75

Rabinowitz, Howard N., 37 n.1, 40
n.22, 42, 109, 156 n.7, 158 n.22,
176 n.12
Race: association of, with other attributes, 78-80, 115; association of,
with political success, 103-05, 114-
15; class structure of, 109 n.20; contemporary mention of, 20-21, 23-25,
30-31, 53-54; influence of, in citizens' reform movement, 28-30. *See
also* Blacks
Railroad Men's League, 18, 73
Rauschenberg, Charles, 56
Reconstruction, 21, 174
Region of birth: association of, with
other attributes, 79, 84-85, 87,
102; association of, with political
success, 125-27, 147-50, 162-63;
association of, with political success and other attributes, 127-28,
131; of candidates, 80-84, 103-05,
157 n.13, 170-71; classification of,
54-55; contemporary mention of,
20, 55-56; political implications of,
174; of population, 110 n.25

Registration rules, 14-15, 170-71
Regression analysis, 10, 156 n.8
Reinhardt, A. M; 64
Religion, 46
Republican party, 14, 19-23, 25, 28-
    29, 40 n.24, 62, 73, 78-79, 84, 99,
    107 n.6, 157 n.15, 162-63, 171
Residence: association of, with other
    attributes, 79, 84, 87-88; associa-
    tion of, with political success, 128,
    152, 157 n.16, 164-65; association
    of, with political success and other
    attributes, 129-30; contemporary
    mention of, 20, 25, 56-57; measure-
    ment of, 68 n.34, 110 n.27; relation-
    ship to human geography, 57-58
Rice, Frank P., 45, 58, 65 n.1, 100
Richmond, J. L., 49
Rings, 13, 16-17, 22
Rossi, Peter H., 175 n.1
Rucker, H. A., 79
Russell, James H., 10, 40 n.26, 57-58,
    87-88, 107 n.4, 176 n.11

Schulze, Robert S., 169
Sciple, George, 15
Scratching, 19, 34, 39 n.20
Smith, C. W., 60
Social characteristics: contemporary
    discussion of, 19, 20, 22; measure-
    ment of, 47, 65 n.6, 158 n.23;
    selection of, 4-5, 46-47, 175
Social filter, 4-9, 11 n.11, 12, 47-48,
    65, 76, 84, 105-06, 114, 123, 149-
    55, 158 n.25, 168, 171-73, 175
Social Register, 65 n.4
Spencer, Samuel B., 24, 74, 134, 136
Standardized discriminant function co-
    efficients, 149, 158 n.24
Star Chamber Ticket, 17, 19
Stockdell, Harry C., 59, 65 n.4

Tax lists, 13, 67 n.20
Thompson, Augustus, 54
Thomson, W. S., 61
Tickets: as ballots, 34; of citizens' re-
    form movement, 26-29; competi-
    tion among, 30, 172; construction

of, 16-19; of Democratic party, 22-
    25; formula for, 23, 73, 107 n.6,
    117, 156 n.5, 161, 171; of Repub-
    lican party, 19-22; union label upon,
    43 n.57; white primary, 31
Trotti, J. P., 57

Uncontested. See Candidates, un-
    contested

Voting. See Elections

Wall, W. W., 54
Ward heelers, 32-33, 44 n.62
Wards, 10 n.5, 13, 41 n.39, 57, 110 n.
    27, 157 n.16, 164
Washington, Booker T., 164
Wealth. See Property
Welch, M. M., 118
West, "Soda Water," 64
West End, 86
White primary, 20-21, 23-24, 29-31,
    37 n.7, 42 n.48, 106 n.2, 163
Wilk's Lambda, 149-50, 152, 158 n.24
Williams, James E., 51
Woodward, C. Vann, 67 n.26, 127,
    175 n.3
Woodward, James G., 15, 30, 51, 73,
    100, 102, 112 n.43, 117, 156 n.5
Wooten, Grigsby H., 40 n.25, 66 n.13,
    107 n.6
Workingclass: candidacies from, 73-74,
    103-05, 161, 169, 171; coalition
    with blacks, 28-29, 170; organiza-
    tions of, 17-18, 107 n.5; political
    activities of, 20, 24, 27-31, 43 n.57,
    49-50, 107, 156 n.4, 160; polit-
    ical handicaps of, 35; proportion of,
    among population, 106 n.3; repre-
    sentation of, on tickets, 22-23, 73,
    156 n.5, 171; social characteristics
    of, candidates, 77-78, 84, 88, 96-
    97. See also Class conflict; Occupa-
    tion
Workingman's Union. See Labor Union
    No. 1

Zald, Mayer N., 55, 169